Dabney Herndon Maury

Recollections of a Virginian in the Mexican, Indian, and Civil Wars

Dabney Herndon Maury

Recollections of a Virginian in the Mexican, Indian, and Civil Wars

ISBN/EAN: 9783337009335

Printed in Europe, USA, Canada, Australia, Japan

Cover: Foto ©ninafisch / pixelio.de

More available books at **www.hansebooks.com**

RECOLLECTIONS OF A VIRGINIAN

IN THE

MEXICAN, INDIAN, AND CIVIL WARS

BY

GENERAL DABNEY HERNDON MAURY
Ex-United States Minister to Colombia

NEW YORK
CHARLES SCRIBNER'S SONS
1894

To My Children

I AFFECTIONATELY INSCRIBE THESE MEMOIRS OF AN OLD
SOLDIER TO MY DEVOTED CHILDREN, WHO FOR TWENTY
YEARS HAVE BEEN THE SOLACE AND PRIDE OF MY
LIFE. AND I WISH TO ACKNOWLEDGE MY SPECIAL
DEBT OF GRATITUDE TO MY DAUGHTER ROSE, WHOSE
ENCOURAGEMENT AND PRACTICAL AID HAVE BEEN OF
THE GREATEST HELP TO ME IN THE PREPARATION OF
THIS VOLUME

CONTENTS

CHAPTER I

CHAPTER II

CHAPTER III

CHAPTER IV

vii

CHAPTER V

CHAPTER VI

CHAPTER VII

CHAPTER VIII

CHAPTER XIV

CHAPTER XV

CHAPTER XVI

CHAPTER XVII

CHAPTER XVIII

CHAPTER I

Fredericksburg, its People and its History — Traditions of George Washington and of the Lees — Anecdotes of Other Famous Men, and Quaint Characters of the Town — Country Homes of the Gentry — General Lafayette's Visit — The Maury Family — Social Life before the War — The Generous Hospitality of the Old Days

REDERICKSBURG, Virginia, is one of the historic towns of America. Founded long before the Revolution, upon the Rappahannock River, at the head of tide-water, it commanded for many years the trade of the opulent planters of all that fertile region lying along the Potomac and Rappahannock rivers from the Blue Ridge Mountains to the Chesapeake Bay. The town was the centre of the commercial and social life of that rich region known as the Northern Neck of Virginia and the Piedmont country, where were born and bred the great Fathers of American liberty. In my boyhood there were many there who had walked and talked with John Marshall, George Washington, George Mason, Thomas Jefferson, James Madison, James Monroe, and the Lees.

For more than a century prior to the Revolution, the sturdy people of that region were often engaged in active war with the great Indian nation once ruled by King Powhatan. In the rebellion of Nathaniel Bacon against Sir William Berkeley two centuries ago, several thousand horsemen marched under his command to assert those principles of popular rights which were proclaimed and

established in 1776. Many of these soldiers were from
Fredericksburg and its vicinity, and it was inevitable that
the descendants of these men should be the very first to
arm against the encroachments of the British crown, and
it was in Fredericksburg that a convention of delegates of
twelve companies of horse assembled and, proclaiming
their purpose to defend the colony of Virginia, or any
other colony, against the king of England, marched,
under the command of Patrick Henry, against Lord
Dunmore in his capital. This occurred twenty-one days
before the famous Declaration of Mecklenburg, and was
therefore the first and most emphatic declaration of our
independence. In 1782, when that independence had
been accomplished, it was a citizen of Fredericksburg
who introduced into the Legislature, which had then
replaced the House of Burgesses, the first resolution for
the emancipation of the negroes, and for the prohibition
of the slave trade, ever offered in America. General
John Minor, who had fought throughout the war, was the
author and advocate of the measure.

George Washington had his boyhood's home in Fredericksburg, and after his public career ended he used to
go there to visit his venerable mother. His arrival was
the occasion of great conviviality and rejoicing. Dinner parties and card parties were then in order, and we
find, in that wonderful record of his daily receipts and
expenditures, that on one of these occasions he won
thirty guineas at loo. Probably it was after this night
that he threw the historic dollar across the river, the only
instance of extravagance ever charged against him. A
dinner party was usually given to him on his arrival at
the old Indian Queen Tavern, where, tradition tells us,
drink was deep and play was high.

It is generally believed that Washington did not laugh

or enjoy a joke. I have often heard Judge Francis Taliaferro Brooke, for many years Chief Justice of Virginia, say
this was not true. Washington often dined at Smithfield,
the home of the Brooke family. It is now known in the
histories of the battle of Fredericksburg as the "Pratt
House." Judge Brooke used to tell of a dinner given to
Washington at the Indian Queen Tavern, at which he was
present. A British officer sang a comic song, — a very
improper song, but as funny as it was improper, — at
which Washington laughed till the tears ran down his
cheeks, and called upon the singer to repeat it.

The Lees frequented Fredericksburg, and Light Horse
Harry was once in prison bounds there for debt. It is
related that from the jail of that town he wrote to his
old friend Robert Morris about his sad case, and asked
him to accommodate him with a loan. The great finan-
cier replied that he was "very sorry he could not oblige
him, because he, too, was in the same condition"! Our
greater Lee, Robert Edward, used to make his summer
home at Chatham, that old, colonial house just opposite
Fredericksburg, then the residence of Fitzhugh. Strat-
ford, where Lee was born, lies on the Potomac, near
Wakefield, the birthplace of Washington. Mrs. Lee
found the place too unhealthy for summer residence,
and moved, with her children, up to the purer air of
Chatham. The estate of Chatham adjoined the land
of Mrs. Washington, where her son George broke the
colt and barked the cherry tree.

Early in this century, General John Minor lived in
the fine old house of Hazel Hill. He was one of the
leading gentlemen of his day, and was remarkable for his
benevolence and generosity. William Wirt paid high
and eloquent tribute to General Minor's consideration
for the young lawyers who were struggling up in the

profession. His negro butler was named Josephus, and was commonly called Joe. Joe had a son whom he named "Jimsephus." General Minor manumitted him, after he had been educated and had been taught the trade of printer, and he was sent to Liberia, where for many years Mr. James Sephas was the able editor of the Liberia *Herald*.

In the fierce struggle between the Federal and States-rights parties General Minor ran for Congress against James Monroe, then a resident of the town. Monroe beat him, but it made no difference in the personal relations of these high gentlemen. General Minor named a son after James Monroe, and Dr. James Monroe Minor entered the Navy as a surgeon. He married into the Pierrepont family of New York, where he became eminent in his profession.

On one occasion, the general went into a shoe store, and found a bright-looking country girl in sharp controversy with the merchant over a pair of shoes. Pleased with the girl's intelligence, he purchased the shoes and gave them to her. On the next Valentine's Day he received this : —

> " If these few lines you do accept,
> A pair of shoes I shall expect.
> If these few lines you do refuse,
> I shall expect a pair of shoes."

She got the shoes. The distinguished law teacher of the University of Virginia, Professor John Minor, is the general's nephew and namesake.

Many of our people advocated negro emancipation and colonization. My grandfather, Mr. Fontaine Maury, manumitted his slaves, and had one of them, a bright young fellow, educated for the law. He was sent to

Liberia, where he became the highly respected Judge Draper,'of Monrovia. President Monroe, then a lawyer in Fredericksburg, was the great advocate of the emancipation and colonization of the negro. The capital of Liberia was named in his honor, Monrovia. Henry Clay, from the neighboring county of Hanover, was also the champion of emancipation, and president of the colonization society.

Commodore Matthew Fontaine Maury also made his home in Fredericksburg, where he married the sister of Captain William Lewis Herndon, that captain who commanded the *Central America* on her last, ill-fated voyage, and who, after he had placed all the women and children and as many as possible of the men passengers safely in the boats, refused, himself, to follow, because he would not desert his sinking ship. Dressing himself in his full uniform, he took his place upon the bridge, and as the vessel sank into the waves, her captain passed, with bowed and uncovered head, into the presence of his Maker.

It was many years prior to this that some good ladies of the town discovered a boy of about ten years in the act of climbing the lightning-rod of old Saint George's steeple to the cross above it. They publicly prophesied that the boy would never come to any good, and doubtless remembered him in their prayers ; and these prevailed, for, long afterward, our country was deeply moved by the thrilling story of the Darien expedition, — of how it wandered, lost in the forests of Panama, many perishing, and of how the survivors owed their safety to this same hero, whose courage and self-devotion made the name of Jack Maury loved and honored forever.

The Honorable Samuel Southard, once Secretary of the Navy, married and lived for a time in Fredericksburg. To his kindness many of our boys owed their commissions in the Navy. A nephew of his by marriage was Jim Harrow, noted for his pugnacity. Jim was a member of the company which marched, in the beginning of the war, to defend Acquia Creek against the United States steamer *Pawnee*. Whenever the *Pawnee* would fire a shot, Jim Harrow would jump upon the parapet, and flap his arms and crow like a chicken cock. He also showed his contempt for the enemy by going beyond the works, and finally took his stand by a persimmon tree outside. A shot from the *Pawnee* struck the tree and cut it down, and Jim Harrow disappeared from view, enveloped in the smoke and dust and *débris* of the explosion. An old cannoneer exclaimed, "Thank God, that infernal fool is dead at last!" The words were scarcely uttered when there was a movement among the branches of the tree, and Jim Harrow emerged, rolling up his sleeves, and calling upon the man who had "thanked God he was dead" to come out, that he might lick him. Three years later, Jim's fights were ended by a Confederate deserter whom he attempted to arrest.

Mrs. Little, a lady of high culture and excellence, presided over the Academy to which the best people of the town and neighboring counties sent their daughters for education. An old planter of the Northern Neck took his darling daughter there. One of Mrs. Little's scholars was a Miss Richardetta H., whose name in the school was inevitably abbreviated to "Dick." The newcomer was enraptured with all her surroundings, and wrote home eloquently about the charms of her roommate, Dick H. Her father was astounded. He had heard much of the high character of Mrs. Little's school. He had also a fearful apprehension of the snares which might be set for a young creature just from the seclusion of her country home, thrown at once into the fashionable vortex of the city of Fredericksburg. So he ordered out his carriage, and posted up to town, to take prompt measures about this business. He found Dick H. a gentle, refined girl, worthy of her distinguished family. She still lives, and is the wife of a prominent ex-general of the Confederacy.

Colonel Byrd Willis was one of the famous characters of his day. Connected with the most influential families of the State, he was the noted wit and *raconteur* of that old town. Weighing over three hundred pounds, he might have played Falstaff without the padding, and in his geniality and kindness equalled Shakespeare's masterpiece. The charming Princess Achille Murat was his daughter. She was an ornament of the court of the third Emperor, and was always the invited guest of the fashionable watering-places of Virginia. After breaking up his home in Florida, Colonel Willis returned to end his days in Fredericksburg. He paid liberally for his board to his landlady, a decayed gentlewoman and kinswoman, of great piety, but ate his meals at the best restaurant; for he enjoyed the pleasures of the table, and old Mrs. Carter's poverty and unthrift were great. He used to tell, how, one day, all of her resources being exhausted, the old lady took to her bed, saying to her housekeeper, "Nancy, there's nothing in the house but mush for dinner. Give that to my boarders. If they are Christians, they will eat it and be thankful; if they are not Christians, it is much better than they deserve."

About 1795 Robert Brooke, governor of Virginia, built his home upon Federal Hill, which looks over Sandy Bottom to Marye's Heights, a thousand yards away. Early in this century, Governor Brooke being dead, Federal Hill became the property of the family of Cobb, since of Georgia. Governor Cobb, of Georgia, and his brother, General Sylvanus Cobb, lived there as boys. In the great battle a Federal battery was placed on the lawn of Federal Hill. General Sylvanus Cobb, for the first time since his boyhood, looked again upon his old home from the stone wall at the foot of Marye's Heights. It was the last time he ever saw it, for a cannon-ball from that battery tore him to pieces.

For many years Mr. Reuben Thom was the postmaster of the town. He was also senior warden of Saint George's Church. Scarcely five feet in stature, he was of heroic nature. Once when the Episcopal Convention was assembled in Saint George's, a dangerous crack was discovered in the gallery of the church, and great apprehension prevailed as to the safety of the building. The senior warden indignantly derided these fears, and, when the convention opened, the amazed congregation saw their warden seated in the gallery, his arms folded, and his back propping the dangerous crack.

He was a man of strictest integrity and absolute sobriety, and was never known to take a drop of strong drink; but his ruddy face was adorned by a prominent nose of flaming and suspicious redness. One day, while admonishing the mail-carrier of King George County because of his tippling propensities, he was silenced by being requested to look at his own nose before he ventured to talk to other people about drinking.

During the bombardment of the town, the old man, then an octogenarian, had his arm-chair moved out into the garden, the nearest place to the cannon of the enemy, and there he sat throughout the day, encouraging by word and example the terrified people of his flock.

It was in 1826 that General Lafayette visited our town,

and was received and entertained with great enthusiasm as he passed on his way to Yorktown. The Fredericksburg Guards escorted him to his destination.[1] One of my earliest recollections is of a pair of white morocco shoes with a portrait of General Lafayette on the instep. This country owes more to that truly noble Frenchman than we ever think of now, and France always found him, in every crisis, a brave and faithful patriot.

While General Lafayette was in Fredericksburg, one of his old soldiers of the Revolution came to town to pay his respects to his former commander. He had a profound conviction of the activity and prevalence of pickpockets, and from the time he entered the streets of the city kept his hand upon his watch. Finally he succeeded, after passing through the crowd, in reaching his general. In his enthusiasm at being greeted so warmly by the great marquis, he seized, with both hands, Lafayette's friendly grasp, and as he turned away clapped his hand again upon his watch pocket, but, alas, it was empty.

Later on I have seen John Randolph's coach with four thoroughbreds, and John and Jubah in attendance, draw up at the Farmers' Hotel; and in the summer season ten coaches at once would drive from that old tavern to the White Sulphur. It was said that one team of thoroughbred sorrels made Chancellor's Tavern, ten miles away, in one hour.

Six miles below Fredericksburg on Massaponox Creek was New Post, the home of General Alexander Spottswood. Great intimacy was cherished between the families of Brooke of Smithfield and Spottswood. Young

---

[1] Colonel Charles Pollard, the great railroad benefactor of Alabama, and most distinguished of all her great citizens for his munificent, pure, and exalted life, was a lieutenant of the escort of General Lafayette on his famous excursion to Yorktown.

Francis Taliaferro Brooke married a daughter of General Spottswood, and their home at Saint Julian, just a mile away, was for many years one of the most charming in the State.

Saint Julian, as I remember it, was one of the most delightful of the many country homes of that fair region. It was seven miles below Fredericksburg, on the right of the main stage road to Richmond, situated in a lovely valley embowered in fine old shade trees, and surrounded by acres of choice fruits and flowers. The vegetable garden was closely guarded by a cedar hedge which a cat could hardly penetrate, while away to the left stretched a meadow bordered by a clear running brook, a tributary of the Massaponox, along which my brother and I, escorted by old John, the carriage driver, used to hunt, with old Orion, a black and white pointer, to help us. A generation later Jackson's infantry and Pelham's guns thundered along that stream until its waters ran red with human blood.

Here my uncle, Frank Brooke, made his home for many years, and my brother and I were ever most welcome guests. Aunt Brooke was a Miss Mary Carter, a beauty of Blenheim, in Albemarle County, and was the most exquisite of Virginia hostesses. Rarely have I enjoyed a table so dainty as hers, with its old blue India china, and handsome silver and napery. Every dish had been the especial care of old Phyllis, the best cook on the Rappahannock. The walls of the parlor were covered by old-fashioned landscape paper, depicting the adventures and death of Captain Cook. Over the mantel hung a portrait of my great-grandfather, Mr. Richard Brooke, in his scarlet coat, buff waistcoat, and lace ruffles, and over the door the portrait of the beautiful Miss Fannie Carter, a famous belle of her day, who married Rosier

Dulany, kinsman of the Colonel Dick Dulany, so well known and loved in Virginia, and so distinguished in the army of northern Virginia for his lofty bearing, gentle nature, and daring courage.

But the charm of Saint Julian was our cousin Helen. Lovely in person and in character, she was the belle of the county, and of Richmond too. She was a little older than I, and her refined, high-bred nature made her my divinity, and she knew it too. Aunt Brooke had a niece, Mary Francis Thompson, whom she adopted as a chosen companion for Helen. She was a sweet, gentle girl, and my brother and she were sweethearts, and when last at Saint Julian on a furlough from the army, I saw on the bark of an aspen tree the big heart carved by my brother, with her initials and his own within it. They had both been dead many years then. When the enemy came to Saint Julian the old family portraits were all carried to Fredericksburg, and stored in the post-office in the care of Mr. Reuben Thom. In the bombardment of the town they were destroyed.

They were a very happy and united family, those Brookes of Saint Julian. In his youth Uncle Frank used to hunt foxes with General Spottswood, and it was after he came home from the Revolutionary War, where he had served on General Greene's staff, that he married Mary Spottswood. He had been her neighbor and lover all his boyhood. After her death, he married Mary Carter. He became a great lawyer, and was for more than forty years on the Supreme Bench, — the Court of Appeals of Virginia. Henry Clay read law in his office, and on his way to Congress used to stop at Saint Julian. Judge Brooke lived to be more than eighty years of age. He lies by his wife in the little graveyard on the hill above their home. The family are all scattered now or dead,

and the dear old place has passed into other hands. It
has become the property of Mr. Boulware, a very well-
known and respected Virginian. It is a comfort to me
that gentle people are there, for it is the dearest place in
all my boyhood's memories.

Johnson Barbour, son of our distinguished governor,
was one of the most brilliant youths of his day, as he has
been for many years the highest illustration of our cultured country gentleman. When about sixteen years of
age he was a visitor in our home in Fredericksburg. He
had been to England with his father when he was our
Minister to the Court of St. James, and the versatility and
readiness of his talk made a great impression upon all of
us, especially upon myself, who felt his superiority to any
boy I had ever seen. We were bedfellows during his
visit, and one night I, wakeful and much impressed by
Johnson's cleverness during the evening, requested him
to examine me on matters of general information. He
complied, and sleepily inquired how many children Queen
Elizabeth had. I gave it up, and the catechism ended,
for Johnson rolled over and went to sleep.

I have recorded these personal anecdotes to illustrate
the character of the community in which our people were
reared. It was a blessed and happy land in my boyhood
and youth. All of the rich bottom lands of the Rappahannock were occupied by prosperous planters, whose
ample estates, with their spacious residences, had descended for generations from father to son. Many of
these were granted by the Crown of England, but very
few are now held under the original grants. The repeal
of the law of entail, brought about by Mr. Jefferson, was
so recent, that in some families the homes were inherited
by the sons, while the daughters were otherwise provided
for. These homes were then the abode of very great

comfort and dignity; a generous and elegant hospitality was universal. The house servants were long and carefully trained in their respective duties, and oftentimes remained for generations in the same families. My children's nurse, "Mammy Lucy," and her progenitors, had been in the family of my father-in-law for five generations, and remained till the Emancipation Proclamation. The usual retinue of the establishment at "Cleveland," my wife's home, was fifteen servants, or more when the house was full of company; and as many as thirty or more of the family and friends daily dined there together for weeks and months at a time.

In Fredericksburg and its near vicinity lived many Scotch families. Every historic name of Scotland is represented among them, and a more worthy class of people can nowhere be found. Their ancestors came over in colonial days, and, curiously enough, became Episcopalians, as were all the population of that region in those days. The history and traditions of the people made them proud, and the religious and literary influences were of a high order. The old College of William and Mary was the Alma Mater of these colonial gentry, while the classical academies of Hanson, and Lawrence, and the Colemans prepared our youth for their higher education there. Following the English system, the study of the classics was the chief aim of these schools. Modern languages were not taught in them, nor mathematics to any valuable extent.

CHAPTER II

N 1824, my father, Captain John Minor Maury, while serving as flag captain of Commodore David Porter's fleet against the pirates of the West Indies, died in the twenty-eighth year of his age. He had been an officer of the Navy since his thirteenth year, and had led a most active and adventurous life; and at the time of his death he was the highest ranking officer of his age in the service. Some years previously he sailed with Captain William Lewis as first officer of a ship bound for China. They had both obtained furloughs for this voyage. Maury, with six men, was left on the island of Nokaheeva to collect sandal-wood and other valuable articles of trade against the return of the ship.

The war with England broke out, and Captain Lewis was blockaded in a Chinese port. Maury and his men were beset by the natives of one part of the island, though befriended by the chief of that portion where ships were accustomed to land, and at last all of the party save Maury and a sailor named Baker were killed by the savages. These two constructed a place of refuge in the tops of four cocoanut trees which grew close enough together for them to make a room as large as a frigate's maintop. A rope ladder was their means of access. Here they were one day, when their eyes were brightened by the sight of a frigate bearing the American flag. It proved to be the *Essex*, Captain David Porter commanding, which had touched at the island for fresh water. Captain Porter had with him a very fast British ship which he had just captured. He named her the *Essex Junior*, and armed her as his consort, placing Lieutenant Downs in command, with Maury as first lieutenant. After refitting they sailed away to Valparaiso, where the British ships *Cherub* and *Phœbe*, under Captain Hilliard, fought and captured them.

Maury's next service was with McDonough in the battle of Lake Champlain, whence he wrote to a friend in Fredericksburg: "We have gained a glorious victory. I hope the most important result of it will be to confirm the wavering allegiance of New York and Vermont to the Union. They have been threatening to secede unless peace be made with England on any terms!" This was in 1815.

About 1822, Porter organized his fleet for the extinction of the pirates of the West Indies. He was allowed to select his officers, and his first choice was of John Minor Maury to be his flag captain. After serving with distinction on that expedition, he died of yellow fever on his homeward voyage, and was buried almost within sight of Norfolk harbor, where his young wife and two little children were anxiously awaiting his coming.

After my father's death his younger brother, Matthew Fontaine Maury, became practically the guardian of my brother, William Lewis Maury, and myself. My brother died at the age of twenty, of heart disease, a victim to the barbarous medical practice of the day.

He was a very handsome, attractive young fellow, and a great favorite in society. The doctors subjected him to the "moxa," a cruel invention of that time. A spot as large as a half dollar was burned into the flesh over his heart. He was bled frequently. It was proposed to bleed him periodically. For several years he ate no meat, and for the last year of his life was kept in bed. Our uncle protested vainly against this practice, which he realized was killing my brother, but the highest medical authorities of the day upheld this system of depletion. At last, after ever increasing torture, he was released from a life which had dawned full of brightness and promise for him, and had become one of continued suffering.

After my brother's death my uncle's interest centred in me, and no son ever had a more tender and sympathetic father than I. As long as he lived this mutual confidence and affection existed unimpaired. He was the most lovable man I ever knew, and he won the confidence of all who came within his gentle influence. He ever used cordial praise and approbation as an incentive to endeavor, and if admonition were needed, he gave it in a manner which left no sting. Oftentimes a playful jest would serve the purpose of his correction. From my earliest boyhood I went to him for counsel and for comfort in all my troubles, and always left him with renewed purpose and self-respect. When I came to him from West Point he said to me, "Well, Dab, how did you come out?"

"Very poorly, Uncle Matt. I graduated thirty-fifth."

He looked sorry he had asked me, but suddenly taking heart he inquired, "How many were in the class?"

"There were sixty of us."

"That was first-rate. You beat me all hollow. I

was twenty-seventh, and there were only forty in my class."

This was truly encouraging. He had a pleasant greeting for every one, but was especially kindly in his way of treating the mechanics and workmen with whom his business brought him in contact. He made them feel he was learning from them, while he never failed to leave with them something instructive about their own branch of work. He was thus learning and teaching all of his time.

In his youth he read Scott and other English classics, and was very fond of Shakespeare, and all his life he read and studied the Bible. I do not think he ever read any novels after he began to develop the great thoughts with which his brain was teeming. His power of concentration was wonderful. Writing upon the subject in which he was interested, in the midst of his family, he would pause, pen in hand, to laugh at some jest or say a word *apropos* of the question under discussion, and return in an instant to his work. He wrote his "Navigation" and many strong papers on Naval Reform, which first attracted attention to him, before he was thirty years old. Mr. Calhoun said of him, "Maury is a man of great thoughts"; and Mr. Tyler was urged and desired to make him Secretary of the Navy.

In 1853–54 I was spending the winter in Philadelphia, when he wrote to me to go and see Mr. Biddle, who had charge of the annual report of the National Observatory, and deliver to him a message relative to it. After our business was ended, Mr. Biddle said to me: "This uncle of yours is a strange man. Here he is publishing, as an official report, the materials for the most valuable and interesting book of science ever produced.

You may tell him from me, that if he does not utilize it, he will have the chagrin of seeing some Yankee bookmaker steal his thunder and reap a fortune from it."

I sat down in Mr. Biddle's office and wrote to him. He replied by next mail that he would take Biddle's advice, and the "Physical Geography of the Sea" was soon published by the Harpers. It created a world-wide interest, and before the war broke out eleven editions had been issued. He used to say to me, "Dab, that is your book."

At the outbreak of the war, he was at the height of his great scientific career, in the most desirable position possible for the exercise of his talents. But he did not hesitate a moment as to his action, but promptly gave up all of his prospects in life for his people's sake, and calmly faced the uncertainties and anxieties of a new career. When his decision became known, the Emperor of Russia, and a little later the Emperor of France, invited him in the most generous terms to come to them and pursue in tranquillity, and in luxurious comfort and ease, those investigations which were for the benefit of all mankind, until peace should once again enable him to resume them at home. He replied, gratefully acknowledging the invitations, but stating that his presence might be of service to his own people, and in their hour of need he could not desert them.

At the age of seventeen I entered the University of Virginia, and enjoyed the life of freedom from home surveillance, and the great pleasure of association with men well reared and educated, matured in their purposes, and studying earnestly in the fine professional schools which then, as now, were recognized as among the highest in the country. Johnson Barbour, Randolph Tucker, Robert Withers, John S. Barbour, Stage Davis,

Winter Davis, Hunter Murshill, George Randolph, Confederate Secretary of War, Honorable Volney E. Howard, R. L. Dubney, and many another who made his mark in life and has gone over the river, were there then.

After leaving the University, where I was in the junior law class, I continued the pursuit of that most exacting study in Fredericksburg. There were twenty-six of us in the class of that year, and our instructor was the venerable and learned Judge Lomax, distinguished alike for his legal attainments and the courteous dignity of his bearing. I fear he realized from the first that I would not prove a bright and shining light in my adopted profession, for he used always to select the easiest questions and present them to me for solution. One day he inquired of me, "Mr. Maury, does ignorance of the law justify the commission of an offence?"

"Certainly, sir," I promptly replied. I noticed that he looked at me with a kind of hopeless forbearance, and as I had by that time begun to have grave misgivings of my own as to my legal qualifications, I went to him and told him that I had decided not to pursue further so inexorable and unjust a profession as that of law.

Of all our class, Shake Caldwell was *facile princeps* in his studies, as he was our "glass of fashion and mould of form." He was the son of Mr. James Caldwell of New Orleans, and the beautiful Widow Wormley of Fredericksburg. They were near neighbors of ours, and my relations with Shakespeare were warm and affectionate till the day of his death. He was one of the handsomest and most elegant gentlemen I have ever known, as he was one of the ablest men of his day. He was so handsome, so charming, so witty, that many people credited him with being a society man only; but, while brilliant in social life, he was steadfast and strong in his affections and duties, with a great capacity for business, so that when he died he was probably the richest man in Virginia, and he used his great wealth as a trust confided to him for the good of his people.

After we parted,— I to go to West Point, and he to seek his fortune, — I knew nothing of his career for six years until he told me of it himself. He went to Mobile to enter upon the practice of law. After a year of almost hopeless waiting for business, his father, who had by that time successfully established the gas works of New Orleans, resolved to undertake similar works in Mobile, and wrote to his son that if he would take charge of the new enterprise, he would give him $750 per annum, which was more than his law practice brought him. After two years of successful management in Mobile, Mr. James Caldwell decided to establish gas works in Cincinnati, and offered Shakespeare the management of these at $2000 per annum. This property so increased in value in a few years that Mr. Caldwell, enriched by the business in Mobile and New Orleans, transferred to his son, for his sister and himself, all of his interests in Cincinnati. Soon after this, having acquired a handsome estate, Shakespeare became attached to a brilliant young girl of Louisville, one of the illustrious Breckinridge family. She was an orphan and an heiress, and had many suitors. His own property was worth about half a million. Their happy married life was only ended by her early death. In 1874 his sister, who had meanwhile become Mrs. Dean, died, and save for a few minor legacies left him her entire fortune, and at his own death his estate was estimated at $ 3,000,000.

When she was young, Shakespeare's sister numbered among her suitors Bob Waring, a member of a wealthy family living in the Northern Neck. As Bob was not very well equipped in his upper story, he was put to work in a dry-goods store in Fredericksburg, where he speedily lost his heart to Sophy Caldwell. About this time Ole Bull came to town to make some music for us, and Bob decided to invite his lady love to enjoy the concert in his company; so he presented himself before her with a request that she would go with him "to hear the old gentleman." She was at first quite at a loss to apprehend his meaning, but finally discovered, from his blushes and hesitating utterances, that he did not consider it proper to pronounce in her divine presence the name of the great virtuoso! Bob and his lady love and the fiddler have gone long ago where I hope they are each enjoying eternal harmonies.

About 1872, Shakespeare established in Louisville an asylum for indigent men who were cared for, without regard to religious creed, by the Little Sisters of the Poor.

In 1875 he came to Richmond, to undertake and organize a similar institution there for the poor of Richmond and Fredericksburg. The endowment of $250,000 was to be under the administration of the Bishop of Richmond, now Cardinal Gibbons. On the day that the Virginia Legislature granted the charter, he was stricken with paralysis, but he soon recovered his mental faculties, and earnestly desired to complete the good work he had so much at heart. But Bishop Gibbons would not permit him to be troubled with business under such circumstances. After two or three months he suffered a relapse, and died in New York city in his fifty-fourth year. He left his great estate to his two daughters, and his generous intentions to his church have been carried out by one of them, who has richly endowed the Catholic University now being erected at Washington.

On relinquishing my arduous pursuit of legal learning, I left Fredericksburg to enter West Point, where I was immured for four years, the only unhappy years of a very happy life, made happy by the love of the truest people, whose interest in me has followed me until this day.   One hundred and sixty-four boys entered the class with me, of whom few had received either social or educational advantages of a very high order.   McClellan was a notable exception to this, being under sixteen years of age when he entered the Academy.   He went at once to the head of the class and remained there until the end, enjoying the while the affection and respect of all.

After six months came the first examination, which pronounced a score or more "deficient," leaving Jackson at the foot of the class and McClellan at the head. Jackson was then in his nineteenth year, and was awkward and uncultured in manner and appearance, but there was an earnest purpose in his aspect which impressed all who saw him.   Birket Fry, A. P. Hill, and I were standing together when he entered the South Barracks under charge of a cadet sergeant.   He was clad in gray homespun, and wore a coarse felt hat, such as wagoners or constables — as he had been — usually wore, and bore a pair of weather-stained saddle-bags across his shoulders.   There was about him so sturdy an expression of purpose that I remarked, "That fellow looks as if he had come to stay."   As the sergeant returned from installing him in his quarters, we asked who the new cadet was.   He replied, "Cadet Jackson, of Virginia."   That was enough for me, and I went at once to show him such interest and kindness as would have gratified others under the circumstances.   But Jackson received me so coldly that I regretted my friendly overtures, and rejoined my companions, rebuffed and discomfited.

His steady purpose to succeed and to do his duty soon won the respect of all, and his teachers and comrades alike honored his efforts and wished him God-speed. His barrack room was small and bare and cold. Every night just before taps he would pile his grate high with anthracite coal, so that by the time the lamps were out, a ruddy glow came from his fire, by which, prone upon the bare floor, he would "bone" his lesson for the next day, until it was literally burned into his brain. The result of this honest purpose was that from one examination to the next he continually rose in his class till he reached the first section, and we used to say, "If we stay here another year, old Jack will be head of the class."

"*In medio tutissimus*" was my motto, and the most valued relic of my many years' study of the humanities; for it kept me safe from disgrace in the examinations, except in those especial accomplishments of the soldier, in all of which I was *facile princeps*. Old Jack was very clumsy in his horsemanship and with his sword, and we were painfully anxious as we watched him leaping the bar and cutting at heads. He would do it, but at the risk of his life. It is to be regretted that any of his biographers should claim for him skill and grace as a horseman, when they have with truth so much of real greatness to tell of him.

In the corps of cadets of that time were many who have become famous beside Jackson and McClellan. There was Grant, a very good and kindly fellow whom everybody liked. He was proficient in mathematics, but did not try to excel at anything except horsemanship. In the riding-school he was very daring. When his turn came to leap the bar, he would make the dragoons lift it from the trestles and raise it as high as their heads, when he would drive his horse over it, clearing at least six feet.

Hancock and Franklin were with us too, and although association of the cadets of one class with those of another was rare, I was much with them, and was intimate with Barnard Bee, that noble South Carolinian who, upon the fatal field on which he bravely fell, gave the name of "Stonewall" Jackson to our hero.

Bee was one of the most admirable young soldiers of that day. Six feet in stature, he was every inch a soldier, and as gentle as he was brave. He was distinguished always for his delicate consideration for others, as for his manly and noble bearing in personal danger. He served with distinction in the Mexican War, and upon the far western frontier, to fall at Manassas in the very moment of our first victory there. About the close of Bee's second year at the Academy, he was court-martialed for some infraction of the regulations, and was meanly sentenced to remain one day behind his classmates, who went off for the biennial furlough. He had the sympathy of all of us in this peculiar punishment, which struck at him through his affections, and I especially strove to cheer and console him. The class notified Bee that as the steamboat passed Gee's Point he must be there, for they would throw over to him a bottle of cocktail to comfort him in his loneliness. Bee liked cocktail, but couldn't swim. I, having promised my mother not to drink while at the Academy, swam for that bottle for love of Bee. For more than an hour I went up and down the Hudson and nearly across it, in vain search for it. It probably broke from its buoy and went down. Poor Bee was in sorry luck that day.

After I had been at West Point a year, my uncle, seeing how my mother pined for me, and being in high favor with the Administration, procured for me a three-weeks' leave of absence.   I joined my mother at the Observatory, and we were all very happy there together. We had then, for commandant, a huge Tennesseean, whose chief aim seemed to be to keep the cadets' hair cropped close.   When I presented myself before him on my return from this leave of absence, he looked at me disapprovingly, and said, "Go and get your hair cut, sir, and report to me."   Joe, our barber, could cut hair quicker and shorter than any living man.   I stepped into his tent, and he ran his shears around my head, nearly scalping me.   In two or three minutes I was back and stood attention.

"Well, sir," said the commandant, "what's the matter now?"

"You ordered me to have my hair cut and report to you, sir."

"Ah!   That's very well indeed, sir."

That evening, at dress parade, I was published a corporal.

The course of study of the second class at West Point was the most difficult.   Bartlett's "Optics" was a fearful book, and the most formidable discussion in it was that called "optical images."   It was a general bugbear to the class; and only the men of the first section were expected to be able to demonstrate it.   The January examinations were close at hand, and all of the men below me had been found deficient save the "immortal section."   I was thoroughly aroused, and being pretty good at a spurt, I made myself master of the course. The "optical images" received my especial attention, for if that were well demonstrated I should be safe.   The week before the examinations Professor Bartlett came into our section, and Lieutenant Deshon of the Ordnance Corps, who was our instructor, ordered, "Mr. Maury will go to the board, and demonstrate the 'optical images.'"

It was a complete success, a perfect demonstration. Professor Bartlett and Deshon were both satisfied, and I got "max" on that fortunate effort of mine, and went up seventeen files in my standing. My classmates, who seemed as delighted as I was, said as the section was dismissed, "Peri, you are safe." I had been called "Peri" since my first arrival at the Academy, in consequence of my inability to accomplish anything in the musical line save that plaintive ditty commencing, "Farewell, farewell to thee, Araby's daughter." I may as well confess that it constitutes my sole repertory unto this day.

Deshon was a very amiable and able man. After the Mexican War we were stationed together at the Academy. He "got off" on religion, and in our rides together used to try to convince me of the truth of his new-found convictions as to transubstantiation, etc. I told him he would end by being a Jesuit, and so he did, having long ago become a member of the great Church of Rome. A purer Christian never lived than he.

CHAPTER III

Graduated at West Point and off for the Mexican War — Operations of the Campaign under General Scott and General Taylor — Anecdotes of these Commanders — Other Officers who became Eminent in the Civil War — The Capture of Vera Cruz — Wounded at Cerro Gordo — In the Hospital — The Journey to Jalapa

N June, 1846, I was graduated, and was attached as second lieutenant to the Mounted Rifles, now the Third Cavalry. General Taylor's victories of the 8th and 9th of May had aroused the enthusiasm of our country, and we listened with intense interest to the letters and reports which came pouring in from that army, — how, when Charley May came trotting up with his squadron of dragoons to capture the Mexican guns, young Randolph Ridgely cried out from his battery, "Hold on a minute, Charley, till I draw their fire"; and how young Kirby Smith, known as Seminole Smith, leaped astride of a Mexican cannon as he sabred the gunners. These and scores of similar incidents we heard as we were girding ourselves to join these glorious fellows. It was then that the Chief of Artillery at West Point, Captain Keyes, came to me and urged me to accept the position of Instructor of Artillery during the ensuing summer encampment. The offer, though kindly pressed, was as firmly declined, as it might cause delay in reaching the scene of active preparations, and I hastened home to make my farewell visit to my mother.

Orders came shortly for me to go to Baltimore and report to Captain Stevens Mason, commanding a squadron of Mounted Rifles about to sail in the brig *Soldana* for the army of General Taylor on the Rio Grande. There were eight commissioned officers and one hundred and sixty men who embarked in this unseaworthy craft of about two hundred tons. All are gone now save the sad old writer of these lines. As we sailed down Chesapeake Bay a gale arose, which compelled all shipping, numbering probably a hundred sail, to harbor in Hampton Roads. The skipper of the *Soldana* was Captain Stubbs, of Maine, well named. Full of the importance of his trust, his ambition moved him to make sail for Mexico before the gale was over. The *Soldana* was the first and only vessel to leave the Roads for the heaving Atlantic on this September morning, and about two A.M. of that same night she rolled her rotten mainmast out and floated a wretched wreck.

Her best hope seemed to make for Charleston, or some other port, and repair damages; but Stubbs went to work with great energy, and rigged up a jury mast, and on the thirty-second day of her voyage, after many storms and calms, having been long reported "lost with all hands," we landed at Point Isabel, every man of us safe and well. The news of Taylor's capture of Monterey had just come in, and the hope of participating in that action, which had induced this squadron of the Rifles to move without waiting for horses, was disappointed.

The Rifles moved on up the Rio Grande to Camargo, whence our colonel, Persifer Smith, then in Monterey, and a soldier of reputation, had us ordered to Monterey as escort to some siege pieces which, under the personal efforts of young Stonewall Jackson, were moving to that city. He worked at them in the muddy roads as he used to do at West Point, and ever did in his great career, and they had to move along. In Monterey were the heroes of the campaign, and some of the War of 1812 and of many an Indian fight.

General Zachary Taylor, a simple and unpretending gentleman, may have been Jackson's model; for he had more of the silent, rapid, impetuous methods, which Jackson practised later on, than any American general save Forrest.

Monterey was a pleasant place for the month or two of our stay there. Grant was then Quartermaster of the Fourth Infantry. I had been badly wounded while hunting near Camargo, so as to disable me from duty while in Monterey, and Grant being also, by the duties of his office, free to go when and where he pleased, we were much together and enjoyed the association. Grant was a thoroughly kind and manly young fellow, with no bad habits, and was respected and liked by his brother officers, especially by those of his own regiment.

In the course of a few weeks news came that General Scott had arrived in the country, and assumed command of the army; that he had changed the line of operations; and that General Taylor's forces would in large part be drawn off to Scott. This caused much talk among us, for Taylor had won the unbounded confidence and love of all of us, while Scott was sneered at as " Old Fuss and Feathers." The expectation was that we should forthwith have an order to trim our hair and beards according to the regulations of the army. With us was General David Emanuel Twiggs, a grand-looking old man, six feet two inches in stature, with long, flowing white hair, and a beard which hung over his broad breast like Aaron's. As I passed his tent one morning early, he was outside of it taking a sponge bath, stripped to the waist.

I had never seen a grander subject for an artist's study.
A few days after I saw him again, shorn of his hoary
locks, hair and beard close cropped, in anticipation of
orders which were never issued; for Scott addressed
himself to the serious work of the Mexican campaign,
which has ranked him so high among the world's great
captains.

General Taylor was ordered to move down to Victoria
with his available forces, where Scott would meet him.
Our route lay along the base of the Sierra Madre Mountains, amid beautiful scenery and through orange groves
and fields of sugar-cane, and was crossed by clear, cool
mountain streams, in which we bathed after our long and
dusty marches. The country people supplied us with
poultry, vegetables, and fruit, and we greatly enjoyed our
march. At Victoria we did not meet General Scott, but
were joined by troops from Camargo. Among those who
returned with General Taylor towards Monterey were
Colonel Jeff Davis and his famous regiment of Mississippi
Rifles, who, two months later, turned the tide of battle
in Taylor's famous victory at Buena Vista. With them,
too, went Bragg's battery. In that battery I met George
H. Thomas, an enthusiastic Virginian then and till the
very moment, many years later, when he drew his sword
against our dear old State. Attached to the battery also
was Lieutenant Bob Wheat, afterwards a distinguished
soldier. Wheat has been somewhat lightly spoken of as
an adventurer in wars, but there was earnest feeling in
him. In all his long and dangerous services he bore
in his bosom the little prayer-book his mother gave him
when he first left home, and on the morning of his last
battle (I believe he fell in the fierce fight at Gaines Mill),
when he had formed his battalion he said, " Boys, before
we move into this fight I will read you something from

this little book." He was listened to with great feeling, and a few hours later he fell dead in the very prime of his career.

We were quiet for some days at Victoria, where no event of interest disturbed us save the stealing of General Taylor's horse, "Old Whitey." Whereupon the general promptly arrested the Alcalde of the town as hostage for the safe and early restitution of "Old Whitey," who was restored next day. Just previous to this Charley May had been sent with his squadron to explore a certain route through the mountains. He rejoined us at Victoria, reporting that he had been beset in a wild gorge by the Mexicans, who fired upon them from the cliffs, and rolled great rocks down on them. He had lost his rear guard under Lieutenant Sturgis, whom he arrested, and who was court-martialed at Victoria. Bragg volunteered to act as counsel for Sturgis, who was entirely acquitted, and came out of the affair with more credit than any one concerned in it. We young fellows, as well as the old ones, were all for Sturgis, who seemed to have been made a scapegoat of.

It was during this march that one of our young officers, Richie, just from West Point, was lassoed and murdered while passing through a Mexican village. We all liked him, and ample vengeance befell that village.

At Tampico we met General Scott and some thousands of troops assembling for the descent upon Vera Cruz. In all there were over 14,000, of whom but few were veterans. All had flint-lock muskets save the Rifles and some artillery companies.

The plains about Tampico afforded ample ground for drill, and here we had, for the first time, drilling by General Scott in the evolutions of the line. As soon as all the transports had arrived with troops and equipments, our whole force sailed for the rendezvous off Lobos Island, whence we sailed for Vera Cruz. More than a hundred men-of-war and transports made up the fleet, which landed at the island of Sacrificios for the attack upon the city. Bee and I were in the same transport, and on the day before the debarkation we paid a visit to a friend of Bee's, the captain of a gunboat. When I was introduced to him he said: "Are you a son of Captain John Minor Maury? Captain Tatnell, who has just left me, declared him to be the finest officer in the United States Navy." To hear this on the eve of my first battle filled me with emotion, and with the desire to be worthy of such a father, and with honest pride that the tribute should be paid in the presence of so noble a friend as Bee.

Our army landed at Vera Cruz, 14,000 strong, in four divisions. The landing was made in whale-boats rowed by the sailors of the fleet. In each boat were from fifty to sixty soldiers, and it was a glorious sight to see the first division, under General Worth, move off at 2 P.M. at the signal from the flag-ship. The fifty great barges kept in line, until near the shore, when General Worth himself led the way to make the landing first of all, and being in a fine gig he accomplished this, and was the first man of the army to plant the American flag upon that shore of Mexico. The Mexicans made no resistance, and the boats rapidly returned for the second division, under Twiggs, which was as quietly transported to the shore. Then the volunteers came, and soon after dark Scott had his whole army in battle order about three miles from Vera Cruz.

Early next morning we moved around the city till we came to the great national road, built by the Spaniards, from Vera Cruz to the city of Mexico. The Mounted

Rifles led in this investment, and C Company was in front when we came out upon the great Camino del Rey, over which at that moment a train of mules, laden with wine and escorted by a troop of Mexicans, was passing. We debouched into the road and fired a few shots at the Mexican dragoons, who fled back to Vera Cruz, firing at us over their shoulders as they ran. When our work for that day was done, we had completed the investment of Vera Cruz. We were very hungry and thirsty. So our Texas guide lassoed a fat beef, a keg of sherry was broached, and we bivouacked upon the northern beach of Vera Cruz, just beyond cannon range of the city, and remained there until, after two or three weeks' bombardment, Vera Cruz surrendered.

While lying there our scouts brought in word that a considerable body of Mexican guerillas had closed up to a bridge two or three miles in our rear. C Company was ordered to go and look after them. We found several hundred of them. They demanded our surrender, and were so defiant and aggressive that we sent a runner back to camp to report the situation. Meantime, we took up a defensive position till our express returned, guiding General Smith and five or six companies of the Rifles. Our company was in advance, and we moved to the attack in company front, occupying the whole breadth of the road. The Mexicans had formed and were awaiting us in ambuscade, and fired a volley at us. They were not thirty yards distant, yet not one of our men was touched. We sprang forward, charged and routed them, chased them half a mile, and marched back in great delight over our first affair. Sergeant Harris, of Winchester, Virginia, was the only man seriously wounded. I won my first compliment in special orders for good conduct.

While we were still bombarding Vera Cruz the news of

General Taylor's victory over Santa Anna's army at Buena
Vista was received. General Scott published it to the
army, congratulating us "upon this great victory of the
successful General Taylor." It was Taylor's fourth deci-
sive victory since May, and was fought with only 4500
men against 23,000. There is every reason to believe
that, had not his forces been diverted to Scott, Taylor
would have captured the city of Mexico at as early a
date as the latter.

After Santa Anna's defeat at Buena Vista, a serious
revolt was organized against him in the city of Mexico.
He moved at once to the capital, restored order, and
marched up rapidly with his army to relieve the siege of
Vera Cruz. Before his arrival Vera Cruz had fallen, and
Scott was prepared to advance upon the city of Mexico.

When the white flag was shown by Vera Cruz we were
overjoyed and greatly comforted, for we had been nearly
three weeks in the sand hills without change of raiment,
our opportunities for bathing were very limited, and the
fleas swarmed over us. I have never seen anything like
those Vera Cruz fleas. If one were to stand ten minutes
in the sand, the fleas would fall upon him in hundreds.
How they live in that dry sand no one knows. They
don't live very high, for they are ever ready for a change
of diet. The engineer officers, G. W. Smith, and
McClellan, slept in canvas bags drawn tight about their
necks, having previously greased themselves all over with
salt pork. Perhaps the fleas did not partake of them,
but they made up for it by regaling themselves on us of
the line who had no canvas bags.

At the sight of the white flag all was gaiety along our
lines ; work and anxiety gave place to pride and comfort.
Our servants brought us fresh clothes from the fleet, and
never had we enjoyed them more. Commissioners were

appointed to arrange terms of surrender, and General Scott selected Captains Joseph E. Johnston and Robert E. Lee to represent us, and nobly they did so. This selection gave great satisfaction throughout the army. In rich uniforms, superbly mounted, they were the most soldierly, as they were the ablest, men in the army. We young Virginians were proud that day to see them, and to know that our two victorious armies were led by two great Virginia generals.

We did not linger long at Vera Cruz, for Scott was eager to press on and capture the capital, and Santa Anna was already preparing to dispute his passage at Cerro Gordo, a strong position three or four days from us. Santa Anna first took position a few days' march from Vera Cruz, near Plan del Rio, on the great national road. Here he entrenched himself, and here we attacked him on the 17th of April, 1847. The Rifles marched at the head of the army, and early in the evening, as we were lying by the side of the road, word came from Lieutenant Gardner, who had been sent up with an infantry picket, that the enemy was advancing to attack us. "Send up the Rifles!" shouted General Harney, and up we moved, and in a few minutes were warmly engaged with the Mexican advance. We drove them steadily back to their fortifications on the high telegraph hill. Our line was halted in the edge of the timber which covered the hill we had just occupied. The Mexican skirmishers rallied and formed in line of battle, just below their fortifications on the opposite hill, whence they kept up a dropping fire upon any of our men who showed themselves. Santa Anna himself, in citizen's dress and mounted on a superb gray horse, was riding about the field, ordering the movements of the troops. He was an able general and a game soldier. Several of my men fired at him, but at such long range as forbade accurate shooting. We were in the undergrowth which crowned the hill, and from here I observed a little body of Rifles, who under Lieutenant Gibbs, had ensconced themselves in a sheltered spot rather nearer to the enemy than our own, and who were in no little danger of being cut off.

I called upon my men to follow, and went down the slope, believing they were behind me; for as I advanced the Mexican battalion fired very actively. Before I had gone a hundred yards a ball shattered my left arm, and turning I found myself alone on that bare hillside. The hill was very steep, and as I turned they opened a rapid file fire upon me, but I managed to reach the cover of the brush, faint and suffering severely. As I did so, a rifleman sprang from behind the only tree affording shelter, and ran to the rear for help. This quickly came in the person of Sergeant Bob Coleman, a gallant soldier and an old schoolmate. He assisted me to a surgeon, who cheerfully said, " You've a very bad arm ; I shall have to cut it off. "

I replied : " There's a man over there whose leg is worse than my arm. When you are ready for me you will find me behind that big rock down the hill." On reaching the rock I found a negro boy, a servant of Lieutenant Stuart, whose horse he had in charge. I mounted it, and set out for Plan del Rio, five miles in the rear, where I knew there were surgeons and all proper accommodations for the wounded. Dr. Cuyler fixed me as comfortably as possible, and said, " We can save that arm, Maury " ; to which I replied, " Do it at all risks. I will die before I will lose it, and I assume all responsibility."

Next morning the battle raged fiercely, but soon came the cheerful strains of " Yankee Doodle " from our band escorting the Mexican prisoners. Scott had won a great victory, and our cavalry was pursuing the flying Mexicans towards the city of Mexico. The Rifles had borne an active part in the battle. Captain Mason and Lieutenants Ewell and Davis were killed; I was severely, and three other officers slightly, wounded. In the long and active service of that famous regiment, every Virginian who entered it was killed, except myself, and I was crippled for life. Generals Jeb Stuart, William E. Jones, and Chamblis, who fell long afterward, were of this number. Loring, our colonel, lost his arm at the gate of Mexico, but that never abated his wonderful activity in many Indian campaigns, in the war between the States, and in the Egyptian campaign against Abyssinia. He served with distinction in the Egyptian wars, and after his return published one of the most interesting books on that country ever written. To the very last his impetuous courage was unabated, and he was one of the most generous of men. He had borne an active part in the Texan war of independence and in the Seminole wars in Florida, having gone from Florida to Texas as a volunteer at sixteen years of age.

While I was being borne from the field, Colonel Sumner, a rough old dragoon who had been temporarily put in command of the Rifles in the absence of our colonel, Persifer Smith, met me, and learning what was going on in front hastened forward, and was almost immediately knocked over by a glancing ball upon his head. As soon after being carried to the rear as he could walk, he came to me and spoke very kindly to me, calling me " my brave boy," which compensated for all the wound and pain and for some previous roughness of manner to me. When we reached Jalapa, Generals Harney, Twiggs, and Riley came to see me, and made me proud and happy by the assurance that good reports of their boy would gladden the hearts of my dear mother and uncle far away in old Fredericksburg.

On the evening of the 17th, as I was making my escape from that bloody-minded surgeon who was so bent upon cutting off my arm, I was a sorry spectacle, covered with blood, pale and faint, one man leading my horse, while Tom, the negro, glad enough to get off from that field, kept close to me with a flask of brandy, and when he saw me about to faint he would set me up with a pull at it. We met General James Shields at the head of his brigade, marching rapidly to go in the fight. He was a fine, manly-looking fellow, and showed me much kindly interest and sympathy. Next morning, in storming a battery, a grape shot struck him fair in the breast, and passed out at his back. Dr. Cuyler said to me, "Maury, I assure you, you can double up your fist and pass your arm through his body." Yet he got well very soon, was severely wounded again at the city of Mexico, and lived to play an important part in making the fame of Stonewall Jackson, and to claim a victory over him at Kernstown. He died several years ago, greatly honored by his people, who might have made him President but for his foreign nationality. I never saw him after that memorable meeting, but have always remembered gratefully his warm and manly sympathy for me.

On the morning of the next day after being wounded, I was removed from the tent to a spacious reed house in the village, quite airy and comfortable. Captain Joe Johnston, just promoted to Lieutenant-Colonel of one of our new regiments, was lying there. He had been badly shot six days before in a daring reconnaissance. During the day Captain Mason was brought in, and lay in one of the rooms opening upon the main hall, where I was. A cannon-ball had torn off his leg, but he was very bright and game. He and I often talked of the fine times we would have at the Virginia Springs in the coming summer. Poor fellow! He never saw them again. Two or three weeks later blood poison set in, and he died soon after being taken to Jalapa. His history was a sorrowful one. The only son of Armstead Mason, who fell in a duel with his kinsman, Colonel McCarthy Stevens, Mason inherited his father's fine estate of Selma, in Loudon County, where he lived extravagantly. A few years before his death he married; his wife died within a year, and after that all went ill with Mason. When his property was all gone, he procured a captaincy in the Rifles, and died bravely, a representative gentleman of the old times.

A few days after being placed in the house, Dr. Cuyler said to me: " Maury, there's a young fellow, Derby, across the street, lying wounded among the volunteers, who says he is a classmate of yours and wishes to come over here. I would not agree to it without consulting you, for he is a coarse fellow; but I don't like him to be among the volunteers." In that war the volunteers were not regarded as they were in the great war between the States.

Of course I cheerfully agreed to his being brought over, and his cot was placed in the hall beside mine. The partitions of the rooms were of reeds wattled together, so that conversations could be heard from one room to the other. John Phœnix Derby was an incessant talker, and uttered a stream of coarse wit, to the great disgust of Joe Johnston, who endured it in silence, till one day he heard Derby order his servant to capture a kid out of a flock of goats passing our door, when he broke out, "If you dare to do that, I'll have you court-martialed and cashiered or shot ! "

In about ten days General Scott, having chased Santa
Anna out of the road, established himself at Jalapa, a
lovely little town on the slope of the mountains, looking
down towards the sea, some ninety miles distant.   Scott
sent litters and a strong escort to move us up into that
delicious climate.   We took two days to make the trip.
All of the second day's march was a race between my
litter and that of a volunteer officer.   We frequently
passed each other and had some pleasant chat.   Two
of my three relays were short men, all of his were long-
legged fellows, so that he could pass my short men, and
I could close up when my tall ones came.   His were all
good-natured volunteers from Tennessee, I believe.   I
said, " I fear you'll beat me ; you have the legs of me."

" Ah, you can't say that," and the poor fellow held up
the stump of his amputated leg.   I had not known before
the nature of his wound.   I privately told my men I
would give them a gold piece or two, if they would get
me into Jalapa first, and so they did.   Mason, Derby,
and I were quartered in an elegant house, where, in a
short time, poor Mason left us.   I went to the Springs
without him.

After Captain Mason's death, from blood poison, the
doctors discovered symptoms of it in me ; but happily
they passed away, and I was permitted to walk about the
city and enjoy the beautiful scenery, the luxurious baths,
the fruits, and the flowers, and nowhere had I seen more
pretty faces than were found among the women of
Jalapa.

Every day I went to see my friend, Colonel Joe Johnston, still ill of his grievous wounds.   He was affectionately
tended by his nephew, Preston Johnston, who was dear to
him as a son.   He was a bright and joyous young fellow,
full of hope and courage, and worthy of the great race

from which he sprung. He fell a few months later while working his gun against Chapultepec. Only a few weeks before General Johnston died, .he spoke to me of the death of this bright young lad, who had been so dear to him. He said, "When Lee came to tell me of Preston's mortal wound, he wept as he took my hand in his."

CHAPTER IV

N my daily visits to Johnston I passed a residence with deep, iron-barred windows. As
I went feebly by one day on the arm of a
friend, Lieutenant Cappee, I heard a sweet,
sympathetic voice murmur, " Pobre teniente ! " (" Poor
lieutenant ! ") ; and, turning, I saw a beautiful young girl,
a perfect vision of female loveliness and sympathy. She
was a blonde, with exquisite features, blue eyes, and curl-
ing golden hair. I passed and repassed there daily, and,
after that, always received a smile and a bow from her,
but our acquaintance never progressed farther. I learned
from an American physician, who had lived twenty years
in Jalapa, that she was the favorite daughter of Santa
Anna, who, though he had never married her mother,
had richly endowed this child, whom any gentleman in
Jalapa would gladly have made his wife. If she be alive
now, she must be sixty years old, and not so attractive
and lovable as she was when I last saw her.

My recollections of Jalapa are the most agreeable of
any I retain of Mexico. We were elegantly lodged and
cared for, and I received much kind attention from the
general officers, who called to see how I was getting on

and to say kind things to me.   Amongst them was General
Benet Riley, who had risen from a private soldier to his
present rank for repeated acts of gallantry.   He was a
man of great stature and fine martial bearing, but entirely
free from any ostentation.   He had the proverbial humor
of his race, and, having lost a part of his palate, his voice
was quite remarkable and added zest to his narrations.
He told me that he had been a shoemaker before he
enlisted in the last war, and that after he acquired the
rank of General, a fellow came to him one day and proposed to get up a coat of arms for him.   He "damned
him" — told him to "Clear out; because, sir, I never
had a coat of any kind till I was twenty-one years old."

Generals Twiggs and Harney of the Dragoons, and
Sumner as well, were all men of great stature and fine
physique.   It was quite remarkable that our dragoons
should have included so many men of extraordinary
size and weight.   In other countries this arm of the
service seeks light and active men.   When Charley
May was married, his groomsmen were his handsome
brother Julian, Sacket, and several others, all six feet
and over.   An English officer, who was present at the
marriage, said to May, "I understand you gentlemen
are all of the light dragoons.   I would like very much
to see your heavies, don't you know."

General Harney, a native of Louisiana, was a very
remarkable man.   Of strong convictions and extraordinary physical powers, he made his presence felt by all
sorts of people.   While serving as Captain of Dragoons
in Florida, he and his company were surprised in their
camp one night by the Seminoles, and all but himself
were murdered as they slept.   They were under their
mosquito nets when the Indians crept upon them.   Two
Indians were appointed to kill each man, and took their

places on either side of him. At the signal, all struck
and killed, save those assigned to Harney, who, finding
themselves too far removed from the company's stores,
deserted their post, that they might be sure of securing
their share of the plunder. Harney, aroused by the
outcry, sprang from his bed, accoutred as he was, and
fled. He was six feet two inches tall and his legs were
well proportioned, and no Indian was able to run with
him. He took the route for the nearest station, some
forty miles distant, through the Everglades, where he
arrived safely. He immediately got together a considerable force, and succeeded in defeating and capturing a
majority of the band which had attacked him. He
told me he hanged all of his prisoners, because the
Indians had a great and superstitious horror of hanging;
for they believe that no man's soul will be received into
the happy hunting grounds that does not pass through the
throat, which is impossible when that route is closed by
a rope; it must seek another road of exit, and all such
souls are rejected at the gates of Paradise. He said a
fine moral effect was produced upon the Indians by this
method of execution.

Early in June I was ordered out of the country to
report when well enough for recruiting service. We went
down to Vera Cruz in a mule litter, the most delightful
of all the modes of travelling I have ever attempted. An
old paymaster, Major Hammond, and I had the litter to
ourselves. We had pillows and lay *vis-à-vis* on a great
mattress. Our light baggage was in with us, and our
books and lunch, and our pistols made us feel safe. We
reached Vera Cruz at midday of a broiling June morning. The yellow fever was raging, and as we passed the
churches, the whole interior seemed occupied by the cots
of the sick. It was a relief, indeed, to get aboard a com-

fortable steamer and breathe the fresh sea breeze. In those days wounded men were rarely seen in our country; therefore, I was an object of interest in Virginia, where I received more than my meed of praise, for I was again complimented in orders and promoted, and the good people of Fredericksburg gave me a beautiful sword, and the lovely Virginia girls carved my chicken for me at dinner and were good to me generally.

The Mexican War was a fine experience for our troops. It was actively pressed, by Taylor and Scott, from May, 1846, to September, 1847, and was a series of victories without check, until the capital was captured and peace was made. From first to last, we had 100,000 men enrolled in our armies, but at no time were over 14,000 engaged in any battle. After the siege of Vera Cruz, Scott's army was much reduced by the expiration of the terms of service of the volunteers, so that he entered the great valley of Mexico with only 9000 men, and received no reinforcements until after the city was taken. By the terms of the treaty of peace, we received from Mexico the vast territory embraced in California, New Mexico, and Arizona, and a full surrender of the disputed territory of Texas, which lies between the Rio Grande and the Nueces. In a spirit of fairness unusual in conquered nations, we gave Mexico $10,000,000 as conscience money. Some years ago when Mr. Hayes was preparing to invade Mexico, the newspapers of that country admonished us that we had to pay Mexico $10,000,000 to stop the last war, and we had better be careful how we again aroused their wrath.

So long a period had elapsed since our last war with Great Britain that a whole generation had passed away, and few of our people had ever seen a wounded soldier, and much interest and kindness were shown to such as reached home. While on my homeward journey, I was detained a day in Louisville. I was at the Galt House, and had occasion to go to a dry-goods store near by for a silk handkerchief for my broken arm. I was followed and overtaken by a kind-hearted Kentuckian, who with much interest asked, " Is it true that you were wounded at the battle of Cerro Gordo?"

" Yes."

" Well, sir, do you ever drink anything?"

" Yes."

" Well, come, please, and take a drink with me." He conducted me into the bar-room of the Galt House and said to the bar-keeper, " Let him have the best you have in the house, no matter what it costs." This was but a faint indication of what was in store for the wounded officers homeward bound.

A rumor of my death had preceded me, and there was great apprehension among my friends lest my mother should hear it before better tidings came. Fortunately, she was spared this pain, for I was her only child and she was a widow. The doctors thought the White Sulphur a fine place for a young soldier with a wounded arm, and there we went for the season and were very happy together.

One day a party of us were playing whist in the bachelors' quarters in Fredericksburg. It was very warm and we had laid aside our coats, when in walked a committee of the citizens of Fredericksburg appointed to present me a handsome sword. Captain William Lewis Herndon, afterwards the hero of the *Central America*, was of the party. The sword was presented with an appropriate speech, and finding myself quite unequal to reply to it, I invited the committee to be seated while I composed a note of appreciation and gratitude. This, with the assistance of Lewis Herndon, was happily accomplished.

There was no railroad to the White Sulphur in those days, but it was, nevertheless, the favorite summer resort with the best class of Southern people. The long journeys over bad roads made four-in-hand teams a necessity, as were baggage-wagons and a retinue of servants and saddle horses. Judges Brooke, Brokenborough, and Robinson, Jerome Bonaparte, of Baltimore, and his brilliant wife, General Wade Hampton, Colonel Singleton, of South Carolina, and Dick Taylor formed the usual coterie every summer. The Hamptons and Singletons built their own spacious summer residences. There were many complaints of the fare, which was considered poor and insufficient, but the dignified proprietor, Mr. Caldwell, consoled his guests by assuring them they paid nothing for their dinners, but only for the wonderful sulphur water which he had discovered about the beginning of the century. During the height of the season one day the crowded dining-room was appalled by a loud cry of " Murder ! " Steward and servants rushed to the victim, who assured them he could get nothing to eat and was dying of starvation. That young man was served well and promptly ever after.

Writing of the White Sulphur, I am reminded of the Ashby brothers. Turner Ashby was one of the most loved of the devoted men of Virginia. He came of a family famed for their expertness in all manly exercises. They were the famed horsemen of the country. Their birthplace and home was in that Piedmont region which had been noted for generations of bold riders, and which was for four years the battle-field of the great armies of the South and North. Turner Ashby and his younger brother Dick were the pride of all that hard-riding countryside. They were devoted to each other and beloved by all. Turner was not tall, but was powerful

and active.   He was swarthy as a Spaniard, with a gentle,
modest bearing and as brave a heart as ever beat.   Men
and women alike trusted and respected him.   One day
a great mountaineer, such as are commonly to be found
in that region of Virginia, came into the railroad store
under his charge and began to bully the youthful clerk,
charging him with being dishonest.   Turner Ashby had
come to the boy's aid when he heard the wanton insult,
and in a moment leaped across the counter, knocked
the bully down, and administered such a thrashing as he
had never before experienced.

The whole of the family connection were manly in
their traits, and the women shared their pride.   The
boys had a sister, Dora.   I well remember her as a
belle of the White Sulphur.   Tall, with flashing black
eyes and gleaming ivory teeth, she was superb, resembling greatly that charming young Virginia matron, who
is still remembered and loved in Richmond as Emma
Gray, now Emma White of Newport.   One day Dora
Ashby was driving with young Herndon, — youngest
brother of Captain William Lewis Herndon, — when
they heard closing up behind them a clamorous uproar
from a four-horse drag.   The young fellows in it were
all cousins or other kinsmen of Dora's, and demanded
that she should give them the road.   Their horses were
almost running; Herndon put his own to their fastest
trot and kept his place.   Finally the drag pushed them
hard and was about to pass them, when Herndon said,
"Miss Dora, shall I give way to the boys?"

"If you do," she replied, "I will never ride with you
again!"   So Herndon plied the whip, and the pursuers
and pursued came tearing through the woods, the
buggy still leading, and the beautiful girl radiant with
triumph.   But, alas, the young rascals suddenly came to

a cut-off, and, whirling into it, reached the hotel a length
or two ahead and won the race.

I used to meet the Ashbys in the summer at the White
Sulphur. Every summer there were tournaments, at
which good horses and good horsemen showed their
power and skill. The Ashbys and the Greenes of Rappahannock and Stafford, their near kin, were always
active in these. Turner Ashby used to ride his thoroughbred stallion at the ring without either saddle or bridle,
and carried it, too ! It was said the young fellows of Rappahannock would not let him enter for the prize unless
he rode without saddle and bridle. Dick Ashby was one
of the handsomest and most winsome men I ever knew.
He was six feet in his stockings, straight as an Indian,
handsome and gentle, and brave as the bravest. He
entered the war as a captain in the cavalry regiment his
brother Turner had raised and commanded. One of the
earliest engagements of this command was a scouting
affair upon the Potomac near Romney, in which Dick
Ashby was killed while acting with heroic courage. His
brother Turner came too late to rescue him, but found
him lying where he had fallen. His body had been
brutally mutilated. From that hour Turner Ashby was
a changed man. A stern sorrow became his controlling
motive, a deep purpose of vengeance possessed him, all
his buoyancy and bright hopes of fame gave place to
grief, and his brief and glorious career closed when
Jackson defeated Banks and Frémont upon the same
day. Ashby had dismounted his command, and sent
his beautiful white stallion to the rear, and drawing
his sword commanded the charge, when he fell dead, a
bullet piercing his noble heart. Such were the Ashbys in
peace and war! They were all gathered at my wedding;
they are all gone now. Their first cousin, brave Wil-

liam Greene, colonel of the Forty-seventh Virginia, fell at Gaines Mill, dying as his cousin Turner had died only a few months before.

I was in the full enjoyment of the daily association with the charming society gathered at the White Sulphur, when orders came for me to report for duty at West Point. I was much disappointed, for my stay there as a cadet had not been a happy one, and I had no desire to return to the Academy; but on arriving there I was persuaded to remain and try the new duties and relations of an officer and professor. There were already some nice young fellows there, and presently there came from Mexico, McClellan, Franklin, Ruddy Clarke, Baldy Smith, G. W. Smith, Kirby Smith, and several others who had washed off the starch of the Academy in two years of war service, and thenceforth we had a very agreeable sojourn together. Our duties were congenial, and we had an excellent mess. The arrival of an old comrade of the war, or of a foreign officer, was enough to start the champagne corks popping; but we were not convivial alone in our pleasures, for we had several clubs where we resumed our riding and fencing and Spanish. We had a Shakespeare club, and a chess club, of which Professor Agnell was president; but best of all was the Napoleon Club. Professor Mahan was president of this, and gave out the Napoleon campaigns to be discussed by each member. Six weeks' time was allowed to prepare the paper. We had ample authorities, both French and English, at our disposal in the library, and worked diligently on our papers. The campaign of Waterloo, by Lieutenant B. S. Alexander, was considered one of the best discussions ever made of that notable defeat of Bonaparte. The campaign of Russia, by G. W. Smith, and of Wagram, by McClellan, showed marked ability. I believe something of this sort has been introduced into the course of study for the cadets.

In this way we spent four years very profitably and happily at the Academy. Remembering how keenly I had felt the restrictions and surveillance of cadet life, I determined to spare those who fell under my charge as much as possible. One night while officer in charge, I came upon a young cadet asleep upon his post. He had leaned his musket against the stair rail, and was fast asleep. I knew it meant severe punishment for him, and he was such a delicate-looking lad my sympathies were aroused, so I wakened him. He was greatly alarmed. I said to him: "If I report this, you will probably be sent away from here in disgrace, your family will be mortified, and you will be seriously injured by it. If you will promise me never to allow it to happen again, I will take no further notice of it." Some years ago a well-known member of Congress invited me to dine with him, and at the table told of this experience with me at West Point. I had often vainly tried to recall the boy and his history, and now for the first time learned both.

Professor Dennis Mahan was one of the ablest of the faculty at West Point. He was a native of Norfolk, Virginia, and had not received a classical education. He told me he was so impressed by the disadvantage of not having studied Latin and Greek, that he had acquired them by hard work after he became a professor at West Point. His was considered a hard nature by the cadets, and he was given to saying sarcastic things in the section room; but I had reason to observe that he was grateful for benefits bestowed upon him, and capable of much real kindness. On one occasion, when a cadet, he made me the victim of his sarcasm. While reciting upon the construction of fortifications, he asked me, "Mr. Maury, what is the height of the breast-height slope?"

"Five feet, sir," I replied.

With that cold manner with which he used to express his contempt for an ignorant cadet, he said, "If it were five feet, Mr. Maury, you could not shoot over it!" As I was only five feet three inches, at that time, this personal allusion was received with a suppressed giggle by my classmates, and for a long time I remembered it against him. Years afterward, he made up for it one night in the Napoleon Club, of which, as I have said, he was president. He came cordially up to me after I had finished reading my paper on the Italian campaign of 1796, grasped my hand with real pleasure, and said: "I congratulate you, Maury. You have discussed your subject in the very spirit of that Italian campaign." I could name many other things about him highly creditable to his warm and generous heart. Some time after the Civil War, at the age of seventy-five years, he lost his life by falling from a steamboat on the Hudson River.

As I recall these memories of my long life, it seems to me people were always glad when I did anything clever, with a sort of surprised gladness, as if they had never thought I could do it. To tell the truth, I was always surprised myself, and delighted in receiving praise, as I winced under censure and that carping criticism which is the refuge and habit of weak and ignorant natures. Fault-finding is the bane of discipline, while just praise is the very life and object of high endeavor. A true soldier strives and lives to win it. A martinet is an unhappy, worthless creature, wretched and mischievous, too. The only consolation is that he is more unhappy than he makes other people.

While the hills and swamps about West Point were fairly good shooting-ground for ruffled grouse (pheasants in Virginia, partridges in New York and Pennsylvania) and woodcock, all of the little mountain streams thereabouts had trout in them. One day, Fitz John Porter, McClellan, and I hired a boat to go a-fishing for perch on the Hudson. We lay at the mouth of a creek which emptied into the river a little more than a mile below the Point. Finding no perch, I sauntered up the creek, searching for trout. In a little over an hour I returned to my still unsuccessful companions with a good creel full of trout; there were over thirty in all, and several were over a foot long. A great sportsman named Warren, brother of General Warren, told me he took over a hundred out of that little stream one day. I met him once coming out of a woodcock swamp with thirty birds in his bag. He advised me not to go in, as he had bagged them all; but having nowhere else to go, I went in, and got eleven more. It was summer, and the birds were breeding. I saw a group of five, not yet feathered. The law should protect the summer birds.

Every winter we had several weeks of good sleighing. One day a party of us drove up to Newburg. While resting our horses there, and sipping something seasonable, one of us read aloud a funny trick of the famous wizard, Herr Alexander, and we unanimously resolved to play it off on Ruddy Clarke, who was always as ready to be the victim of a sell as we were to practise it upon him. At that time, Franklin and Ruddy Clarke occupied a tower room in the new barracks, with a chamber behind it, and it was our habit to adjourn over there for social enjoyment. Besides Ruddy and Franklin, were usually John M. Jones, Pull Hawes, Frank Clarke and Mac and I. So, after dinner, on our return from Newburg,

I told Ruddy that I would bet him a bottle of champagne that he might go into the other room, shut the door, and assume any position he chose, and I would tell, from our room, what his position was. After much doubting and questioning, he finally went into the darkened room, struck an attitude, and called out, " What position am I in?"

I replied, "In the position of a great ass." He looked it when he came out, amidst our laughter, into the light. We induced him, by adroit investigation, to describe to us his exact attitude. It was truly absurd for a professor.

We had a very jovial and humorous set of young officers stationed at the Academy for several years after the Mexican War, and great kindness of feeling prevailed. We played whist, dime points, and faro, and brag at the same moderate rate. It was noted that at faro we almost invariably broke the bank. One winter I was laid up for many weeks by an injury to my leg, received while riding, and my room, during all that time, was the gathering place after dinner. The card table was drawn up to my bed, and I played my hand till tired and sleepy. One night we were playing brag, and I becoming tired and drowsy, little Frank Clarke said he would play my hand for me while I slept. When I awoke, next morning, I found the greatest amount I had ever won at cards under my pillow. I reflected that it was a demoralizing amusement; that avarice, the basest of human passions, was its moving impulse; that often, at the card table, I observed some show of feeling that left an unpleasant remembrance against a comrade, and that none of us could afford to win or lose even a few dollars; so I ceased all play for money, and have been glad of it ever since.

During my stay at West Point as an instructor, Baldy Smith and I were room-mates, and occupied a cottage overlooking Kosciusko's Gardens. We were popular as "Subs," and our pupils used to manifest their appreciation of our efforts in their behalf by paying us long and frequent visits. Our sensations during these well-meant and oft-repeated calls may be best described in the language of a witty Frenchman who was invited to make a cruise on a man-of-war, and afterwards wrote of his experiences there. He said: "Sometimes I would dine with the captain in his cabin, sometimes with lieutenants in the wardroom, and sometimes with midshipmen in the steerage; and my recollections of the conversations of those midshipmen make my blood run cold to this day!"

No one seemed to have discovered the opportunities for good shooting, until I came along with my setters and pointers. These dogs were a great comfort to me and to my pupils; for they always accompanied me on my inspections, going before me, and giving due notice of my approach, and they were cherished accordingly by the cadets.

Captain Alden, Robert Coleman, Fitz John Porter, and I made several shooting excursions over the mountains into Orange County, where the Warwick Woodlands, famed by Frank Forrester, gave us fine sport. We took up our quarters with a plain farmer upon the turnpike, named Dickerman, who made us comfortable. He had a very handsome and cultivated daughter, who was not only the maid of all work, but who in the evenings, after our day's hunt was over, would entertain us in the parlor. She was an excellent musician, and an expert in the art of greasing and polishing our hunting-boots after a hard day's tramp through the mud.

Sometimes Porter and I would ride over to the home of Mr. Peter Townsend, and spend the night, returning next morning in time for our day's work. Mr. Townsend was a most agreeable country gentleman of New York, and had a vast establishment in Orange County. His wife and three daughters made up his household, and a charming family it was. Mrs. Townsend was very dignified and attractive, and her daughters were all bright, cordial, and handsome, and were great favorites with the young officers at West Point. One of them married General Meagher, the gallant commander of the most distinguished Federal brigade in the battle of Fredericksburg, that Irish brigade which charged, and charged again, Lee's line at Marye's Hill, until eye-witnesses have told me that they could walk along its whole front, and step every step upon the bodies of its dead. After their final repulse, a young soldier named Kirkland, a private in a South Carolina regiment, having obtained permission of his colonel, climbed over the famous stone wall, and, under heavy fire, went out upon the field, bearing canteens of water to the wounded, to all of which he ministered. Unhappily for his country, he did not survive the war ; we cannot afford to lose the breed of such men. Another of Mr. Townsend's daughters married General Barlow of New York, a warm personal friend of General Dick Taylor, and a well-known gentleman of New York. I was the recipient of much graceful hospitality from Mr. Townsend's charming household, and time has not dimmed my remembrance of the many delightful hours for which I was their debtor.

CHAPTER V

The Rifles ordered to Oregon — Captain Stuart's Tragic Fate — Reminiscences of McClellan — His Capacity and Character illustrated — His Comments upon Foreign Campaigns — His Popularity with his Troops — A Criticism of the Crimean War — McClellan and Grant contrasted — Generals Franklin, Hancock, and Meade — Young Jerome Bonaparte

MONG my friends of those far-away days was Captain Stuart, who was the son of an able editor of the Charleston *Mercury*, and was a great-nephew of Sir John Stuart, who won the battle of Maida and who at his death was the nearest survivor of the royal family of Stuart. He served with me in the Mounted Rifles, and was one of the most interesting characters I have ever known. Handsome, and gentle as a woman, no soldier of our army surpassed him in courage and daring, and after two years of active service the commanding general said in his report of the last battle of the Mexican War, "Lieutenant Stuart of the Rifles, leaping the ditch, was the first American to enter the city of Mexico."

When the Mexican War was ended, and after I was ordered to West Point, our regiment made ready for service in Oregon, marched across the great plains, and occupied for the ensuing four years that wild and unknown region where there were then only a few venturesome people of the American and British fur-trading companies. At the end of its term of service, the Rifles

were destined for the frontier of Texas, while the First
Dragoons and other troops took their place in Oregon.
The officers and non-commissioned officers were sent by
sea back to the States, while our horses and the private
soldiers, of whom not many remained, were transferred
to the dragoons. Captain Phil Kearney, afterwards General Phil Kearney, who fell in the disastrous defeat of
General Pope at Manassas, was selected to conduct the
transfer of our horses, etc., and to aid him in this work
he chose Captain John G. Walker and James Stuart. If
there was any officer in our regiment equal to Stuart in
conduct, it was Walker, and the two were close friends.

This interesting march seemed an indulgence and a trip
of pleasure. The weather was fine, there seemed nothing likely to disturb them on the route, and their service
being ended when California was reached, they, Stuart
and Walker together, would return to their homes in the
States, where Jamie hoped to find the lady of his love
awaiting him. Their road to California lay through
the country of the Rogue River Indians, but they were
not known to be hostile, and every prospect seemed
pleasant to these two comrades. The worst of their
journey was over, when one night Walker was aroused
by Stuart, who shared his tent. It was after midnight,
and Stuart said he had not been able to sleep at all because of a conviction that his death was at hand. He
could not rid himself of the feeling, and he wished
Walker to see to it that the wishes he now desired to
impart would be carried out.

In vain Walker tried first to laugh away all this as a
sort of nightmare. Stuart agreed that it might be so,
but he urged his friend to listen and to promise him to
be the executor of his last request, to which Walker at
last assented, little suspecting the catastrophe hanging

over them. The next day's march justified Stuart's anxieties; for they found that the Rogue River Indians had begun hostilities, and came upon the trail of a large Indian war party, and preparations were immediately made to follow it and punish the hostiles. At their breakfast next morning, Stuart told of a vivid dream which had troubled him, — how an Indian warrior appeared at the door of the tent, drew his bow upon Walker first, and then changing his aim to Stuart, shot him through the body.

Kearney divided his command for the march and fight that day into two bodies, sending Stuart with his party down the river on the opposite side, where they came up with the enemy, charged, and scattered them. The chief seemed to surrender to Stuart, who ordered him to drop his bow, and to emphasize the order tapped him upon his head. Instantly the chief drove an arrow through Stuart's body. He lived a few hours in great agony; his grave was made under a tree at the forks of the road, and carefully marked.

· George B. McClellan, to whose cadet days I have already briefly referred, came to West Point at the age of fifteen years and seven months. He bore every evidence of gentle nature and high culture, and his countenance was as charming as his demeanor was modest and winning. His father, the celebrated Dr. McClellan, and his elder brother, Dr. John McClellan, were two of the ablest and best-educated men of their day, and he had been reared in their presence. I remember that it was about the middle of June, 1842, when we first met in the section room at West Point. The class was at first arranged according to alphabetical order, and our initial letters placed us for a brief space side by side. For a very brief space it was, for he pushed at

once to the head, while I plodded along in the middle
— that easiest and safest of positions — through all the
long four years of my cadetship. At the end, Mac went
into the Engineer Corps, and I, as I have said, into the
Rifles. After the Mexican War, while we were both at
West Point as instructors, we were, of course, daily
associated together for several years, and a happy association it was. A brighter, kindlier, more genial gentleman did not live than he. Sharing freely in all the
convivial hospitality of the mess, he was a constant
student of his profession. Having been instructed in
the Classics and in French before he came to the Academy, he learned Spanish and German there, and before
he was sent to Europe to study and report upon the
cavalry service of the great military powers of the world,
he had acquired sufficient knowledge of the Russian lan
guage to enable him to make a satisfactory and valuable
report. The excellent saddles and horse equipage ever
since used in our service were introduced by him from
the Cossacks. He was an excellent horseman, and one
of our most athletic and best swordsmen. We rode
and fenced together almost daily. His father gave him
a handsome thoroughbred mare, and I had brought from
Virginia a very fleet race mare. So long as my arm was
in splints, she ran away with me whenever I rode her.
Nobody else would ride her; but she threw me only
twice in the four years, once by carrying me under a
limb which swept me off over her tail, and again when
she reared and fell over on me, which didn't hurt me,
while it gave great amusement to the crowded company
of passengers on the steamer *New World*, before whom
I had tried to "show off" as I galloped down to the
wharf on my beautiful thoroughbred mare, arrayed in my
best suit of cavalry clothes.

Mac and Mac's mare had no such foolishness about them. One bright, but bitter cold Christmas Day, he and I decided to escape the wassail of the Academy by riding over the mountains to Newburg. A heavy snow covered the ground, and the road was so slippery we had to lead our horses part of the way. About 11 A.M. we reached a little country church where Christmas services were being held. A number of handsome sleighs about the door bespoke a congregation of the gentlefolks of the county, and we decided to enter and join in the service. Over our uniforms we wore the heavy blue overcoats of the cavalry soldier. There were but few people in the church, so we modestly took our places in one of the many empty pews upon a side aisle. The service was progressing when the sexton, evidently indignant that private soldiers should intrude themselves into such a company as his congregation, marched us out of our position and back into one of the pauper pews of the church. We noticed that the rector paused on seeing this blunder on the part of his subordinate, and afterwards we were told how annoyed he had been by it. To us it was only a funny incident of a cold tramp.

We got back just at dusk, as the mess were sitting down to a rich Christmas dinner. We had seen nothing to eat or drink, save a glass of something hot at Newburg. Had that aristocratic congregation known it was the future general of the Army of the Potomac who was with them in their Christmas service, we might not have been so hungry and thirsty when we opened the mess-room door and called, "Newel, give us some champagne." Old George Thomas was then president of the mess, and a more genial and kindly president we never had. Everybody loved him, and he was at that time

a Virginian before everything else. Franklin and
Ruddy Clarke, Kirby Smith, G. W. Smith, Neighbor
Jones, John M. Jones, W. P. de Janou, and a score of
others were round that Christmas board, and joined in
the burst of welcome as we broke in. I well remember
that it was one of our jolliest, as it was our last, Christmas together; for before the year rolled around, we were
scattered to our distant posts, never to meet again.

McClellan had the happiest faculty of acquiring
knowledge I have ever known, and unlike most men
who store up learning, he knew well how to use it when
the occasion came. He would often sit late with a
jovial party, and then go to study while we went to bed,
and be up in the morning, bright as the brightest. His
report of his observations in his inspections of the military establishments of Europe was of great value. He
was present with the allied armies in the Crimea, and
had the best opportunities of observing the relative
position of the troops and their generals. He considered Omar Pasha the ablest of all those generals. It is
well known that when the allies arrived on the field,
Omar had already driven every Russian across the Dan-
ube, and left nothing for the allies to do. But in a
council of war of the commanding generals, it was resolved that the eyes of Europe were upon them; that it
would never do to let that infidel dog have all the
credit; and that they must do something to eclipse the
glories of the Turk. They resolved upon the invasion
and occupation of the Crimea. We all remember how
sad and unfortunate was the conduct of the affair,—
how England, especially, showed so little aptitude for
field operations against well-commanded and well-
organized European troops, that she lost her prestige;
and it was said the Emperor Napoleon had brought her

into that business, in order that her inferiority as a war power might be demonstrated before the world.

Lord Raglan sailed for the Crimea with about twenty-six thousand troops. The debarkation of his army upon the Crimean coast occupied six days; and then he was several days' march from Sebastopol, without any transportation for his supplies or one dollar of current money. McClellan had been with Scott when he landed fourteen thousand Americans within three miles of Vera Cruz in six hours, invested that city by the morning of the second day, and captured it in two weeks' time. McClellan could only find in the splendid constancy of the British troops in the battle of Inkerman a justification of their claim to superiority. In marking out the lines of attack upon Sebastopol, the French took to themselves the right of the line, which, McClellan observed, was much more difficult to entrench than the left of the line, which the English occupied. Yet, upon the signal for assault, when the French, with MacMahon at their head, with his cap upon his sword, swarmed over the Russian defences, the English, having several hundred yards of open ground to pass before reaching the Redan, were repulsed with heavy loss, until the French achieved such a position as enabled them to break the Russian defence and let their allies into the works. The capture of the city and works was but a small part of what lay before the allied army. The defences of the north side seemed unassailable. McClellan believed that the death of Nicholas enabled his son, Alexander, to make peace when the allies had made their last effort, and thus the English army, under brave Sir Colin Campbell, was enabled to reach India in time to save that empire. The Sepoy revolt is now believed to have been the result of Russian machination. McClellan thought so then.

He was in the Crimea when the charge of the Light Brigade took place. So also was Colonel Jerome Bonaparte. He was captain of cavalry and aide-de-camp to General Meurice, who commanded the French cavalry upon that field. From McClellan, from Bonaparte, and from the contemporaneous newspaper reports, we learned of that affair, as follows. A short time before this date, the allied cavalry was drawn up in column, probably of squadrons, watching a heavy demonstration of Cossack cavalry. The British Heavy Brigade, under the command of General Scarlet, was in front of the column; next came the Light Brigade, Lord Cardigan; and Lord Lucan commanded the whole British division. The French cavalry, also in column of attack, was in rear of the British when the Cossacks charged the infantry line, a regiment of Scottish Highlanders, part of Sir Colin Campbell's command. The Highlanders poured a heavy fire from their line of battle upon the Cossacks, which staggered and confused them. At the same instant Lord Lucan ordered General Scarlet to "Charge those Cossacks with the Heavies," which was promptly and handsomely done, and the Russians were driven away. Lord Lucan was an impetuous commander, and in his hot courage joined in the charge and sword play of the "Heavies," leaving his Light Brigade standing without orders. Cardigan felt he could not take the responsibility of moving without orders, and because the Light Brigade did not move, the French cavalry behind it could not, therefore the Cossacks got off with only the punishment administered by the "Heavies." There was much chaffing of the Light Brigade by their comrades, because of this incident. On Lord Raglan's staff was a clever, ambitious cavalry major, Nolan, who was the apostle of the power of light cavalry. He had written a very clever book we young officers used to enjoy, which proved that light cavalry could deal with any sort of troops. He was greatly grieved by this lost opportunity. A short time after, Lord Raglan ordered an attack by all the British troops, and gave Major Nolan the paragraph from the order, saying, "The Light Brigade will charge and recapture the English guns." Some time before, the Russians had captured an English battery which was at this time parked with some twenty other field-pieces in front of where Lord Lucan's cavalry was drawn up. The story goes that Nolan galloped off delighted, all too hastily, and gave the order to Lord Lucan, who, looking at the array of cannon about a mile away, exclaimed, "Charge what?"

"That," Nolan replied, adding bitterly, "Shall I show your lordship the way?" as he took his place at the head of the squadron. Lord Lucan, swearing no man but himself should lead his command, dashed past him and ordered the charge to be sounded, and away went the seven hundred fine British horses over the plain at a smashing gallop. The Russian batteries poured a heavy fire into them, and the Russian cavalry and infantry picked up such of them as got through the guns. General Meurice exclaimed: "That is magnificent, but that is not war! Go, Bonaparte, ask Lord Lucan what it means, and how I can help him."

At the same time several French squadrons were deployed, which drove back the pursuing Russians and covered the retreating English. Bonaparte found Lord Lucan in a great rage. "Means, sir!" he said. "It means that my brigade is destroyed, my son is killed, my nephew is killed"; and as some bearers carried Major Nolan's body by, he added, "And it is well for that poor young man he lies there, for he would have a heavy reckoning with me for this day's work. But tell him, by God, sir, I have the written order for it! Here's the written order for it."

And so ended this famous charge, the result of a blunder. Fifty-two men and six officers were killed, and the usual proportion wounded out of about seven hundred.

While McClellan's sympathies were with the Southern States, in which were his kindred and warmest friends, he never wavered in his natural allegiance to Pennsylvania. Several years before the outbreak of the war, and soon after his return from the Crimea, he resigned his captaincy in the army to accept the presidency of the Mississippi Central Railroad, and in the winter of 1860–61 wrote me, then in Santa Fé, that while he knew the South was being wronged, and feared that war was inevitable, he would fight, if fight he must, for Pennsylvania, his native State. I could not blame him, for I, too, felt my paramount allegiance to Virginia. I confess I was surprised when, on my anxious and perilous journey home, I was met upon the plains by the tidings of McClellan's victory in West Virginia, and his proclamation terming us "Rebels." But he was a high-toned, humane gentleman, and no words or acts of cruelty were ever attributed to him. After the war, we soon resumed our friendly relations, which were only terminated by his untimely death.

McClellan was no politician. He was a gentleman and a soldier of a very high order. Every feeling and instinct of his nature was averse to the character and war policy of the administration. Lincoln and Stanton required that the army should always be interposed between them and the Confederate capital. McClellan in vain pointed out to them that to capture Richmond, the army should operate from below it. Grant, three years later, urged the same base of operations, but Mr. Stanton replied that he must attack from the Washington side. Grant said, "If I do, I shall lose one hundred thousand men." Stanton assured him he should have them to lose. And now we know that he did lose over eighty thousand before he placed his army where he ultimately took Richmond.

McClellan possessed in a remarkable degree the confidence and love of his troops. This was manifested in an extraordinary manner when he came to General Pope's routed army; it was in utter disorder. Generals Pope, McDowell, and the mob of defeated soldiers, were all crowding along the road to Alexandria, when "Little Mac" appeared. At once a change came over the soldiers. They knew Pope was no general, and they had more confidence in "Little Mac" than in any man alive. His assumption of command spread hope and joy throughout their ranks, which at once assumed shape and order, and in a few days McClellan had the Army of the Potomac in hand, and was marching it with precision and order to hinder Lee's invasion of Pennsylvania. The army of northern Virginia encountered and defeated them, destroying three corps, and crossed the Potomac with all the rich stores captured in Pennsylvania, and moved on to new fields of glory. But the Capital was saved, and McClellan had saved it, and was then deposed. The army and the people followed him with their confidence and love. He ran for the Presidency upon a platform that was pacific and just, and would have spared our country the cruelty of Andrew Johnson's reconstruction.

It is difficult to compare McClellan with Grant; both men were kindly in nature, both were brave. While

McClellan was personally as brave as Grant, and of a higher spirit, he seemed to lack that inflexible decision of opinion and purpose which bore Grant to his great fortune. While McClellan would be, and was, eminent amongst the highest characters and in the greatest affairs of peace or war, Grant seemed suited only to such a terrible occasion as brought him from his tannery into fame. But for the war, he would possibly have pursued to the end of his life his early calling.

Pennsylvania has in every war furnished many able soldiers to our armies, and it has been my good fortune to know some of them well, and to retain their friendship until this day. General William B. Franklin is of the highest class of Pennsylvania gentlemen. Like McClellan and Hancock, he was well born and educated, and combined the versatile capacity and attainments of the former with the sturdy character of the latter. We were both stationed at West Point as instructors, and our acquaintance ripened into a friendship which in its warmth and congeniality has often reminded me of that which united Warrington and Pendennis. It has survived through all the chances and changes of a lifetime. Franklin's father was an able clerk of the House of Representatives, and by a happy lot he married the daughter of Matthew St. Clair Clarke, who succeeded his father in office, holding the position for many years. Such an illustration of congenial marriage as theirs is rarely seen. All these years they have together trod their journey, joying and giving joy to the same friends, having the same memories and the same firm faith in their life to come.

Hancock, a native of Pennsylvania, and Meade, who came of a Pennsylvania family, but was born in Spain, were high-toned gentlemen and great commanders. In fact, no State in the Union has produced so many great soldiers as Pennsylvania, save Virginia. And there are so many points of resemblance, and so many identities of soil, climate, character, and history between Virginia and Pennsylvania, that it seems as if we ought never to have been a divided people or separate communities. In times long gone we co-operated in our common defence. When Braddock marched to free Pennsylvania from a cruel enemy, Washington was the pioneer of his army through the wilderness, while Ben Franklin was its purveyor. A generation later, when that scheme of civil liberty which blesses all mankind to-day was announced, it was cradled in Pennsylvania, and Pennsylvanians died in Virginia, and Virginians in Pennsylvania, to establish it. The same climate blesses our whole territory, and the waters which fertilize the fields of Pennsylvania and bear her cereals to the sea flow through Virginia, too. And those blue mountains which beautify and have built up the prosperity of the one State, sweep down through the other as well. In both of these States no slavery can ever exist again, and all conditions impel them as one great people to co-operate for the common good of our common country.

Among those whom I found when I returned to West Point after the Mexican War, was young Jerome Bonaparte. He is a grandson of King Jerome who, when in Baltimore as a lieutenant in the French navy, married the beautiful Miss Patterson, a reigning belle of that city. The Emperor Napoleon disapproved of his brother's marriage to one not of royal rank. Colonel Bonaparte's father, Mr. Jerome Bonaparte, for many years a distinguished member of society in Baltimore, was the only issue of the first marriage of King Jerome.

In 1854, Colonel Bonaparte was graduated at West

Point, and entered C Troop of the Mounted Rifles, then serving at Fort Inge, Texas. After one or two years of frontier service, the Emperor Napoleon III. summoned him to France. He served in Algiers, in the Italian campaign, through the Crimean War, and in the war between France and Germany. On his return from the Crimea he came to Carlisle Barracks and paid us a visit; he had seen his first service under me in the Rifles. It was then that he gave me many interesting details of the military operations there which came under his personal observation, and to which I have briefly alluded. Colonel Bonaparte's commanding appearance, the grace and gentleness of his demeanor, and his fine intelligence win for him the admiration of all who know him. He was held in high esteem by Louis Napoleon and his beautiful and unfortunate Empress.

CHAPTER VI

General Stonewall Jackson — His Remarkable Character — Married at "Cleveland" to the Eldest Daughter of Mr. Wiley Roy Mason — Anecdotes of General Burnside — On the Texas Frontier with the Rifles — The Life at Fort Inge — Mrs. Maury's Journey to the Post — Promoted and transferred — Sent Home on Sick Leave

NE day while at West Point we were surprised by a visit from young Major Stonewall Jackson, who had been serving since the war with an artillery company on duty in New York harbor. At that time he was convinced that one of his legs was bigger than the other, and that one of his arms was likewise unduly heavy. He had acquired the habit of raising the heavy arm straight up so that, as he said, the blood would run back into his body and lighten it. I believe he never after relinquished this peculiar practice, even upon the battle-field. He told us he had procured a year's furlough to try a professorship which had been offered him at the Virginia Military Institute. He remained there until the outbreak of the war between the States brought him before the world as the great Christian soldier of his time.

His was the most remarkable character I have ever known. Cold and impassive of aspect, he was tenderly affectionate and full of fire. Filled with conscientious scruples, he was at times cruelly unjust. His arrests of Hill, Winder, and General Richard Garnett, three of the noblest officers in our service, were inexcusable, espe-

cially that of Garnett, whom he arrested for not charging
Shields' victorious army with the bayonet when his ammunition failed! Jackson permitted him to remain in
this painful position for many months, and when Garnett
finally succeeded in obtaining a trial before a court-mar-
tial, he was acquitted upon Jackson's own testimony!
The court yielded to Garnett's insistence that his treatment had been so unjustifiable as to make it only right
that he should place on record the testimony for the defence. Poor Garnett! He fell in the front of his brigade
at Gettysburg, loved and mourned by all who knew him.

The arrest of General Charles Winder was another act
of unreasoning harshness, which General Dick Taylor,
who had great influence with Jackson, induced him to
revoke. Twice he arrested that noble soldier, A. P.
Hill, whose name was the last upon his own lips and
those of Lee. General Lee was deeply pained by this
inharmony between two of his ablest officers, and summoned them before him with a view of causing a recon-
ciliation. After hearing their several statements, Lee,
walking gravely to and fro, said, " He who has been the
most aggrieved can be the most magnanimous and make
the first overtures of peace." This wise verdict forever
settled their differences. Jackson unhappily died at
Chancellorsville in the zenith of his great fame, and in
the grandest victory of Lee's army. Hill, more fortunate, fell by the last hostile shot at Petersburg, and both
were spared the misery of the surrender and its cruel
consequences. Hill's was a very gentle, affectionate
nature, full of courage and of high ambition. The noble
monument, recently unveiled in Richmond, designed by
the Virginia artist, Shepherd, is the perfect presentment
of this distinguished soldier.

Just before going to the Mexican War, I went with my

mother and sister to the Warrenton Springs, then a favorite resort of the tide-water Virginians. The day after our arrival there, as I was descending the steps, I met a party of young ladies coming up. As they reached the top, one of them missed the step and fell. I assisted her to rise, and we were introduced; she was Miss Nannie Mason, and from that day we became very warm friends. The exigencies of the service demanded my departure from the springs after some weeks of delightful association, and we only met briefly and casually until time and opportunity favored me, and we discovered we had lost much happiness.

Soon after the execution of King Charles, many of his adherents came to this Virginia, among them two brothers, John and George Mason. The great George Mason, the author of the Bill of Rights, was descended from one of these brothers, and Judge John Y. Mason, once our Minister to France, was descended from the other. My wife's father, Mr. Wiley Roy Mason, was remotely akin to the judge, and they were close friends, and in their day no higher or more congenial gentlemen than these two were to be found in all our land. Mr. Roy Mason had gone into King George County with his young wife, to seek his fortune. He was without property or money in 1830, and had built up the largest law practice in all that region, and acquired real estate which yielded him annually more than his practice. Such was the confidence in his integrity and ability, that it was said of him that he had done away with litigation in the court of King George County, because when people had a disagreement about rights of property, they went to Roy Mason's office and left the case for him to decide, with entire confidence in the uprightness of the decision, and escaped big fees and court charges.

Mr. Mason kept open house at "Cleveland," his country home, and my marriage with his eldest daughter was made the occasion of a generous hospitality which was long remembered in the county.   There were eight bridesmaids and groomsmen, and I asked McClellan and Franklin to be of the number, but distant service prevented them from coming, and Burnside and Reno, of the Ordnance, took their places.   Neighbor Jones and Seth Barton came to represent the army, and many score of gentlemen, schoolmates, and friends, — Turner Ashby and his noble brother Dick, and many another destined soon to fall in defence of our homes.   My wife had three sisters and three first cousins, who followed her example, and married army officers.   They were all remarkably handsome and attractive girls, and General Sherman finally predicted, "Those Mason girls will break up the army."

Burnside was the life of many a jovial incident of that long-remembered wedding.   The festivities lasted a week, and he had never before enjoyed an occasion so entirely to his taste.   He remembered in the day of his power the kindness he had received at "Cleveland," and when Mr. Stanton sent an order for the arrest of Mr. Mason, Judge Lomax, Colonel Washington, Dr. Stuart, Mr. Thomas Barton, and other old and prominent gentlemen of the Northern Neck, Burnside forbore to execute it, and he gave Mrs. Mason a safeguard for her home and property, which were never molested until after his removal from the command of the army and district.   Then a regiment under the command of Sir Percy Wyndham, an Englishman, " looted " " Cleveland," carried off a great store of choice old wines and brandy, the finest in the county, many household and personal effects and private letters, and my family Bible.   When Mr. Mason returned from

Fredericksburg that day, he found his house had been thus invaded, and went in person to see the colonel, who caused the return of the Bible. But of his wines, etc., he never saw more, except about a quart of his Tinto Madeira, which one of his old servants brought him when he came home wet and chilled that night. It had been poured into her cabin pail by a good-natured soldier, who had no turn for such thin tipple after the choice old brandy.

About 1856, Burnside was stationed at Tucalote, a Mexican village some twenty miles west of Fort Union. The Apache Indians were not friendly, and on the occasion of some grievance came into the village with insolent and threatening deportment, fully armed, and ready for a fight. At this time Burnside's battery had no rifles or revolvers, — only the artillery sabre, and there were but forty men, all told, for duty. These he marched to where the Indians were daring an attack. After some inconclusive discussion, the Indians ended all further talk by a discharge of arrows. Burnside charged them at once, broke and scattered them, and chased them for some miles over the open prairie towards cover. His horses enabled his party to overtake the flying Indians, but the blows of the dull sabres glanced from their shining skulls almost harmlessly. He then gave point with fine effect, so that some twenty of the hostiles were killed before they reached the shelter of the timber. Soon after this he resigned and joined McClellan in his railroad business, until the war between the States brought them both again into service.

After the war, Burnside remembered the good people he had met and known in Virginia, and, learning that a young lady, who was one of the bridesmaids at my wedding, had been turned out of her office as a clerk in one of the departments, he left the White Sulphur Springs and posted to Washington, and had her reinstated. He was an excellent officer, but he knew his measure and felt his unfitness to supersede McClellan, whom he had long and justly looked upon as his superior. He protested against the change of commanders, made as it was after McClellan's most signal service.

At the end of my furlough, I joined my Company H of the Rifles at Fort Inge, on the Leona River, a beautiful little stream which gushes out of a deep, bright pool, well stocked with fine, black bass. There were no settlements between us and the Rio Grande, ninety miles away, and only occasional bands of marauding Indians passed along there. These were mostly Lipans, who made frequent incursions into the country about San Antonio and the lower Rio Grande. For several years the Rifles were occupied in scouting for these depredators, and occasionally a band was caught and scattered. When hard pressed, they would separate and make their way singly across the Rio Grande into Mexico, where they were safe from our pursuit. These Indians had their resting-places at Fort Worth, upon the upper Brazos, near where the Second Dragoons were stationed, and they always kept the peace with them. Evidently they regarded us as a separate tribe, for whenever they were about to make a raid down our way, they would tell the dragoons that they had " war with the Rifles " and gravely bid them " Good by."

In those days the quarters for officers and troops, upon the frontier, were only such as the soldiers could construct of the materials at hand. At Fort Inge they were made of poles set in trenches close together, the many open chinks being daubed with mud. The roofs were thatched, and the floors were of coarse boards sawed by hand. All was as unsightly as it was comfortless. Fortunately, the climate was so mild that we had no occasion for fires except for cooking. Game of every sort abounded all about us. Deer, wild turkeys, ducks, partridges, were to be had for the seeking. San Antonio, ninety-eight miles to the eastward, was our nearest town; from thence our mail came by courier once a week.

Colonel George Crittenden, then commanding Fort Inge, one day killed ten deer in nine shots. He used a little, small-bore rifle, muzzle-loader, of course. He was a wonderful fisherman, and spent day after day floating along the Leona, catching black bass. One day he took a bass which weighed eight pounds. He said he had often seen one which weighed ten pounds, but never could catch him. When at guard-mounting the orderly would daily report to him, his formula was, " Do you know how to catch minnows? "

" Yes, Colonel."

"Then take my bucket, go to the creek, and catch some." When he had accomplished this duty, the colonel would say, " You may go to your quarters."

He had early gone to Texas, and was one of the Mier prisoners who had to draw for the black bean when that ill-conducted invasion came to grief. One out of every ten Americans captured was shot. The colonel told me that one day while in prison in Matamoras, he examined the well of the prison, and discovered a fish in it. I said, " I'll bet you caught him." He laughed, and replied, " Indeed, I did. I got a pin, made a hook, found a piece of twine, and fished for that fellow till I caught him." He told me he had on one occasion fished in the Tennessee River two days without getting a bite, and enjoyed it as much as any fishing he had ever had.

Colonel Crittenden was one of the most honorable and truthful gentlemen I have ever known, and was a son of the distinguished John J. Crittenden, long United States senator from Kentucky, whose influence was most potent in preventing the secession of his State. His father's course greatly distressed Colonel Crittenden. He told me in Santa Fé, at the outbreak of the war, " I am sure I shall find my father altogether with the South when I get home." The unfortunate affair at Fishing Creek, where the Confederate force under his command was badly worsted, ended his career in the field. He lived many years after the war, and enjoyed the good-will and respect of all who knew him.

The only other officer at Fort Inge was the Assistant Surgeon, Dr. Getty. The Indians were quiet and we led a very uneventful life, our chief interest being the care of the horses sick with the glanders. At least one-third of the troop had glanders or farcy. Some died, some we shot, but most of them entirely recovered. Many escaped the loathsome disease, which was quite remarkable, for we had no separate stabling or pasturage for them.

In the course of that year, young Jerome Bonaparte joined us, and I was enabled to go to New Orleans to meet my wife and bring her to Fort Inge. It was a comfortless abiding-place for one reared as she had been, but then, as ever, her home was with her husband. It was some years before she ever met any of the wives of the officers of the Rifles. Now whole regiments are together in completely comfortable and handsome residences, but it was very different then. I found my wife at the home of Dr. Wedderburn, a well-known physician of the city. The yellow fever was raging, and quinine and opium were his especial prescription for it. I think he gave as much as thirty grains of quinine and four grains of opium in bad cases of yellow fever, with unfailing success, he said.

The fever increased in violence, and we soon made haste to leave, taking passage on the steamer *Fashion*, Captain Baker commanding. She was a very frail vessel, such as no quartermaster would dare to send troops or stores in now, but her captain was well acquainted with her ways and the ways of these seas, and had kept her going for many a year, until, not long after our voyage, even his skill could not prevail against the power of one of our Gulf storms, and the *Fashion* was wrecked. Captain Baker's sons were gallant officers of the Navy, and for many years one of them has been the able editor of the *Times-Democrat*.

There were several officers and families going out on this trip, and we made the journey from San Antonio in ambulances, keeping together for sociability and safety. I well remember Colonel Morris, an old infantry officer, who was going with his family to the Post at Eagle Pass, then Fort Duncan. The first night out we stopped in Castroville, at the hotel kept by Madame Tardee, a typical French hostess. Our party was large enough to occupy the whole of the second floor, the ceilings and partitions of which were all of thin cotton cloth. We only realized the force of this economical arrangement after some unguarded conversation had set the entire party to suppressed giggling and whispering. There were young men and maidens along, and we had altogether a very pleasant journey. I remember Colonel Morris and his family as being especially kind to us. He was an old veteran, who had seen much service, and gave my wife much good advice as to her frontier life, which at Fort Inge was rough enough.

The only event of interest to me while commanding H Company at Fort Inge was a riotous outbreak on the part of some of the men. The company, from long idleness and isolation, had become quite careless of duty, and many of them would drink at the sutler's more than was good for them.   They were encouraged to indiscipline by the laundresses of the company, of whom there were four of the lowest specimens of their class east of the Rio Grande ; and their houses were often scenes of the most outrageous disorder.   One night about eleven o'clock the first sergeant, a huge ne'er-do-well, came to my quarters in great excitement and reported that a number of the worst men in the troop had taken possession of one of the laundresses' houses, were drunk and violent, and threatened to kill any man who attempted to enter.

I snatched up my sabre and revolver and hastened with the trembling sergeant to the scene of the outbreak, where I found the rioters had beaten off the guard and had scattered to their quarters, except one violent fellow named O'Donnel, one of the worst men in the troop, who had gone in the other direction.   Taking a corporal with me, I went in pursuit of him.   The moon was full, and the sky was clear, and we soon found our man crouched in a potato patch several hundred yards below the stable. As I hailed him and ordered him to come in, he arose and started to run.   I fired and he dropped at the shot, and when I reached his side he was as ghastly a picture of a dead man as I have ever seen.   He lay upon his back with fixed and staring eyes, gasping in a dreadful way. My feelings were fearfully wrought up, and I would have given my right hand to recall the last half minute.   I turned him over, and examined him to find his wound, when, to my great joy, he said, "You haven't hit me bad, Lieutenant," and showed me the slight mark of my bullet. As he started to rise, he caught his foot in the potato vine and fell prone, with his stomach fair upon the sharp stump of a sapling, which knocked the life out of him for the time. I had him carried to the hospital, and never again had any trouble with that company. Next day all of the laundresses were put into a wagon and hauled away, bag and baggage, and deposited at a settlement far beyond the limits of the government reservation.

In the course of a few months, I was promoted to be first lieutenant of B Company, then stationed at Fort Ewell, the most unhealthy and comfortless of all our frontier posts. I took my wife down to San Antonio, then the most populous and attractive town in the State, and leaving her there in the care of that able and excellent man, Dr. Heerf, who still stands at the head of his profession, I set out in sad spirits for my place of banishment. The route lay for more than one hundred miles over a very desolate region, then scarcely inhabited, and frequently traversed by bands of hostile Indians. I had no escort but one smart young Rifleman, who took care of my horses. The quartermaster gave me a wagon, the teamster of which was the most extraordinary coward I have ever met with. He died many deaths between San Antonio and the Nueces.

Two or three traders from Camargo on the Rio Grande came to me on setting out and proposed that for mutual defence and sociability we should travel together. We should then have a party of five well-armed men, not counting the teamster, and in those days five well-armed Americans were a match for five times as many Indians, who had no weapons but bows and spears. It often happened out there that one or two white men kept bands of Indians at bay till succor came, or the Indians abandoned the attack. They would lose many warriors for a good herd of horses, but not one for only a few. I had with me then a very fine bay mare and also a very fleet black Spanish horse. I rode that mare once ninety-eight miles in twenty-four hours, galloping all the way. We rode into San Antonio fresh as daisies, the mare and I.

At the Rio Frio I fell ill, and my fellow-travellers left me there, for they cared not to tarry in that dangerous locality.   As I grew worse, I sent my Rifleman on to Fort Ewell, thirty miles, for the doctor and remedies, while I lay all night at the ford of the Rio Frio with no help or companion but that white-livered teamster, whose fright was so ludicrous as to amuse me in spite of my sufferings. During the night a lion came prowling into our little camp, and the teamster retired to my tent, where I induced him to fire my gun, which sounded as loud as a cannon.   At last I grew so much worse that I decided not to wait for the doctor, but set out at daylight for Fort Ewell.   The road was bad, but I travelled in the wagon, being unable to sit my horse.   The teamster cracked his whip and struck a trot, looking all the while around the horizon for Indians, and never slacked his gait until we met my Rifleman hastening back to me with a buggy.   There was no ambulance at the Post, and the surgeon could not leave, so he sent his buggy for me with medicines and a kind letter of advice.   The buggy was a delightful change from the hard-going wagon, the remedies acted promptly, and the arrival of a reinforcement in the person of the Rifleman revived the teamster's spirits wonderfully, and we soon trotted over the distance to Fort Ewell.   In all my experience, I have never seen so desolate and uncomfortable a place, and my heart was light, when, in a few days, the doctor sent me back to San Antonio with a sick certificate, whence General Persifer Smith sent me home on sick leave.

CHAPTER VII

Philadelphia Hospitality — The Wreck of the Steamship *San Francisco*
— An Expedition to New Mexico under General Persifer Smith —
Incidents of the March — The Beauty of the Wild Rose Pass —
Hunting Adventures — Peculiarities of the Game of the Country
— Encounters with the Apaches — Odd Characters — Arrival at
Laredo

E went to Philadelphia, where my wife was, under the care of the great and good Dr. Meigg, who was not only chief of living physicians, but one of the most charming of *raconteurs*. His visits were tri-weekly; but when he came he was prepared to sit nearly an hour with us, entertaining us with his instructive and delightful talk. I remember, as an evidence of his thoughtful kindness, that he brought one day from his own house an exquisite Madonna to brighten my wife's room, and hung it where she could see it from her bed. When our stay in Philadelphia was ended, I went to his house and asked him for his bill. He showed a desire to make no charge at all for his services, but finally said in a pleasant way: "I know how proud you army men are, and you will be angry if I charge you nothing. I am in great need of a twenty-dollar gold piece, and if you have one about you, I will thank you for it." I had one and many more which I had expected to pay him.

People were very kind to us in Philadelphia, especially the families of Biddle and Gilpin. During our stay there the lamentable wreck of the steamship *San*

Francisco occurred. A widespread anxiety prevailed in our whole country, for upon her was a whole regiment of United States artillery, *en route* to California round the Horn. By the breaking off of the upper deck, Colonel Washington, Captain Taylor, and several hundred officers and men were swept away. The hull was left drifting, with hundreds of the men, women, and children of the regiment,— where, no man could say.

My uncle, Lieutenant M. F. Maury, had then announced his theories about the wind and currents of the sea, and was at the head of the National Observatory. Humboldt had declared him the discoverer of a new science. On him the Secretary of the Navy called to locate the position of the *San Francisco*, and direct the course of the ship to be sent to her rescue. I well remember the honest pride with which he wrote me how they found the wreck just where he showed it ought to be, and saved the hundreds of survivors ; among them Lieutenant Frank Murray, who won grateful acknowledgment for his heroic conduct and gentle care of the helpless women and children, in recognition of which the people of Philadelphia gave him a service of silver.

I took my wife to her home at " Cleveland," her father's country seat, and went my way to Texas again, arriving at Corpus Christi in time to join General Persifer Smith on his expedition up into New Mexico. He had an escort of one hundred Riflemen, made up of ten men from each company, under the command of Captain John G. Walker. I commanded the artillery, viz., one mountain howitzer and twelve men. Lieutenant E. A. Carr, lately promoted to brigadier, Lieutenant Alfred Gibbs, aide-de-camp, and Assistant-Surgeon McParlan completed our command.

General Persifer Smith had been our first colonel, and

all who remember him at Monterey and on "Scott's line" from Vera Cruz to the city of Mexico will agree that he was a fine specimen of a soldier and a man. In the day of battle he perhaps had no superior in our army. His courage was of the highest order, his attainments were varied, his professional information was excellent, his judgment was sound, his plans were always formed promptly and executed boldly, and he had under all circumstances complete control of his resources. Those who knew General Smith only after disease had sapped the vigor of his faculties can form little idea of him as he was when first appointed colonel of the Rifles. He was then the illustration of a brave and hardy soldier, and courteous, high-spirited gentleman. Had he no claim upon history beside Contreras, he would still rank with the best commanders America has produced. His success in that affair was achieved by a small force over the Mexican army in strong position. His confidence in his troops and in the soundness of his plans was strikingly illustrated by the composure with which he drew out his watch as he saw his Rifles moving to the assault, and when the last Mexican had left the redoubt or surrendered, announced to the officers around him, " It has taken just seventeen minutes."

He marched with a large wagon train to carry forage for our horses, for we were to be gone nearly four months, and could not expect to find adequate pasturage along our route. We arose at 3 A.M., marched at 4.30, and halted for camp on the best water we could find, averaging thirty-three miles daily throughout the march.

One day, having missed our watering-place, we continued the march till 10 P.M., camping on Lympia Creek, in the mouth of the Wild Rose Pass. At Fort Davis, upon the Lympia, we halted, where was a great spring of fresh, delicious water and excellent grass. From this camp General Smith went off toward the Rio Grande.

Soon after Baldy Smith proposed to me to take a good escort and make up a party of officers and go down the Pass to the Sierra Prieta, a lofty peak which rose at the mouth of the gorge above all the surrounding mountains. Game abounded all about us, and I well remember that Lieutenants Dodge and Cole and myself killed over eighty ducks, mostly blue-winged teal, that day, so we had a bountiful supper. Dr. Guild was one of our party, afterward chief medical officer of the army of northern Virginia. All was quiet outside our camp during the night, while in the great Sibley tent we passed a jolly time.

Early next morning, leaving a strong guard in camp, we commenced the ascent of the mountain along whose base ran a deep trail made by the Apaches on their way to and from their permanent camp, twenty miles distant. The ascent was the work of several hours. We rode until our horses could go no further, and then dismounting, we all, seven in number, raced for the top. I forbear to say who first waved his bandanna from the summit. Around the crown of this singular peak arose a precipice of basaltic rock some thirty feet high, after surmounting which we found ourselves upon a smooth plateau nearly a mile across. Upon it were grass and herbs, and a rabbit bounced up here and there and scudded away from us. To this day I have never been able to decide how those rabbits got up there, or why.

Baldy Smith pointed out to us the Apache camp, in which two years before he, with William Henry Whiting, Dick Howard, and Policarpio, their guide, were carried prisoners, and held until the chiefs decided whether to kill them or not. Happily, after a solemn council it was determined to release them. "Polly," as he was known, was a famous Mexican guide and hunter, as brave and faithful as any man upon the plains. When last in Texas I heard of him as an eloquent Baptist preacher.

When we descended, we found in the trail the fresh pony-tracks of two Indian scouts, so we kept very quiet in camp till after full dark, when we harnessed up and drove ten miles on our homeward way as fast as we could go, and halted for the night in the road. Once during the night the sentinel quietly called us. Some animal, probably a grizzly, was moving along the mountain side not far above us. We were astir early next morning, and were soon back in our camp upon the Lympia. The First Infantry had arrived by this time and established itself in Fort Davis, situated in a beautiful cañon in the mountains, with a deep, cold, gushing spring just at its mouth.

The next party that went down that Lympia Cañon did not fare as well as we did. Like ourselves, they went partly for the pleasure of the trip and partly to report as to the whereabouts of the Indians, but none of them came back to recite the incidents of the expedition; for they were surprised in their camp and all murdered by those Apaches.

I have never seen anything in America more beautiful than the Wild Rose Pass, where for near twenty miles the bright Lympia finds its way along the base of the precipices, over one thousand feet high, or through lovely meadows which stretch away for miles over slopes dotted with patches of fine timber. The morning we first entered it, Baldy Smith and I rode together, and noted with delight how the morning sunshine touched the tops of those high cliffs, and bathed them in innumerable tints of crimson and violet and gold. We used to believe when we visited the Dusseldorf Gallery, and noted the landscapes hanging there, that such coloring was the invention of the painter ; but no painter yet has ever equalled nature, and in the Wild Rose Pass she has spread her most beautiful colors. I remember once to have heard an artist of merit discussing this very question of the inadequacy of the painter's palette to reproduce the hues of nature. " People are prone," he said, " to criticise landscapes and say they are exaggerated in color, but if any one will try to reproduce a sunrise or a sunset he will realize the difficulty of portraying upon one small canvas the brilliant and beautiful tints which nature continually spreads out before us."

We rested well and long in that delightful camp upon the Lympia. I was the hunter of our mess, and was often tempted to stray too far from camp alone. I had a great ambition to encounter a grizzly, as we called the fierce, brown bears of that region, and one evening I had gone alone down into the cañon in search of partridges and teal. One barrel of my gun was charged with number six, and the other held nine buckshot for Indians. I had gone some distance down into the cañon, when I observed that the sun was low and I must hasten back to camp. On my homeward way I came upon the track of a huge grizzly, who had crossed the road only a few minutes before, and must at that moment have been within two hundred paces of me. When I viewed that footprint, two feet long, and knew the foot that made it was close by, I quickened my own pace for camp, and did not feel that I was called upon to "project" with bears like that. I had several times caused apprehension by long absences alone, and at last Walker insisted that I should not go out again without an escort, and gave me two fine young Riflemen, Bryan and Davis, for my companions, who were good hunters, and added much to my pleasure and comfort.

One day while hunting alone on some lagoons seven or eight miles from the camp, I crawled upon some geese and bagged three with one barrel while they were upon the water, and two with the second barrel as they rose. They flew half a mile and settled upon the bare prairie, whither I followed them and got three more, and hastened back to camp with my horse covered with geese and ducks, which I liberally distributed among the ladies of the First Infantry, who had just arrived from their long march to occupy Fort Davis. This was probably the best game they had tasted for a month or more.

Soon after this we set out for El Paso, and on the second or third day were met by a man who told us with great vociferation how the Indians had run off fifty head of his cattle from Eagle Springs, and begged the general to aid him in recovering them. His nickname was "Talking" Campbell. In those early days of Texas, men were named from some personal peculiarity, and we had then living " Big-foot " Wallace, a tremendous, good-natured fellow from Rockbridge County, Virginia. On my first introduction to him I could not perceive any unusual size in his feet, and was informed that he acquired his cognomen honestly in battle, having slain a famous Indian chief known as "Big Foot." Then there was "Deaf" Smith, who once, when General Houston ordered his army to lie down that they might be the better protected from the Mexican cannon, looked around him, and, seeing the smoke and flame of the Mexican guns and all his comrades prone upon the ground, did not tarry there a moment longer, but, turning, fled and reported all killed but himself. It was said that for years "Deaf" Smith was engaged in single combats because of this experience in his first great battle. Few men dared to mention San Jacinto or Sam Houston in his presence.

Then there was "Stuttering" Lane, a capital good fellow from San Antonio, who had many funny jokes upon himself suggested by his infirmity. When asked why a certain lady did not marry him after promising to do so, he stammered out that she was going to marry him, till a certain "damn-fool-busybody" told her he stuttered! Another was our friend then present with us, and no man who ever met "Talking" Campbell ever had occasion to inquire why he was so called any more than he would have had in interviewing "Stuttering" Lane. But "Talking" Campbell was full of fight, and delighted when Captain Walker with forty Riflemen was ordered to follow and recover his cattle; he insisted upon going along. Young Frank Armstrong, General Smith's step-son, afterwards a very distinguished general himself, also obtained permission to go, and Lieutenant Carr was of the party.

The Indians had more than twenty-four hours' start, and had driven the cattle at headlong speed and left a broad trail straight to their stronghold in the mountains, whither Walker followed and found them in their village, where a sharp fight ensued. One Rifleman was killed, and Carr was wounded with an arrow in the abdomen, as was Captain Van Buren, who died of his wound on the seventh day after he received it. It seemed a mere incision, so slight that neither Van Buren nor the surgeons felt any anxiety about it. He was sitting up, laughing and talking with his comrades, and apparently well, when an artery burst, and he died in a few minutes. This made us anxious about Carr's wound, but he soon recovered from it and lived to be mainly instrumental in defeating Van Dorn at Elk Horn in 1862. The cattle had been cut up and distributed, and all Walker could do was to kill a few Indians and destroy their village.

We pursued our march, and he rejoined us in the course of a few days. Campbell's herd was of fifteen hundred head, which he was driving across to California. The night of their halt at Eagle Springs very few of them got any water, and they were driven on to the Rio Grande, thirty miles distant. At fifteen miles from the spring we came upon the first dead cattle. When within sight and smell of the river, they made a grand rush for the water, and lay dead in piles. We afterwards heard that he got safely to market with the balance and made a good profit. We never saw "Talking" Campbell again, or any man equal to him in his peculiar line.

We reached El Paso in the very height of the grape season. Never had we tasted such delicious grapes, and the wine made from them was very good. But our relish for it was not enhanced when we saw the process of its manufacture. Under a dirty shed a bull's hide was hung by the legs. In it were put many bushels of grapes, and also a dirty, bare-legged Mexican, who, stripped to his knees, was actively pressing the juice with his feet, which had not been intentionally washed before in a long time, not since the last grape season. We were assured it was the best way to make good wine, but we did not try any of that. From El Paso we went up to Fort Fil-more, where for the last time I met my friend, Barnard Bee. When we parted, he gave me a very curious and massive ring made of several different colors of the gold of that country. It was stolen out of my dressing-case soon after his death.

We then retraced our route to San Antonio, laying in a good supply of grapes and watermelons for our mess and a good store also for the wife of Captain Granger, who had entertained us very kindly upon our upward march. Captain Granger commanded a small detachment of infantry, twenty-eight men, stationed at a famous Indian crossing on Devil's River. There was no defence whatever, and an Indian arrow could at any time have pierced the cotton walls of Mrs. Granger's tent, but she seemed secure and contented in her isolated home. There was not a white man within hundreds of miles. Soon after we passed, a soldier was shot dead with an arrow, close to her tent, but no other casualty occurred there until a year or two later. General Hood, then a lieutenant, had a hard fight with a band of Indians thereabouts. He and several of his men were wounded, and some were killed; the Indians got rather the best of the cavalrymen that time. Hood was a very daring and ambitious man, but very unfortunate as a commander. Devil's River was far too beautiful a stream to have so bad a name. It was very like the Shenandoah in the great valley of Virginia. It was clear and very grateful to the sight and taste of the weary and thirsty men and horses who sought it from far and wide.

While we were at Fort Inge, Colonel Crittenden marched, with two or three squadrons, up the Nueces, scouting after a large body of Indians. The weather was very hot and dry; the springs were gone, and water could be found only in the larger streams. He marched from the Nueces across to Devil's River, and for three days neither man nor horse had one drop of water. As they approached Devil's River, they rode amongst some thousands of wild turkeys, trotting along the same road after water. Their wings were hanging off from their bodies, and their mouths were wide open. They paid no attention to the troops, merely opening out to let them pass, and the men had no desire to molest them. Neither man nor horse died of that terrible suffering, and never was Devil's River more welcome, than when on the morning of the third day they rode into its pleasant waters.

We saw many upland plover upon our march, and found them always on the burned places of the prairie. They found in them the roasted grass seed upon which they love to feed, and on which they grow fat and delicious in flavor. For the first time, I shot the black partridge, the *moreno*, the best of the five varieties of that bird I found in this region. Their crops were always filled with small nuts resembling beechnuts, which they find at the roots of a grass growing upon the mountain side. They are very game, lie close and fly strong, and are tender and juicy, being one or two ounces heavier than the Virginia partridge.

Our march ended at San Antonio, where I turned in my artillery and went to join my company at Fort McIntosh, Laredo. The headquarters of the regiment were there, with one squadron, also seven or eight companies of infantry and one company of artillery. Laredo, a Mexican town, was a mile away. Occasionally, Colonel Loring, one of the kindest and best and bravest of men, gave a fandango at his quarters, and invited some of the *élite* of Laredo to meet our officers and their families. But there was no cordial association possible between people who did not understand each other's language. My resource was hunting, and, a few days before Christmas, Colonel Loring proposed that we should make up a party and go thirty miles or so away, where we could find plenty of deer, and bring in some venison for Christmas. Captain Tom Claiborn and Lieutenant Tom English were of the party.

In every company there were several hunters, who scouted the country for game, and sometimes brought in reports of Indians. In our party there were seven of us, who in four days killed thirty-six deer and a lion, all of which we shot with the Mississippi rifle. In one day we brought in sixteen deer and the lion. We lived upon the tid-bits and fore quarters of the deer, which Tom Claiborn knew well how to cook over a camp-fire, while he seasoned his culinary efforts with racy anecdotes of his experiences in Oregon and on the great overland route of the regiment.

Late one afternoon, we had all come in from our day's hunt, when we heard partridges whistling close by. Lieutenant English had a handsome black setter puppy, which he had taught some tricks of a poodle, and which he had named Toots. Claiborn took Toots with him and went in pursuit of the partridges. He had a fine Manton gun, and before sunset he bagged twenty-two birds, without missing a shot. Toots behaved so well that Claiborn convinced English that he ought to give the dog to me, which he did, only stipulating his name should not be changed. For more than ten years, he was one of my family. He had his mouth on every kind of game that ever wore fur or feathers. He fought with my greyhounds in many a wolf hunt, whipped every bulldog that ever attacked him, was bitten by a rattlesnake, and sprinkled by a polecat, and had as much sense as many men, and more principle. It was while he was hunting with me one day that he was bitten by a rattler. I burned the place with gunpowder, and carried him as quickly as I could to a doctor. Toots had never seen him before, but he allowed him to cut away the flesh and burn him with caustic, only whining softly from the extreme pain. Some months after this, he got into a fight and was bitten on the same foot. I was away when it happened, and he went by himself to that same doctor, and sitting upon his haunches, as he had been taught to do, held up the injured foot for the doctor's inspection and treatment.

CHAPTER VIII

Big Game Hunting in Texas — Encounter with an American Lion —
Exciting Fight with a Wild Bull — Pierced with Cactus Spikes —
Fierce Battle with a Wounded Cow — On Recruiting Service at
Carlisle Barracks — New Tactics for Mounted Rifles — The May
Family — Sad Results of a Duel

AFTER this Christmas hunt, I found occupation in scouting and drilling, and in making a new system of tactics for mounted troops. The general introduction of the revolver and long-range rifle called for such changes in cavalry tactics as would enable the men to dismount quickly and use their rifles on foot, and demanded also single-rank formations. The working out of these problems occupied my thoughts and interests for a long time, and I had favorable opportunity for testing every movement, having charge of the instruction of my company, and the good-will of my intelligent brother-officers, though occasionally a sneer would reach me from some leather-head of the old dragoon *régime*, who did not wish to have to learn new tactics (they generally didn't know much of any). But I persevered with my work, won friends to it of all who saw it tried, and had the satisfaction of having it adopted by the Secretary of War, John B. Floyd, who, being a great hunter and rifleman himself, knew that weapon could only be used effectively on foot, and that the time had come for moving horsemen to where they could be dismounted and could thus render efficient service.

By this new system of tactics, a troop of Mounted Rifles could be moving at the gallop, and when the trumpet sounded, "Dismount to fight," could halt, link their horses, and be handling their rifles in line of battle in seven seconds. McClellan, who had been inspecting the cavalry systems of Europe, wrote me warm congratulations upon my great success. The tactics were used in both armies during the Civil War, and have been universally adopted in the Indian fighting upon the plains, and have very recently been embodied in the New Tactics.

As I have said, hunting was my only pleasure in Texas. In that day there were no settlements upon that vast region between the Nueces and the Rio Grande. It was a great pasture for thousands of wild horses, and wild cattle, deer, antelope, and every game bird we know of, and every sort of predatory beast. The tigers, or great, spotted panthers, as large sometimes as Bengal tigers, and the tawny, maneless lions, and many small varieties of the cat tribe abounded there. Nowhere, save in South Africa, were such quantities of large game to be found.

One day while patrolling that region, we encamped on sweet water in a grassy valley, and in the evening I went out for venison, having told the guide, Juan Galvan, a famous Indian scout, to follow me. When about a mile from camp I saw a deer and two fawns, as I thought them to be, enter the chaparral before me. I galloped rapidly around to the other side of the timber, to get a shot at the game as it emerged from it, when what was my delight to see a large lion come sauntering out on the prairie, moving up the wind with his nose

well up and his long tail brushing the grass as he walked
slowly along. The breeze blew fresh and the grass
muffled my horse's tracks, as I cantered up to within
fifty paces. Then I halted and drew a fine sight upon
him behind his shoulder, but my horse moved, and I
had to lower my rifle. I had just quieted him and taken
aim again, when the guide with a clatter came galloping
up behind me. The lion, surprised, wheeled toward
me, when I dashed at him with a shout which made him
turn and bound away. I tried to close, and get a running shot, but he outran my slow troop horse and went
away with great leaps till he reached the chaparral. Had
my rifle been a Winchester, or had I been upon my
own horse, I would have dismounted and taken a sure
shot, but on a previous day this brute had run off from
me when I dismounted to shoot, and I did not feel justified in being left alone to encounter that great beast
with a Mississippi rifle. I was greatly provoked with
the guide, but he had run up to help me, was a very
daring fellow, and very fond of me.

Soon after this, the grass near Fort McIntosh being
used up, it was necessary to send our horses down the
river for fresh pasturage, so that they might be in condition for the summer scouting. Tom Claiborn was
captain of B Company, and Llewellyn Jones, captain of
F Company. Claiborn's wife and children were domi-
ciled in the garrison, and Jones' health was infirm, so I
took the squadron two days' march down the Rio Grande,
where we made a comfortable camp, and grazed our
horses and hunted for more than a month. We were too
far from the fort to draw our fresh meat and rations.
Wild cattle abounded about us, and each company had
good hunters, and every night they brought in fat beeves,
unbranded and as wild and savage as any other wild

beasts in that region.   When Mexico dethroned the last Emperor, Iturbide, and established a republic, the garrisons in what is now Texas were all withdrawn. The Indians then poured in upon the large ranches, murdered the people, and turned the stock loose. These had increased and multiplied till the whole of the region between the Rio Grande and the Nueces swarmed with wild horses and cattle, and one day I encountered a small herd of wild asses, as wild as zebras and very active.

I had heard so much of the fierceness and activity of the wild cattle, that I desired to be able to tell by experience about the truth of these reports; so one morning, at daybreak, I set out with Juan Galvan and two Riflemen with pack mules to bring in the meat we expected to kill. Juan soon found the fresh trail of an enormous bull. His tracks were easily followed, for amidst the thousands his were larger than any. It was about eleven o'clock when Juan, who was riding at a fox trot just in my front, threw up his rifle and fired at a huge, white bull who broke out of the brush and ran off at a rapid gait. After two hours of hot pursuit, we came up with this monarch of the herds in a thick clump of bushes, where Juan and I dismounted, and, running up to within thirty or forty paces, fired into his great, white body. The brush was too thick for us to pick our shots. He ran out near the Riflemen, both of whom fired at him, but he kept on his way at a swinging gait. The blood in great splashes fell upon the broad cactus leaves, and made the trail easy to follow, and excited us, as the sight of blood will affect any hunter.

Again, after half an hour's pursuit, we came upon our bull, and as before, Juan and I dismounted and ran up to put two more balls into him. There was more blood now upon the trail, and we were more eager, so that when we found him the third time at bay, I resolved to make a sure shot, and, running closer to him than ever before, delivered it. Old Juan was too smart to dismount, though I had not observed this. As my rifle cracked, I heard the bushes rattling, and the men cried out, "Look out, Lieutenant! He is charging you!" I wheeled and ran for my horse, but the bull was too close for me to stop to mount, so as I heard him close at my heels, I turned suddenly towards a huge cactus I was passing and sprang into it, struggling through it and tumbling flat upon the ground upon the other side. In all my life I had never been so terrified, and I was so tormented by the great cactus spikes which had pierced my body, that for an instant I would have welcomed the bull or anything else that would have relieved me of my misery.

After some moments, I ventured to arise and investigate the whereabouts of that animal, an action which I immediately regretted; for he instantly saw me and made another dash for me, the men crying as he did so, "He's charging again!" I whirled through another cactus, the twin of the one I had just left, and lay as flat and still as a dead man; and I almost wished that I was dead, for in my flight I had acquired a second supply of cactus spikes, which left no part of my body unprovided for. They are of the size of a large darning-needle, with barbed points, and when one is pulled out it leaves the barb in to mark the place.

Juan, having more sense and experience with bulls than I, had never taken his foot out of the stirrup, and now dashed off after my horse, which had availed itself of the opportunity to run away. The Riflemen, too, had retired to a safe distance, so that when, after a longer delay than before, I arose very cautiously and inspected the field, I alone remained upon it. My rifle was empty, and all of my friends were gone, and, utterly demoralized, I stood wondering what had ever induced me to imagine that I wished to hunt a wild bull. One cheerful fact gave me courage: the bull was gone with the rest, but alas! the cactus spikes remained.

I reloaded my rifle, picked out some of the most accessible of them, and tried to rally my spirits and look cheerful as Juan rode up, leading my horse and crying out in a gay voice, "Vamos!"

"Vamos where?" said I.

"Por el toro."

"Damn the toro," I responded heartily, as with a poor assumption of lively acquiescence, I took my seat where the late General Pope had his headquarters. As a good many spikes still remained, that saddle was far from being a downy pillow. But I wriggled and twisted and managed to keep up, and we soon emerged from the chaparral into a grassy glade where a herd of cattle had been startled by our approach. We drew up all abreast, and fired into the herd. I struck a great brindled bull, but permitted him to pass on, for just then bulls were a drug in my market. Juan, however, dashed off, whirling his lasso, and returned in ten minutes, saying, "We got him." Two of our shots had struck a beautiful, young sorrel cow, breaking her fore leg. Juan having lassoed her and tied her to the big, swinging limb of a mesquite, proposed going on after the bull, but I preferred to remain and look after the safety of the cow, and I told Juan that before following up the bull, I desired him to examine the rope and make sure the cow was securely tied. As we approached, she charged madly at us twice, but being thrown violently back upon her haunches, she ceased this and remained sullenly quiet. At last Juan slipped off his horse and went carefully around the tree, followed slowly by the cow. Moran, one of the Riflemen, a large, handsome fellow, had dismounted, and stood leaning against his horse, holding Juan's rifle and his own in his hand. Old Dewey, a very phlegmatic Vermonter, was sitting lazily in his saddle, his rifle across his pommel. I was quite alert, and ready to move on short notice, should the cow decide to charge again, which she suddenly did. The rope broke and she dashed at Moran, goring his horse in the flank. He dropped his rifles, and sprang up a tree. She then struck old Dewey's horse, lifting him so that his rider pitched over his head and, turning a somersault, landed upon his feet, rifle in hand. Turning, he delivered a quick shot in the cow's face, and then made for a tree, which he lost no time in climbing. The cow now had the field to herself, for by the time Dewey was safely ensconced, I was a rifle-shot away, where a three-legged cow could not catch me. Finally, Juan slipped down from his perch and gathering up his rifle mounted his horse, and, riding up to the animal, shot her in the curl and ended the battle.

We butchered her, and, packing the mules with the meat, sent the men back to camp with it, while Juan and I took another turn at our bull. We bounced him out of a thicket a little before sunset, ran him a mile, and then gave up the chase, and set out for camp ten miles away. It was ten o'clock before we got in, and I was occupied until a late hour getting rid of the cactus. Next morning I looked as if I had the measles, and felt as if the small-pox had me. So I declined to resume the chase that day, and kept my headquarters in my tent, letting the indefatigable Juan go out with a fresh party, which found the bull where we had left off. He charged them many times, and finally fell by the nineteenth ball. He was an enormous beast, entirely white, save his jet-black horns and hoofs. I had his great hide for a tent floor. It was all we got of him, for his wounds and heated contest had spoiled his great mass of fat meat. But it was certainly the most exciting contest and chase I ever enjoyed. I discovered that day that when a bull charges, he puts his head down, shuts his eyes, and goes straight for his enemy; but when a cow makes the attack, she keeps her eyes wide open and can't be dodged.

Soon after this, we were coming into camp late one evening, when suddenly we heard a wild bull come moaning towards us. It is the wildest sound imaginable in a lonely place. Juan and I leaped from our horses and hastened to meet him, concealing ourselves behind a bush that bordered his course. As we waited, we could hear him drawing nearer and nearer, moaning, and crushing the gravel under his heavy tread. He had come within ten paces when as his fore shoulders emerged into view, I whispered, "Now!" We both fired behind his shoulder, and Juan immediately ran for a tree, while I, being clad in a light coat, threw myself flat down behind my bush. As I lay there, I could hear the hurried tramp of the bull, whether in advance or retreat I could not decide, and the uncertainty was painfully alarming. Happily, he had wheeled and run back at our shot. The night closed in dark, and Juan could not follow him till the moon rose, when he found the bloody trail, but gave up the chase, very properly ; for we were in a dangerous neighborhood.

After three years of this sort of frontier service, I was appointed recruiting officer at San Antonio. General

Albert Sidney Johnston, commanding the department of Texas, was our next neighbor there, and a very good one he was. That accomplished soldier, Don Carlos Buel, was also stationed there. General George Mercer Brooke, one of the bravest men and highest gentlemen in the service, died there. He was my friend and our only kinsman in that wild country.

While in San Antonio, Major Dick Howard and I purchased a cattle ranch on the Cibolo River, about twenty-five miles from the town. The house was an unusually good one for that time in Texas, being built of hewn logs, well plastered and floored. It stood upon a hill in a fine grove overlooking the road from San Antonio to the Gulf. We had fifteen hundred head of breeding cattle, and proposed to send into Mexico for one hundred mares, and to raise mules, and I intended to resign and live on the ranch. But my wife's health and spirits so gave way under the affliction and exhaustion consequent upon the death of our little daughter, that I decided, instead, to accept a detail on the recruiting service which took me to Carlisle Barracks, Pennsylvania. When the war broke out I sold my ranch, doubling my money in Confederate gold bonds.

On arriving at Carlisle, then our only cavalry school, Colonel Charley May, the commandant, appointed me the superintendent of instruction and commandant of the Post. The duty and station were agreeable and comfortable. All of the young cavalry graduates from West Point reported to me for duty, and I thus became well acquainted with many of the brightest young men of the army. Fitz Lee, Averill, Lomax, Big Jim Major, "Red Jackson," and many others were there, whom it was my fortune to serve with or against in the great war, which none of us then realized was so near at hand.

The shooting about there was very good. Mr. Johnston Moore, an excellent gentleman, a real sportsman, and the owner of many farms in the vicinity, was often my companion. A comfortable dinner at his town residence, with a bottle of good champagne, made an appropriate ending to many a pleasant day's sport. At that time he had a beautiful daughter, who was a great favorite socially, especially with the young officers. No man's lot seemed happier than his. Twenty years afterward I met him at the Virginia Springs. Time and sorrow had written deep lines upon his manly face. His daughter was dead, his son had fallen in the war, and many griefs had been his portion, but the gentle, affectionate nature was with him still, and I was tempted to go with him once again over the green fields and wooded hills of the Cumberland valley, where so often, with our guns and dogs, we had borne each other company. But it would not have been the same, for sorrowful memories of the years which lay between would have dimmed the sunshine of the reunion for us.

While at Carlisle I was authorized by Secretary of War Floyd to prepare and publish the "Tactics for Mounted Rifles." Major Buel aided me to procure personal interviews with the Secretary, who entered earnestly into a system which facilitated the mounted riflemen in going effectively into action; and at that time all of our so-called cavalrymen were mounted riflemen. My clandestine interviews with the Secretary were not discovered in the Red Tape Department until the "Tactics" was adopted and published, when the admonition was administered from the chief of that department to "observe the prescribed channels of correspondence in future." This much amused Buel and me.

This suggested to me the expediency of merging the

five regiments of mounted troops in one corps. The three senior regiments united in a memorial to Congress to arrange us accordingly, but it was not done till the great war put aside all personal considerations, for expediency's sake, and in both armies the mounted troops were all classed as cavalry,— a misnomer, if by cavalry we mean soldiers who fight on horseback ; for it is well known that the troopers of Stuart and Hampton, Van Dorn and Forrest, all dismounted to fight. Sabres have long been laid aside except by holiday soldiers, not one in fifty of whom is a swordsman. It was usual for our men in the Rifles to put away their swords whenever they went upon a hostile expedition, and in our great war, in which many thousands of men were killed and wounded, our surgeons were rarely troubled by sabre cuts.

Colonel Charley May, our commandant, was a " Light Dragoon," although, being six feet four inches tall and of tremendous frame, he was fitter for the heavy cavalry. His brother Julian was in my regiment, and was a remarkably handsome man. He, too, was over six feet in stature. Those Mays were extraordinary men in their physical and mental characteristics. Five of the brothers averaged over six feet three inches in height, and all were men of marked character. The Honorable Henry May, a member of Congress from Baltimore, was a man of ability, and of most kind and courtly manners. In the exciting times incident to the disrupting of the government, Mr. May stood up manfully for the rights of the people. I believe he was imprisoned for it. I was thrown intimately with Colonel May for two years, at Carlisle Barracks, and on me devolved the sad duty of paying the last honors of a dead soldier to his brother Julian.

Julian May's history was a very sad one.   He was
the youngest of the sons of Dr. May, a leading physician of Washington in his day.   Before he was twenty-
one, Julian became involved in a difficulty with young
Cochran.   Both were connected with well-known families in Washington, and the duel was the recognized
mode of settling personal difficulties between gentlemen.   This barbarous custom had the sanction of the
highest men of our country in those days, and it was
considered inevitable that these two youths should
resort to it.   So they crossed the river into Virginia,
and fought with rifles at forty paces.   Cochran was shot
in the head, and died instantly, and Julian May became
a fugitive, his life and happiness ruined.   Those who
knew him best realized that he never recovered from
this terrible experience.

General Jackson had then retired to the shades of the
Hermitage, where he was passing the evening of his
days.   He was a friend of the May family, and naturally sympathized with young Julian in his sad position.
At his request, the position of lieutenant was given the
young man in the regiment of Mounted Riflemen, then
just organized in time for the Mexican War.   From
1848 to 1860, when his death occurred, Julian May was
in all the vicissitudes of the service of that regiment,
and his genial and kindly nature made him a favorite
with his comrades throughout the army.   His remarkable personal beauty was enhanced by a courtly breeding
and bearing which distinguished him in every circle he
entered.   He died suddenly at Tucalote, while returning
from Santa Fé to his post at Fort Union.   We laid him
in the little soldiers' cemetery on the hillside overlooking the Post.   I commanded the escort at his funeral,
and read the service of the Church at his grave.

Charley May had long been married to a daughter of Mr. George Law, of New York, when the war broke out. He then resigned from the army and retired to private life. While his sympathies were with his own people in the South, he could not array himself against the people of his wife, who was a very admirable lady, to whom he was much attached.

William May, of the Navy, was the only one of the brothers not over six feet in stature. He was highly esteemed in the service, and had the manhood of his race. Captain William Lewis Maury, of the Confederate cruiser *Georgia*, who was his shipmate in the old Navy, told me that on one occasion May was sent off in command of a boat which was wrecked upon a reef. They found refuge upon the rocks, to which they clung till a launch from the ship came to their rescue. There was not room in the launch for all of the men to go at once, so May and part of the crew got aboard of her, but as she pulled away from the reef, he saw some of his men still on the rocks, and before he could be prevented he sprang overboard and swam back to cast his lot with them. They were a gallant race, those Mays; the men handsome and proud, and the women beautiful.

While at Carlisle, I was appointed a member of a board of cavalry officers, which decided upon a uniform style of horse equipage for the army. Colonels Joseph E. Johnston, Robert E. Lee, Andrew Porter, and several others, were members of the board of which Colonel Philip Saint George Cooke was president. After six or seven weeks of careful examination of every item, we adopted the Cossack saddle brought over by McClellan, and now known by his name. It has stood the test of all these years of service, and is generally used by all frontiersmen.

CHAPTER IX

EANWHILE the Rifles had been transferred to the department of New Mexico, when I was appointed regimental adjutant, and ordered to Fort Union, the headquarters of the regiment. A number of officers *en route* to their commands, and two hundred cavalry recruits from Carlisle went along with us, and at Fort Leavenworth a remount of four hundred horses was turned over to me, to be distributed to the companies at Fort Union. We remained at Fort Leavenworth just long enough to organize our command and prepare it for the difficult duty of convoying nearly five hundred young cavalry horses across the desert and through the range of predatory Indians for eight hundred miles. The recruits had been in active drill at Carlisle for some months, and we had a fine set of young officers not long from West Point, who were assigned to duty with the squadron, which was mounted on the best broken of the remount horses, so that everything was soon in fair marching order. The horses which were not under saddle were driven out in strings, each string being made up of thirty animals and placed in charge of its own squad of men. The picket rope of the string was secured to one end of the wagon, in which was hauled the tent of the squad, with their clothing and rations, etc. A pair of heavy, steady wheel horses were hitched to the wagon and driven by the teamster. Then came the led horses in spans, each secured by a short halter to the picket rope. The string was led off by a pair of steady leaders, hitched by a swingletree to the end of the picket rope, the whole thus presenting a team of about twelve or fifteen pairs of horses. The management of this team required no little skill on the part of the drivers and outriders of the squad. In the party there were a dozen or more of these strings, and they made the Indians' mouths water, I suspect, but they never got a horse.

In this respect we were more fortunate than an expedition which had preceded us the year before, under the command of Colonel Cooke. When he reached the Comanche country, old Mancho, the chief of the tribe, rode up one day, making overtures of peace, and requesting an interview, which Colonel Cooke granted. Mancho inquired of him by whose permission he undertook to travel across the country, and what his object there was. Cooke replied that he came by permission of the Great White Chief in Washington, and that he only wished to travel across the country that he might show it to his young men. To this Mancho retorted that it was *his* country, and neither the Great White Chief nor anybody else had the right to ride over it without his permission, but, if Cooke would give him a supply of provisions and whiskey and tobacco, he was willing to allow him to proceed. Cooke coolly told him to "go to Guinea," or its equivalent, adding that he would give him nothing, and would ride over the country as often as he pleased; and so the interview ended.

That night, while all the camp was wrapped in slumber, the Comanches swooped down upon it, dashing their horses through it at full speed, shaking their blankets and buffalo robes, and howling like demons. As a matter of course, every animal in Cooke's command, rendered frantic by the uproar, stampeded, and next morning he found himself on foot in the midst of the plains. He remained there until able to collect enough horses to pull his wagons to Fort Union, and he probably remembered Mancho in wrath until his life's end.

Such an experience would have been especially unfortunate for us, who had in our party women and children; for several families of officers living in New Mexico had joined our command. Happily, as I have said, we made the trip in safety, and we marched away from Fort Leavenworth before the middle of July, in fine health and spirits. Our route lay through Kansas, then in the full richness of its summer verdure, across the Kansas and Kaw rivers, across the Walnut Creek, Pawnee Fork at Fort Larned, the Arkansas at old Fort Atkinson, and thence by the Cimarron to Fort Union.

I had bought in St. Louis, for the use of my family, one of those excellent carriages constructed for travel on the plains, and the quartermaster at Fort Leavenworth gave us all the wagons we needed for transporting our furniture and supplies. After we got beyond the settlements, wood was very rarely seen, but for fuel we had an abundance of "buffalo-chips." Our water supply was far from what we should have desired, but we had to take it as we found it, one day out of a river and the next out of a mud hole. We were, fortunately, well supplied with charcoal filters, and at night we would set a bucket of muddy water on the table, drop the charcoal ball into it, and convey the rubber tube into the mouth of a demijohn on the floor, which was sewed into a blanket cover and always kept thoroughly wet. Next morning the bucket would be empty, save for a liberal supply of dirt, and the demijohn would be filled with clear, cool water.

Our march across the plains was very interesting. There were six or eight travelling carriages for the families of the married officers. These followed the advance guard, and were followed in their turn by the Mounted Riflemen, close behind whom came the strings of horses, and then the rear guard. The herd of cattle and the milch cows were sent ahead early in the morning, under the care of a small escort. Extraordinary vigilance was necessary, for any Indians, after passing the Kaws and Osages, might be hostile, and four hundred fine young horses, besides some hundreds of mules, would prove a great temptation. We had some grouse shooting, until Council Grove was passed, where we saw the last inhabited prairies and entered fairly upon the great American Desert, the home of the buffalo, the wolf, the antelope, and the wild Indian.

Orton, the wagon-master, a six-foot plainsman, was a good hunter, and my constant companion in my many excursions out upon the flanks of the column. My rifle was a three-grooved Harper's Ferry barrel, mounted by the gunsmith at Carlisle, in a common shot-gun stock, with a wooden ramrod and horn sights. One day I surprised Orton by cutting down a fine antelope at a great distance. I told him to step it off, because his legs were long and would leave no occasion for cavil at short measure. Orton paced four hundred and seventy-five paces to the antelope. Next day I brought down a wolf at two hundred and twenty paces.

One morning Orton got off before I could leave the

command. We were then in the Comanche range, and must needs be as alert as possible. When at last I was ready to set out, I rode a long way to look for him, but could see nothing of him. Suddenly I saw three men galloping towards me from the direction of the column, and, supposing they were messengers sent for me, I went to meet them. We were in a rolling country, and as I rose on each ridge I noticed that the horsemen veered off from me. My horse, Black Jack, a famous hunter, became much excited. He quickened his pace until he seemed to devour the ground. At last, as I mounted a ridge, I came upon three Indians crossing it at full speed, about two hundred yards from me. I did not pursue them, but dismounted, and fired at the only antelope I had seen that day. He was several hundred yards off, and I was flustered by the Indians, and by the necessity of reloading before they could get to me, but on glancing towards them I saw that on hearing the crack of the rifle, they had plied their quirts and heels, and were making all speed in the other direction.

I then hastened to where I saw, several miles away, the dust of our column, and was surprised to learn on reaching it that nobody had seen the Indians, nor had Orton returned. So I rode out again to look for him, and finally found him, but he had not seen the Indians either, until I pointed them out to him, dismounted, on the crest of a ridge some miles distant, whence they watched our column. Observing our herders in charge of the milch cattle resting on a hill not far off, we joined them, and found the Indians had been after them. The lazy rascals had put their rifles into a wagon, and were sauntering along at ease, when all at once the Indians came down upon them, and insulted them by rubbing their arrows under their noses, turning their pockets out, taking their tobacco, handkerchiefs, etc., and were galloping off triumphantly when they found me in their path. That night we doubled our guard about camp, but saw no more of them until we came to Walnut Creek, where we found them shooting buffalo.

Our first view of the buffalo was very exciting. There were thousands of them, and we were marching through them for three days, at thirty miles a day, and all day and all night the air resounded with their bellowing. The first one I shot lay down to die, and as I desired to get his tongue out, I dismounted, and was marching bravely up to the young bull, when all at once he sprang up and dashed at me. I turned and ran toward my horse, and as I mounted I saw the bull flat on his back, his legs quivering in the air. Being dead sure enough this time, I got his tongue without any further trouble or fright. Many buffalo hunters had this experience with their first bull.

John Omahundro, of Louisa County, Virginia, was an active scout for General Jeb Stuart during the late war. After the war, he went back to his wild life upon the plains. He was a remarkably handsome and pleasing young fellow, and very expert with his lasso and arms. He went about the country with Carver, the shooter, and was widely known as "Texas Jack."

One night in Montgomery, Alabama, General John G. Walker, "Texas Jack," and I were seated together, talking of our experiences on the plains, and found we had all had the same with our first buffalo. Jack had leaned over his and struck his knife into him, when the beast sprang up and chased him to the wagon, against which he put his head and fell dead just as Jack had succeeded in putting it between them. Unlike the ox or the horse, the buffalo springs upon all four feet at once.

We had with us a smart young sergeant, Bowman by name, who was my companion on this run, and requested permission to go with me when I should make another. Next morning I saw a herd of buffalo grazing not far off from our camp, and was about to ride after them when Sergeant Bowman came up and, touching his cap, asked, "Will the Captain permit me to go with him?"

"Certainly, Sergeant, I would like to have you with me." He then inquired, "Will the Captain permit Alphonse to go, too?"

"No," I said. "He can't manage his horse or his pistol, and he may shoot himself or some one else." But Bowman urged that he would keep close by him, and look after him, and finally I unfortunately yielded, and said, "Well, let him come on." Bowman was a very bright, pleasant, young fellow, attentive to his duties, and a favorite with all the officers. Alphonse was a little French soldier fresh from Algeria. He was amiable, alert, and wholly ignorant of the English language, and full of the excitable enthusiasm of his race. He was very vain of his equestrian accomplishments, supposed to have been acquired during his African campaigns, and having been recently unhorsed in the presence of his command, his Gallic honor was now at stake, and he felt the importance of vindicating among the buffaloes the horsemanship of France.

As we cantered towards the herd, first one and then another of the young officers galloped out from the column, and joined us, until, to my regret, I found our party increased to eight, nearly all inexperienced hunters, and most of them mounted on wild horses hardly less excitable than themselves. Alphonse was perched on the back of a big, hard-mouthed, powerful horse, and in his hand was an army revolver, which he had cocked before he was in cannon range of the game. His eyes gleamed with an eagerness that filled me with apprehension, and my prophetic soul misgave me as I looked at him. I halted my party in a hollow nearest the buffalo, pointed out to them the great danger from so large a party as ours running at once into the herd, ordered Alphonse to uncock his pistol and return it to the holster, and cautioned the others against either drawing or cocking until they should have closed in upon the buffalo.

Then, with an inward wish that I was well out of the affair, I led the way at a gallop over the ridge and straight for a thousand buffalo grazing four hundred yards away. The nearest bulls wheeled with a loud grunting as soon as we cleared the top of the ridge, and the whole herd went off at a full gallop, we dashing after at the speed of our horses. I was still in the lead, and had closed to within fifty yards of the hindmost of the herd, when suddenly a pistol cracked behind me, and a ball went singing through the air. I knew at once it could only be the Frenchman, and reining in my horse, I, like Mazeppa, "writhing half my form about, hurled back my curse" at his infernal carelessness. As I reined in my horse, the Frenchman tore past me, his eyes wide open with excitement, as he tugged at his bridle with both hands, in one of which was that pistol cocked again. Close by his side rode his friend, Bowman, as if trying to help him. They turned off toward the right, and I pushed my horse after the herd.

I had shot two or three buffaloes, when a pistol shot on my right attracted me, and, as I looked hastily in that direction, I saw Bowman toss his arms wildly in the air. I felt he was a dead man, but being in the thick of the run, it was not till some seconds had elapsed, and his riderless horse, pursued by Alphonse, had galloped far off into the prairie, that I was able to follow back the trail to where my poor sergeant lay. He was the most ghastly picture of sudden death I have ever seen. He lay with his head thrown back, his wide-open eyes staring at the sky, and his clenched hands full of grass. There was not a spark of life left in him; all had gone out in that sudden wild toss that I had seen. The ball had entered his breast, and had gone straight through his heart. I dismounted, and leaning my head upon my horse's neck, I wept like a child. Only two or three minutes before he had passed me, looking so full of life and generous earnestness to rescue his friend, and now he lay with that friend's bullet through his heart. For we could only account for it by believing that, as he leaned over in his effort to check Alphonse's horse, the Frenchman, in his excitement, had discharged his pistol.

By the time I reached Bowman's side, all our companions, absorbed by the chase, had disappeared, and only the dead man and I were together on the wide expanse of prairie. After half an hour I was relieved to see Alphonse galloping toward me, leading the sergeant's horse. His success in accomplishing this feat filled him with inward satisfaction, which beamed from his face when he came up to me; but it was instantly replaced by a look of amazed horror, when I said, "Did you shoot this man?" Evidently he was unconscious of having done so. Indeed, I do not believe that he knew his pistol had gone off at all. On examination, I found two barrels were empty. I met Alphonse not very long ago, and talked with him of this sad occurrence. He says the sergeant shot himself, and evidently believes it. Having at last succeeded in attracting one of the young officers who had come within hail in pursuit of a cow he had shot, I rode off to seek the column and get an ambulance. After galloping several miles, I returned with the surgeon and such assistants as he required, and placed the sergeant's body in his charge. By this time all our hunters had assembled save Lieutenant, now General, Frank. One of the party reported to me that he had seen Lieutenant Frank's horse throw him over his head, and then gallop off with the buffalo, and that, though he seemed considerably shaken up, he was evidently not seriously hurt, for he had gone on in pursuit of his horse. Having no confidence in the woodcraft of any of our party, I ordered the ambulance to be driven to the top of the highest ridge near us, to serve as a landmark for my return, and then galloped off in the direction I had been told Frank had taken. After going at a rapid pace for two or three miles, I overtook that young gentleman striding along over the prairie, pistol in hand, right away from his friends. The soft grass of the prairie deadened the sound of my horse's hoofs, and I was close behind him before he knew it.

"Hallo, Frank!" I shouted, "where are you going?" He wheeled around with an expression of intense relief, and replied that he was making for camp.

"Where is your horse?"

"Oh, he went off with the buffalo two hours ago."

"Is your pistol loaded?"

"No, by George! I forgot that."

"Well, old fellow, you are in a very bad neighborhood for an empty pistol, and you are making straight

for the Pawnee camp. Load up as quick as you can
and jump up behind me, for we must lose no time in
getting out of here."

Black Jack was a generous horse, and soon bore us
back to where we found the melancholy group on the
hilltop anxiously watching for our return. We overtook the column at Walnut Creek, and in a sequestered
little nook, formed by a bend of the river, we prepared
a grave for our comrade, and just as the sun was setting
I read the service of the Episcopal Church over his
body, and we left him to his rest.

In the department of New Mexico the Rifles had many
affairs with the Indians, some of them brilliant. In
one of these, Captain Alfred Gibbs was desperately
wounded at the conclusion of a most energetic pursuit
and action which had been a complete success; for the
Rifles killed every Indian in the band, and took from
them all their plunder and property. But our last
Indian affair was perhaps the most important and creditable of all our encounters with these gentry. Colonel
George B. Crittenden, having ascertained that the Comanches were in great force within two days' march of
Fort Union, organized with secrecy and dispatch a party
of about eighty-five Riflemen, and moved with great
rapidity in pursuit of the Indians, who had, however,
gone towards the Cimarron before he could reach their
late camping-ground. He pushed on after them, marching over a country previously unknown to any but the
Indians, and the Mexicans who trade with them. The
road was difficult and rough. It lay through the mountains, and the weather was bitterly cold. Still he went
on, travelling night and day, and enduring every privation, and using every precaution to avoid discovery.
On the morning of the eighth day, about seven o'clock,

they galloped into the Comanche camp, of about one hundred and fifty lodges.

The surprise was complete. Many of the warriors were still rolled in their buffalo robes asleep when the first rifle cracked. Three hundred of them were absent, hunting buffalo, but over two hundred of them remained, and these were fearful odds against Crittenden's attacking force, which was only sixty Rifles, the remainder being left with the packs. A sharp fight ensued, but a few minutes sufficed to leave the Rifles in possession of the village. The women and children, to the number of four or five hundred, fled to the rocky hillside at the first alarm. The warriors fought only long enough to cover their retreat, and then followed their example. The Rifles remained in the village about eight hours, actively occupied all the time in destroying tents and stores, and maintaining a desultory fire with the Indians on the rocks above them. The results of this operation were thirty-five warriors killed, more than a hundred and fifty lodges with a large amount of stores destroyed, and forty horses captured. Not a woman or child was hurt. Four of the Rifles were wounded, none very dangerously. Soon after the Comanches sued for peace, and their request was favorably considered by the commander of the department.

Perhaps no regiment in the service was in its day more distinguished than the Rifles. In Mexico, during nine months, we engaged the enemy eighteen times, losing in killed and wounded, sixteen commissioned officers and several hundred men. Commencing with the Rogue River affair, in Oregon, detachments of this regiment had fifty-six successful encounters with the Indians of that State, of Texas, and of New Mexico, losing in these eight commissioned officers and many men killed and wounded.   So that from the day of our landing at Vera Cruz to the beginning of the late war, a period of fourteen years, this regiment, or portions of it, had encountered the enemies of our country more than seventy times, and had lost in killed and wounded twenty-four commissioned officers and a proportionate number of its rank and file.

CHAPTER X

AFTER Sergeant Bowman's death, we continued
our march without any incident of note,
although, as I have said, we were in hourly
danger of attack or molestation from our red-
skin neighbors. When within two days' march of Fort
Union, we reached the Point of Rocks, where a sad
tragedy had been enacted not many months before.
We watched the ominous spot with anxious eyes, as
its outlines became clearer before us, and felt relieved
when we had left it and its sorrowful associations far
behind ; for even the children of our party were familiar with the sad details of the savage barbarities which
had been enacted there.

Some time before we reached it, a gentleman from Virginia, named White, was making his way to Santa Fé,
where he had business matters awaiting him, carrying
with him his young wife and little child. They had left
Fort Leavenworth in company with a trader's train, with
which they journeyed for protection until within two days
of Fort Union. Their travelling companions were rough
and undesirable associates, and the sojourn together had
been so disagreeable from these causes that they decided

to shorten it as far as possible, and just before reaching the Point of Rocks said good by to the rest of the party, and pushed on towards the fort. The place, as the name implies, is a rocky point which juts out from the neighboring mountain range, and served to conceal the Indians sheltered behind it, who awaited there the coming of their victims. From the time a train left the settlements it was constantly under the espionage of its watchful enemies, and no detail which might afford them an opportunity for murder or robbery escaped their vigilant observation.

The Indians sprang upon the Whites' little party and killed him and the driver of the carriage, carrying Mrs. White and the baby off with them. The dead and mutilated bodies of the two men were found beside the empty vehicle by their late travelling companions, who sent couriers on to the Post to give the alarm. A party of the dragoons, commanded by Captain Greer, and guided by the famous Kit Carson, immediately went in pursuit of the marauders, who had fled to the mountains. It was two days before Greer could come up with them, for they had the advantage of thirty-six hours' start. On the evening of the second day, just at dusk, as the command was winding along a rocky defile, Kit Carson suddenly halted them, saying he heard a child crying. They stopped and listened, but no repetition of the sound met their ears, and they pushed on. Again he called a halt and listened, and again nothing could be heard.

Every moment was of value, and, deciding at last that it was the cry of a wildcat which had deceived them, they continued their rapid march, and finally surprised the Indians in their camp. Their fires were lighted, and they felt so secure from molestation that they had taken no precaution against it. At the first volley they fled, making no attempt at a stand against Greer's men. Mrs. White had been bound to a tree, whether for torture or greater security will never be known, but most probably for the latter reason. Just before Greer, who led the attack, reached her side, an Indian, flying before him, turned and, with cold-blooded barbarity, transfixed her with an arrow. With such means as he could command, Captain Greer prepared a grave and laid her body in it, and then the command set out for its homeward march. There was no trace of the little child to be found in the camp, and they were forced to the conclusion that the Indians had carried it off in their retreat, although this was unlike their usual method of procedure.

They had left the scenes of their late encounter several hours' march behind them, and had arrived at the wild mountain pass where they had tarried the night before to listen for the cry which had reached them, when suddenly Kit Carson reined in his horse and pointed down the rocky side of the defile along which the road wound. There among the boulders lay the dead body of the child. The savages, finding it troublesome, and doubtless annoyed by its cries from hunger and fatigue, had snatched it from the arms of the agonized mother and thrown it down the precipice beside them, leaving it there to perish from cold and starvation or to fall a victim to some prowling beast.

There were many such heartbreaking scenes enacted in those days upon our frontiers, and no Indians were oftener the participants in them than the Apaches and Comanches, with whom we had to deal. After a man has been brought face to face with them in many years of frontier service, he is inclined to agree unreservedly with General Sheridan's verdict regarding a " good Indian."

We reached Fort Union in good time and with all of
our horses in fine condition.   It was then the regimental
headquarters, but only one troop of Mounted Rifles
remained there, the others having been sent out upon
an expedition against the Indians, who had been making
threatening demonstrations.   It was during this campaign
that an incident occurred, which evidenced the coolness
and courage of one of our young officers, whose name
is recognized to-day wherever lovers of fine horses are
found.   I allude to General William H. Jackson, of
Bellemead, or, as his old army friends still call him,
" Red Jackson."   At the time of which I write, he was
a lieutenant in the Rifles, and was out after the Comanches, with his company.   Of course, on a scout of
this sort, all hunting and shooting was strictly forbidden.
One day a grizzly came down from the mountains and
crossed the route of the column.   Jackson coolly rode
out to encounter the animal, armed only with his sabre.
His horse was blind in one eye, and, by keeping that side
turned to the bear, Jackson was able to get close to
him.   At his approach, the grizzly, nothing loath, rose on
his hind legs ready for a fight, and Jackson cleft his skull
with his sword.   It is doubtful if such an exploit was ever
elsewhere attempted or accomplished.

We found Major Simonson, Captain Morris, Dr. Baily,
Lieutenant Julian May, and several other officers on
duty at Fort Union when we reached there.   I was
Regimental Adjutant, and we had the regimental band,
but very little to occupy us beside the usual routine
of a frontier cavalry post, which allowed us plenty of
leisure for hunting and wolf-chasing.

Captain Shoemaker was the officer in charge of the
ordnance stores.   He was a kindly gentleman, well
known and respected in the army, and kept a fine

pack of greyhounds. His dog Possum was a cross of a breed left with our regiment, by Sir George Gore, some years before. He was the tallest and longest dog I have ever seen, and of great fleetness and power. He always led the pack of ten greyhounds, which I was enabled to make up and keep in the Commissary's corral, under charge of Corporal Thomson, a bright young Virginian and an ardent hunter. Three times a week in the season we would have the pack out to kill a wolf. As the prairie sloped gently up to the edge of the Turkey Mountains, some five miles distant, we had a good course in full view of the garrison, and almost always caught the wolf before he could reach the timber. Otherwise we didn't get him, for the hounds would not run in cover, and the coyotes seemed to know this, and always made for it from the start. Possum, invariably in the lead, would thrust his long snout between the wolf's hind legs as he closed on him, and toss him over his back, where he would hold him until the rest of the pack came up, when he was soon killed. Sometimes the riders would be up in time to beat the dogs off and tie up the wolf, taking him home for another day's run. Occasionally we would get an antelope, and Possum always threw him in the same way. No animal is so fleet as the antelope, with a good start and a fair field before him. Like the hare, however, he is timid, and, when headed off or turned, becomes bewildered, loses his running, and is easily caught.

Thus it was that Toots one evening started an antelope, and was running him along the little valley of the creek that watered Fort Union, when I galloped to head him where he would come out upon the prairie, over which the ten greyhounds were spread out "breasting." These, seeing me running, all took up the run in the same direction, and as the antelope came out upon the plain he saw a circle of enemies closing around him, and hesitated, bewildered. Toots was close behind him, and, seizing him by the leg, swung on to him until I rolled off Black Jack, caught him by the horn, and killed him before any dog of the pack had reached him. Toots was a wonderful dog, occasionally too zealous, as when one day he killed a polecat in our kitchen, and we had to vacate the premises for a week, taking refuge with our good friends, Dr. Baily and his wife.

Not long after, Corporal Thomson and I took the dogs out after a wolf. We ran one four miles, but he finally got into the brush of Turkey Mountains and escaped us. We were returning slowly, the hounds trotting behind the corporal's horse, and Toots, as usual, ranging out on the prairie, when all at once I saw him come running in towards us, his ears thrown back in alarm, and behind him came wabbling in pursuit a polecat, with tail erect, ready for action. Toots had learned something about polecats in that momentous encounter in our kitchen, but the greyhounds had yet to be initiated into the mysteries of that animal, so when they lifted up their eyes and saw this one coming, they gathered about him and with one consent rent him asunder. Then began high jinks; such tumbling and whining and rubbing of noses and general gymnastics no ten dogs ever set up at the same time. The corporal and I nearly rolled off our horses with laughter, and Toots sat off beyond polecat range, laughing as if he would split his sides. Evidently, he enjoyed the joke more than any of us.

Toots was the only setter that ever lived to take hold of a buffalo. One morning, after Sergeant Bowman's death, I was riding at the head of the column, eagerly watching Lieutenant Tracy, who was running a cow with a six-months-old calf. The cow suddenly charged Tracy, whose horse stampeded and ran away with him for a mile or more before he could check or turn him. The calf also stampeded and ran straight for me until it was within about fifteen yards, when I turned upon it and rolled it over. Toots sprang from the carriage where he was having a ride beside the driver, dashed past me, and swung to the calf while it was yet struggling upon the ground. Long afterward, near Fort Wise, I shot an ante-lope and broke his hind leg. Toots chased him with me for fully two miles, and caught and held him until I seized his horn and knifed him. Game was so plentiful then on the western frontier that there were few days in which we could not have good sport. My own expe-rience in the field convinced me that there was no animal so wary, so enduring, and so dangerous as the wild bull of Texas. I except the grizzly bear always, who has not his equal for fierce and aggressive courage in all the cata-logue of wild beasts.

One day at Fort Staunton a horse guard came gallop-ing in and reported to Captain Claiborne of the Rifles, that an old she-grizzly and two cubs were in the timber near the horse pasture. Claiborne, who was a great hunter and a fine shot, snatched his rifle, and, accompanied by a friend, hurried out to meet his savage game. They soon found them and rolled the she-bear over, but the cubs, about the size of setter dogs, climbed up into some trees and went out upon the limbs, where no one could get at them. Claiborne's object being not to kill but to capture them, it was decided to shoot the limbs, cutting them away with rifle-balls until they would no longer bear the weight of the cubs. Being capital shots, this was soon accomplished, and they had the satisfaction of securing alive fine specimens by this novel plan for cap-turing grizzlies.

We passed one year at Fort Union, at the end of which we heard the news of John Brown's capture of Harper's Ferry. Then the Indians cut off mail communication, and we heard no more for many weeks, when by a system of escorts between the Rifles and the First Cavalry our mail-route was re-established, and a sergeant brought me a letter from Lieutenant Jeb Stuart, congratulating me upon my promotion to a captaincy in the Adjutant-General's department, with orders to repair to Santa Fé, then the headquarters of the department of New Mexico. This was a great gratification, as it was a position of high trust and importance, and carried with it assurance of a comfortable and permanent residence.

There were many officers stationed at Santa Fé, and the city, being the headquarters of the department, was much visited by officers from every part of it, and we all got on very cordially together until the quickening excitement of the approaching war separated us. Before the year was out we had to be upon our guard in our intercourse with each other; for, whereas we seemed to be in accord before the hostilities began, and nearly all were Southern in their sympathies, when the time came to prove the faith, there were but few who gave up the certain pay and emoluments of the established government of the United States for the uncertainty of one yet to be created. I remember that at our last Christmas dinner in Santa Fé, we carefully selected our guests according to their avowed intentions in the coming crisis.

At last the blow fell for which we had so apprehensively been watching. In these days of telegraph and rapid transit, it is hard to realize the suspense and anxiety from which we suffered as the days dragged their slow lengths along from the arrival of one mail to the next. We could only expect news once a week, and not

then if the Indians chose to interfere with its trans-
mission, which they frequently did. As the mail-day
would approach, our impatience would increase with each
hour of suspense, and I well recall the anxious group
which gathered in our parlor one evening in May, 1861,
to await its arrival and distribution. There was Loring,
our colonel, who had fought through two wars, and was
again to win distinction in another, and Lieutenant John
Pegram, who in the coming struggle would rise to the
rank of general, and die bravely for his home and people,
and Grason of Virginia, and several others, who with my
wife and me awaited with ill-concealed anxiety the coming of the orderly with the mail-bag. The mail for all
the department came to my office, and had to be assorted there, but at last we were able to seize the papers
and turn to the telegrams. Usually it was our home
letters, with news of our dear ones far away, which were
opened first, but that night these were cast aside un-
noticed, while we read of the fall of Fort Sumter. Even
then it was some time before we could grasp the details.
One after another we took the sheet and tried to read
aloud its contents, and each voice, broken with emotion
in the effort, refused to do its owner's bidding.

The die was cast. The great war which was to bring
to us and to our people ruin and desolation was upon us,
and we must go to meet it. It was in no light or unap-
preciative mood that we sat looking at each other in the
silence which followed the reading of the telegrams; for
we realized the greatness of the sacrifice expected of us,
and it was with sad hearts that we turned our backs upon
the friends and associations of a happy past, and faced
the issues of a future which had little to offer us save the
consciousness of duty loyally performed. At last I awoke
once more to the excitement of the moment, and to a

realization of the great crisis of which we alone were informed, and, seizing the papers, I ran out into the street and made my way to the officers' quarters, shouting aloud as I went that Fort Sumter had fallen, and war had begun !

CHAPTER XI

S soon as the news of Virginia's secession from the Union reached me, I sent in my resignation, and prepared to follow it to the States. No one. had ever doubted that such would be my course, and all my friends regarded it as the only proper one for me to pursue.

The Navajoes had become hostile, committing many depredations that fall, and we had fitted out a formidable expedition to invade their country during the winter. It was placed under the command of Colonel Canby, who pressed it with severity. While the troops suffered much from the great cold and deep snows, the Indians perished in numbers. They are less savage and more thrifty than any other wild tribe, having permanent homes, flocks and herds, and some manufactures, and are therefore more assailable. They paid a heavy reckoning that winter, for their homes were destroyed and their herds taken from them, and it was said that they dared not stay long in any one place, and that all the children born to them during that campaign perished. They soon and earnestly sued for peace, and kept it too, until recently hostilities have been renewed in their region.

Canby did his work effectually, and returned to Santa Fé just as I was about to leave it for Richmond. He, with his wife, was our guest there, and I carefully explained to him how and where I had distributed the troops of the department, of which he showed his approval, and I then transferred to him my office and my house. Just four years afterward, I left him my office in Mobile, he and I having closed the great war after the long-contested battle of Mobile, with mutual respect for each other.

During the fighting with the Oregon Indians, in which Jamie Stuart was killed, Walker's command captured a young Indian little more than a lad. The Rifles had scattered a band which took to the river, and as our men were examining the banks in search of fugitives, one of them saw a pair of bright eyes shining through the roots of an overhanging tree, and stooping, caught an Indian boy by his legs, and hauled him out. They took him along for some time, until near where he could make his way to his people, and then set him free. It would have been better for all if the young reptile had been shot then and there. Years afterward, Canby was murdered by the celebrated Modoc chief, Captain Jack. He was the Indian boy caught by Walker thirty years before, and set free, and in relating the history of his life just before his execution, Jack recited the incidents of his capture and of his liberation. The Post chaplain who ministered to him in his last moments felt it his duty to prepare him for his fate, and to reconcile him to it by descanting to him upon the good company who would greet him in the eternal home, to which Jack replied: "I don't know none them peoples. They your friends. I give you ten ponies you tak' my place to-morrer!"

I sold out my household goods of every sort in Santa Fé, and hired a wagon of the first train to cross the plains, and the quartermaster furnished me with an ambulance and team. At Fort Union, where we halted to make up our party, every consideration and respect was shown us. Lieutenant Enos, a big-hearted young fellow from New York, had been much with me and my family, and showed deep emotion on parting from us. Lieutenant Gay, another manly young officer, took me to one side and said: "You may need a good horse before you get through. I present you with that Navajo mare of mine. I picked her out of a drove of five hundred we captured. She is yours." Webb, the sutler, pressed upon me as much money as I would accept. I assured him I was well supplied, but told him of another of our Southern officers who needed money, and he gave him as much as he could be induced to take.

At every Post upon our route the same kindly feeling met us, and at parting we were told: "I hate to lose you, old fellow, but you are perfectly right. If I were in your place, I would do the same thing."

The season was late, and the grass for half of our journey very bad, and we were forty-five days in our wagons, a wearisome time of suspense and anxiety to us. Our escort consisted of about seventy men, who had just served the term of their enlistment, and were on furlough. With two exceptions, they all intended on reaching the States to join Northern regiments for the approaching war.

As we proceeded, rumors of the coming struggle flew thick and fast toward us, and each day the danger of arrest and detention seemed more imminent, and our anxiety for the helpless women and children of our party increased.   When within two or three miles of Council Grove, we met three rough-looking men in an open wagon, who called out to us as they passed: "You had better look out in Council Grove! They are going to give you hell!"

Captain John G. Walker was in command of the party, and he and I took counsel, finally deciding that he should close his command well up on the rising ground above the village, while I would ride on into it and report if there were any hostile demonstration or purpose to hurt or hinder us.   We knew that Jim Lane and the Kansas roughs had been notified of our coming and of our position towards the government of the United States, and that we were now entering the most advanced outposts of the "Jay Hawkers."   I rode up to our carriage, and asked my wife to let me have the children's old shoes, telling her I would ride on ahead and buy some new ones, as we should not halt in the place.   As she gave them to me, she also let me understand that she knew my real object.   I rode forward, and stopping at the largest store, where some horses were hitched, went in and got the shoes.   A group of men standing there greeted me sociably, and were inclined to be chatty, and I rode back and told Walker to come on, as there was no danger.   We marched rapidly through the town to our camp, four miles beyond, and felt relief at having escaped any trouble.   One of our objects in going beyond the village was to prevent the men from obtaining liquor if we could, for it was the Fourth of July, and after their long enforced sobriety upon the march they would be the more apt to indulge themselves too freely now.

Our camp had been pitched, and I was stretched out

on my cot resting after the hard, hot ride, when I was aroused by a disturbance near the guard tent. As I looked out an old Rifleman, named Kearns, knocked the sergeant of the guard down. I have never seen a man knocked as he was. He went tumbling fifteen feet before he rested on his back. Kearns stood, pistol in hand, defying arrest. He was six feet two inches in height, and was known as the bully of the regiment. When he was sober, he was an excellent soldier, but now he was maddened by whiskey. He laid his loaded rifle at his feet, and swore he would kill any one who attempted to arrest him, and, holding his revolver in his hand with his thumb on the hammer, he was ready to make good his word.

Walker, at about forty paces' distance from Kearns, was attempting to cap his Colt's rifle and shoot him down where he stood; for he thought it was the signal for a general uprising; that it meant violence to us and to our wives and children. I snatched up my six-shooter, and ran to Walker, urging him not to shoot Kearns, adding that I would disarm him. Mrs. Walker at the same time clung to her husband, imploring him not to shoot, while I, holding my cocked pistol behind me, advanced rapidly towards my man, striving to keep the while between Walker and him. As I approached him, I held out my left hand for his revolver, and said a few earnest words to him about the helpless women and children he was endangering, ending by ordering him to go at once to the guard tent. He handed me his pistol, saying, "Captain Maury, I've always uphilt ye fer a gintleman, if ye are a Southern man, and I'll do just as ye bid me," and turning he went to the guard tent and lay down.

Next morning when I came out of my tent I saw

Kearns sitting in front of the guard tent, looking the picture of woe. I beckoned him to me, and gave him his arms, and begged him not to drink again upon this march. With very deep feeling he said, "Sure, I'll never forgit your treatment of me as long as I live, and ef iver ye need a friend, ye'll find him in me." He showed sincere emotion, and he kept his word, for he never drank again, and he seemed always on the lookout for an opportunity to help me or to serve me in any possible way. Nor did the insubordinate characters who had encouraged Kearns to his riotous outbreak ever transgress further, though they would have gone to any length had he not yielded.

Two of them were on my tent detail, and the morning I rode away from camp into Leavenworth they stole my revolvers. I was greatly concerned when I heard it, and, after I had reported to the commanding officer, set out for the encampment of our escort with a vague hope of recovering them. I saw a man approaching me, whom I recognized as the rascal I suspected. When he saw me he changed his course, and, as I still approached him, broke into a run. I did likewise, and as he stepped into a little ditch and fell, I sprang on top of him, demanding my pistol, which he relinquished. By that time the sergeant of the guard had come hastily up, and, taking out my memorandum book, I called the number of the pistol. The sergeant said, "It is yours, Captain," and handed it to me. I then ordered him to take the man to the guard tent and hand him over to the officer with my compliments, which was done forthwith. One of the officers had already recovered the other pistol for me, and I thus received another of the many evidences proffered us of the good feeling of our brother-officers towards us, who were so soon to be widely separated from them.

At Topeka, Kansas, the morning papers contained the order announcing that "Captain Carter L. Stevenson, Captain Dabney H. Maury, and Lieutenant Edward Dillon are hereby stricken from the rolls of the army for entertaining treasonable designs against the government of the United States." From that time we naturally doubted if we would be permitted to proceed on our journey southward.

On our homeward march, we crossed the Arkansas at Bent's old ford, and followed the river down its course for many days. Walker had brought with him a huge and savage dog, half mastiff, half bloodhound, of whom everybody was afraid. He was more tolerant of me than of any one, because I used to take him with me on my hunts. But on this particular evening old Cy was very cross, and as in passing I patted him on the head he tossed up his mouth and seized me by the arm with a savage growl. I knew it was war to the death, and I kicked him heavily in the ribs, drawing my knife as I did so. The brute crouched and sprang at my throat, and I caught him fair in the breast with my knife. He drew back, casting a reproachful look at me, and, staggering to the river, rolled over dead. I called out to Walker that I had killed his dog, expressing my regret at having been forced to do so; to which he replied that he was glad I had done it, and that I had no other course, as he certainly would have killed me if I hadn't him.

Our camp was near Fort Atkinson, about which we found some two thousand Indians assembled. They were Arapahoes and Cheyennes, who were awaiting the annual distribution by the Indian agents of presents, etc. About ten minutes after old Cy's death, I observed a number of Indians gathered about his body, and finally

an old squaw emerged from the crowd, exultingly holding aloft one of old Cy's hind quarters, as she went to
her tepee shouting in wild Indian fashion. As the
group dispersed I went down to the river. They had
left nothing of the dog save a little blood upon the
grass. They had had no fresh meat for some time, and
dog is an Indian's dainty dish.

On our last night out we camped within eight miles
of Fort Leavenworth, and very early next morning I
rode into the Post, expecting possible arrest, and intending to pass on to Louisville and await my family there,
if I found there was any intention to stop me. I rode
to the sutler's store just as the morning flag was running
up, and found there old Colonel Rich, one of the most
respected and beloved of the old-time sutlers. His son
was already in the First Missouri Regiment and in the
field on the Southern side. Poor lad! He fell gallantly
fighting at Shiloh.

I was clad in an old corduroy hunting-suit, and had
not been shaven or shorn since I left Santa Fé, and the
old gentleman peered curiously into my face as we
walked out of hearing before he said, "Why, it's Maury,
isn't it?"

"Yes."

"Well, I'd never have taken you for a gentleman.
What are you doing here so early?"

"I am here to learn if they intend to arrest me."

"No, indeed; they will treat you more kindly than
ever you were treated in Fort Leavenworth." And so,
indeed, they did.

I hastened back to meet the column and come in with
the other officers and report to the commander of the
Post, Colonel Prince. After cordially welcoming us, he
said, "Maury, here's an order interesting to you and

Stevenson," and gave us the order we had seen a few days before at Topeka. I then turned to the paymaster and asked if a month's pay was not due me. He said, "Yes; and I would like to pay it to you, but here is an order just received requiring that it shall be paid to you only in Washington." It has been paid me since.

Our stay in Leavenworth was brief, and when we came away a young kinsman of mine from Virginia, who was employed in the paymaster's department, joined us. His name was Francis Berkeley. He entered a Virginia regiment, shouldered his musket, and played his part like a man, and now lives, highly respected, as Captain Berkeley of Staunton. One of our Virginia regiments was known as "the Berkeley regiment," because the colonel, the lieutenant-colonel, the major, and the adjutant were all Berkeleys, akin to each other.

The record of the Virginians everywhere, when their State seceded, is full of pride and honor. Many were in distant parts of the army, or on remote stations in the Navy, or otherwise enjoying positions of credit and emolument. . Yet, with a promptness and devotion never surpassed, they surrendered every benefit which long and distinguished service had earned for them, and made their way home through dangers and difficulties, from a noble sense of duty to their State and to their people.

Of those who finally decided to bear arms against the South, George H. Thomas easily leads in point of ability and attainments as a soldier. He was born in Southampton County, Virginia, was greatly distinguished in the Mexican War, and was voted a sword by his native State. No man was ever more devoted to his own people, and they greatly loved and honored him. In

the Virginia Convention, which was greatly opposed
to secession until Lincoln declared his purpose to march
an army across the State to coerce South Carolina,
Thomas was thought of as the commander-in-chief of
the Virginia forces. Neither Lee nor Johnston had yet
declared his purpose in case his State should secede,
while Thomas had proclaimed that he would retire from
the Federal army and enter the service of Virginia in
the event of her secession.

He had active friends to support his claims, and he
applied early for an appointment in the Virginia forces,
and Governor Letcher held an important office awaiting
his resignation from the United States army. With this
in his pocket, as it were, he went to New York to sever
his connection with the service of the United States, and
bring his wife back to Virginia with him. She was a
woman of fine character. Her kindred and her property were in New York, and through her influence he
delayed his action until he had received from General
Scott orders to an important post; and like other great
soldiers of history and good men everywhere and in all
times past, he was conquered by a woman.

When General Fitz Lee, *en route* to Virginia, after his
own resignation, called to see Thomas, he said at parting, "Well, Major, I suppose we shall meet in Richmond in a few days?"

"Yes," replied Thomas. His wife — a handsome
woman she was — remarked, "He thinks he will."

Thomas' purposes were as well understood as those
of any other man whatever in his position. He made
them a matter of record by his official applications for
service, which were published and well known before his
death. Had he followed his natural inclinations and
allegiance, and accepted the commission which Gov-

ernor Letcher held in reserve for him, his native State would have been the better off by one more able and brave commander.

We reached St. Louis with great anxiety, for party-feeling ran high there, General Lyon being especially vigorous in his course against the secession party. Camp Jackson had been captured and some citizens had been shot. We regretted the fact that we were compelled to remain all night in the city, and could not cross over into Illinois until next morning. Some of our late escort had travelled along with us thus far, and among them a corporal who said he intended to have me arrested. He was an Englishman, and was one of those who had instigated Kearns to his violent outbreak. I had decided to avoid the fashionable hotels in St. Louis, where I might be met and recognized, and went to a quiet house, where such was not so apt to be the case. While registering my name, a man came up beside me to register his, and turning I found myself face to face with the corporal. I gave him a nod of recognition, which he received with an insolent and triumphant air, as I fancied, at having me at last in his power. It was already midnight, and no arrests could be made then, and we were to cross the river before sunrise in the morning, so I said to myself, "If that fellow does not go over into Illinois with us, we are safe." As we stepped on the ferry-boat, one of the very first men we saw was this rascal. I had not been so alarmed since leaving Fort Union. Two trains were waiting the arrival of the ferry-boat, one bound for Chicago, and the other for Louisville, and to our great satisfaction the man took the former, and we saw him no more.

The conductor of our train was a remarkably gentle-manly man, and said, pointing to our servants who had

gone with us to New Mexico: "I presume these are
your slaves, and I wish to tell you not to be anxious
about them.   I have carried more than four thousand
slaves over this line, and have never lost one."   I was not
uneasy on that score, for ours were more afraid of losing us than we were of losing them; but it was with a
feeling of general relief that I gathered my little party
safely around me in the Galt House in Louisville, and
took a julep.

CHAPTER XII

E reached Richmond on July 19th, where all was in active preparation for war. I reported to the governor and to General Lee, commanding the forces of Virginia. I was much impressed by the grave and anxious aspect of General Lee, and remarked to Commodore Maury that it surprised and depressed me. He, too, had observed it. I was appointed Colonel of Cavalry of the Virginia forces, and ordered to report to Adjutant-General Cooper. The same day I received my appointment as Captain of the Regular Cavalry of the Confederacy, and Lieutenant-Colonel of their provisional army.

I told General Cooper that I would take my family to Fredericksburg, where my mother, whom I had not seen for two years, was living, and he replied that he would send my orders there.

The Sunday that I spent in Fredericksburg, we could hear all day the distant firing at Manassas. No orders had yet come for me, but I took the first train for Richmond. I had been apprehensive lest my wife or mother should hinder me from going into battle, but I never again had any anxiety on that score, for they seemed as solicitous as I that I should be in time for that engagement. On arriving at the adjutant-general's office, I found that my orders had been sent to the Spottswood Hotel, where I had never been at all. But for this mistake, I should have reached Manassas in time for the great battle, for I was assigned to General Joseph E. Johnston, as his adjutant-general.

On my way up, I met people at every station who were full of the news of the great victory. President Davis was on the down train, and had been in the battle, and from the platform of the car made a stirring speech to the exultant multitude. When I reached the field, the Federal dead were not yet all buried, and I remember well the horrid spectacle of near one hundred red-breeched Zouaves who lay about where the Confederates had captured a Federal battery, their swollen bodies and blackened faces making a ghastly contrast with their bright scarlet uniforms and gay trappings.

On my arrival, I immediately presented my orders to General Johnston. As he read them, he exclaimed with great emphasis: "This is an outrage! I rank General Lee, and he has no right to order officers into my army." Of course I was deeply mortified, and after an interval sufficient to allow him to grow calmer, I asked him to let me speak to him. He cordially assented, and, walking off from ear-shot of those about him, and placing his arm affectionately on my shoulder, said, "Maury, you know, or you ought to know, that I would rather have you in this office with me than any other man in the army, but I cannot accept any orders which will acquiesce in so unlawful an assignment of rank of the Confederate generals as has been made." As he spoke, he passed his arm over my shoulder, and showed great feeling for me.

I said: "I know nothing of this, and my position is a very embarrassing one. With your permission, I will go at once to Richmond and request assignment elsewhere." Which I did forthwith.

General Johnston recovered from his wounds at Jalapa in time to enter the valley of Mexico with General Scott, and bear his part in those battles. At Chapultepec, while leading his battalion, he was severely wounded again, making the ninth shot received by him in battle. On the disbandment of the voltigeurs, he was restored to the Topographical Engineers, where he served until 1854. When two new regiments of cavalry were added to our regular army, he was appointed Lieutenant-Colonel of the First, and Lee Lieutenant-Colonel of the Second. In the course of four or five years, Johnston was made Quartermaster-General, with rank and pay of Brigadier-General, and the Senior Major promoted to his vacated Lieutenant-Colonelcy. The Confederate Congress made a law that all officers should hold rank in the Confederate army in accordance with that held in the United States army, and Johnston, as the only brigadier-general who came south, felt that he was entitled to be the senior general of the Confederate forces. But it was ordered that he should take position as if he had been a lieutenant-colonel. This placed him below Sidney Johnston, General Cooper, and General Lee, making him fourth in rank instead of first, and was naturally very galling to him, conscious as he was of his great powers and remarkable services.

I subsequently learned that after our interview at Manassas, General Johnston wrote to President Davis, protesting against the injustice of the existing state of affairs, and saying that he would raise no protest now, nor until the independence of the Southern Confederacy should be achieved, when he would use all lawful means to have his rank rightfully established. The gauntlet then thrown down was accepted as a gauge of battle between the President and General Johnston, ultimately causing his removal from the command of the army of Tennessee and the downfall of the Confederacy, as many now believe. Johnston was critical, controversial, and sometimes irritable by nature, very exact in his statements, and possessed of a wonderful memory. Few men read so much as he, and none I have ever seen retained so accurately facts and impressions, or were so careful in the selection of the words to express their views. It is not probable that any man in our country had ever studied the histories and biographies of wars and warriors as had Johnston.

I find among my papers the following letter from General Johnston, which is interesting as giving his account of the campaign preceding his removal from the command of the army of Tennessee : —

MACON, GA., September 1st, 1864.

My Dear Maury :

I have been intending ever since my arrival at this place to pay a part of the epistolary debt I owe you. But you know how lazy it makes one to have nothing to do, and so with the hot weather we have been enduring here, I have absolutely devoted myself to idleness. I have been disposed to write more particularly of what concerns myself — to explain to you, as far as practicable, the operations for which I was laid on the shelf, for you are one of the last whose unfavorable opinion I would be willing to incur.

You know that the army I commanded was that which, under General Bragg, was routed at Missionary Ridge. Sherman's army was that which routed it, reinforced by the Sixteenth and Twenty-third Corps. I am censured for not taking the offensive at Dalton — where the enemy, if beaten, had a secure refuge behind the fortified gap at Ringgold, or in the fortress of Chattanooga, and where the

odds against us were almost ten to four. At Resaca he received
five brigades, near Kingston three, and about 3500 cavalry; at
New Hope Church one; in all about 14,000 infantry and artillery.
The enemy received the Seventeenth Corps and a number of garrisons and bridge guards from Tennessee and Kentucky that had
been relieved by "hundred-day men."

I am blamed for not fighting. Operations commenced about the
6th of May; I was relieved on the 18th of July. In that time we
fought daily, always under circumstances so favorable to us as to
make it certain that the sum of the enemy's losses was five times
ours, which was 10,000 men. Northern papers represented theirs
up to about the end of June at 45,000. Sherman's progress was
at the rate of a mile and a quarter a day. Had this style of fighting been allowed to continue, is it not clear that we would soon
have been able to give battle with abundant chances of victory, and
that the enemy, beaten on this side of the Chattahoochee, would
have been destroyed? It is certain that Sherman's army was
stronger, compared with that of Tennessee, than Grant's, compared
with that of Northern Virginia. General Bragg asserts that Sherman's was absolutely stronger than Grant's. It is well known that
the army of Virginia was much superior to that of Tennessee.

Why, then, should I be condemned for the defensive while General Lee was adding to his great fame by the same course? General
Bragg seems to have earned at Missionary Ridge his present high
position. People report at Columbus and Montgomery that General Bragg said that my losses had been frightful; that I had disre-
garded the wishes and instructions of the President; that he had
in vain implored me to change my course, by which I suppose is
meant assume the offensive.

As these things are utterly untrue, it is not to be supposed that
they were said by General Bragg. The President gave me no
instructions and expressed no wishes except just before we reached
the Chattahoochee, warning me not to fight with the river behind us
and against crossing it, and previously he urged me not to allow
Sherman to detach to Grant's aid. General Bragg passed some
ten hours with me just before I was relieved, and gave me the impression that his visit to the army was casual, he being on his way
further west to endeavor to get us reinforcements from Kirby Smith
and Lee. I thought him satisfied with the state of things, but not
so with that in Virginia. He assured me that he had always main-

tained in Richmond that Sherman's army was stronger than Grant's. He said nothing of the intention to relieve me, but talked with General Hood on the subject, as I learned after my removal. It is clear that his expedition had no other object than my removal and the giving proper direction to public opinion on the subject. He could have had no other object in going to Montgomery. A man of honor in his place would have communicated with me as well as with Hood on the subject. Being expected to assume the offensive, he attacked on the 20th, 22d, and 28th of July, disastrously, losing more men than I had done in seventy-two days. Since then his defensive has been at least as quiet as mine was.

But you must be tired of this. We are living very quietly and pleasantly here. The Georgians have been very hospitable. We stopped here merely because it was the first stopping-place. Remember us cordially to Mrs. Maury. Tell her the gloves arrived most opportunely. Mine had just been lost and it would have been impossible to buy more, and they are lovely. Just before I left the army we thought the odds against us had been reduced almost six to four. I have not supposed therefore that Sherman could either invest Atlanta or carry it by assault.

Very truly yours,   J. E. JOHNSTON.

Major-General Maury.

When Johnston took charge of the great army of Tennessee, which had been defeated and disorganized before his arrival to its command, it was in wretched condition. Most of the general officers were in open hostility or avowed mistrust of the general commanding, and indiscipline prevailed throughout. When Johnston came, the change was instantaneous, and henceforth no army of the Confederacy ever equalled Johnston's in drill and high discipline.

General Carter Stevenson was one of the division commanders of that army, a man of the largest experience and military accomplishments. He had served in every army of the Confederacy, and actively in all of our wars since 1834. He told me he had never seen any troops in such fine discipline and condition as

Johnston's army the day he was removed from its command. General Randall L. Gibson had been in constant action in the Western army. He it was who closed an honorable record by his masterly command of the defences near Spanish Fort, on the eastern shore of Mobile Bay, in the last great battle of the war between the States. He says that when Johnston assumed command of that army, it was somewhat demoralized, but when the campaign with Sherman opened, the worst regiment in it was equal to its best when he came to its command. A Missouri soldier of Cockrell's brigade, which Johnston declared to be the best body of infantry he ever saw, was on his way back to his regiment after recovery from a wound. I asked him, "What do you all think of the change of commanders?"

"Oh, sir, we are mightily cut down about it. The bomb-proofs and the newspapers complain of his retreats. Why, we didn't miss a meal from Dalton to Atlanta, and were always ready for the fight. We never felt we were retreating."

Just after Johnston's removal, General Wigfall passed Mobile, and sent a request to me to come down to his steamer, for he wanted to have some talk with me. He was just from the army of Tennessee, where he had been with Hood, Johnston having gone away. He spoke with his accustomed vigor relative to the change of commanders, saying: "Mr. Davis' favor was no less fatal to its objects than his animosities. That young man Hood had a fine career before him until Davis undertook to make of him what the good Lord had not done — to make a great general of him. He has removed General Johnston and put Hood in his place. He has thus ruined Hood, and destroyed the last hope of the Southern Confederacy."

Several years after the war, the Legislature of Virginia ordered General Johnston's portrait to be painted by Elder and hung in the capitol of the State. I was asked to be present at the sittings, to keep him in conversation that the artist might have the advantage of the play of his features. The first day he discussed Napoleon, Marlborough, and Wellington. Ranking Napoleon above all great commanders since Cæsar, he criticised him with great animation for more than half an hour. Marlborough he ranked as the greatest commander and statesman England ever produced. He inveighed bitterly against the partisanship of Macaulay, who accepted as authority contemporary disparagement of Marlborough, while he rejected the same authority as unworthy of credit when it assailed King William. The next day he discussed Lee, Jackson, and Forrest, and according to Lee and Jackson the full measure of their fame, he pronounced Forrest the greatest soldier the war produced. These discussions occupied each day the whole time of the sittings. He spoke uninterruptedly. Elder and I listened, and always regretted that his words and emphasis could not be recorded and preserved. The portrait is a good one, and it hangs in the rotunda with those of Lee, Jackson, Maury, and many another of Virginia's sons from colonial days till now.

At Seven Pines, when assured of victory, Johnston was stricken down by the severest injury he had ever received. A shell burst near him, breaking three of his ribs, and at the same time a rifle-ball pierced his shoulder-blade. He fell from his horse, and was borne from the field to the residence of his friend, Mr. Cranshaw, where he lay until somewhat recovered from his eleventh and last wound. While lying there, he was the object of great interest and affection to all our people, who felt we were deprived, at a most critical time, of our great leader, who up to that time had evinced every capacity of a general, while Lee had not yet achieved success in the field. During this period, an old gentleman of Richmond called to pay his respects and express sympathy for our general. He said, "General, I not only deplore this because of the suffering it entails upon you, but I consider it a great national calamity." To his great amazement, Johnston suddenly raised himself upon his elbow, and with his peculiar energy of expression said: "No, sir. The shot that struck me down is the very best that has been fired for the Southern Confederacy yet. For I possess in no degree the confidence of our government, and now they have in my place one who does possess it, and who can accomplish what I never could have done,— the concentration of our armies for the defence of the capital of the Confederacy."

Dr. Fauntleroy, his medical attendant and the chief surgeon of the army, was present at this interview, which he related to me many years after, when Johnston was running for Congress, and when the opposition papers were daily disparaging him. Fauntleroy told me this while I was on my way to the White Sulphur, where General and Mrs. Johnston were established for the summer. I urged Fauntleroy to publish this characteristic anecdote in the Richmond *Dispatch*. He demurred, but I insisted that he owed it to the general to remind our people of those days when he endured so much for them, and he finally agreed to do it, stipulating that he should not sign his name to the story.

Accordingly, it came out in the next issue of the *Dispatch*, signed "Medicus." I went on my way to the Springs, well pleased with the part I had borne in this tribute to the old man. A few days afterward Johnston returned from his canvass, and was very bright and well-satisfied with the progress of his contest. He hunted me up about dinner-time, and said he had some fresh mint and good brandy at his cottage, where we would go, and his wife would make us a julep. On our way across the lawn, he was so cheery and pleasant that it seemed to me a favorable time to tell him of Fauntleroy's publication, and if he seemed greatly pleased I would impart to him my share in this friendly service. As I proceeded with my narrative, I observed an ominous silence come over him, with an increasing redness about his face and a peculiar twitching of his neck, premonitory of an explosion. Suddenly he stopped still, and in a fierce tone said, "Don't you think it an infamous outrage, sir, to publish a gentleman's name in the newspapers without his permission?" I did not remind him that his name had been daily for many months published in the newspapers without his permission, nor did I think it worth while to allude to the part I had borne in this "infamous outrage," but just went right along. In fact, I rather acquiesced in his views, and changed the subject, till Mrs. Johnston with her delicious juleps and hearty cordiality made us forget all the outrages of the world.

I have never known two people more devoted to each other than they were. Her health was not robust, and he watched over her in her illnesses with the greatest tenderness, and at all times paid her the delicate attentions of a lover. I believe they had been married more than fifty years when her death occurred. It left him very desolate. They had no children, which was a great cause of regret to him, for he was very fond of children and was especially so of mine. He told me one day with much feeling, "You are certainly blessed in your children."

One day, while living in Richmond, Mrs. Johnston stopped her carriage and asked me if I could tell her where her husband was. I went to seek him, and told him "the handsomest and brightest woman in Richmond was looking for her husband." Drawing himself up, he said: "There is but one woman in Richmond who answers to that description, and she is my wife. Where is she?" Soon after, he fell and hurt his leg seriously. When I went to see him, I found him with his crippled leg supported by a chair, and Mrs. Johnston, sitting by his side, was chaffing him. I told her she ought not to treat a husband so who adored her as he did, and related his compliment of a few days before. She laughed heartily at us both, saying he would never have said it if he had not known that I would tell her.

She was very bright and jovial and loved to banter him, and he enjoyed it all quite as much as she did. One summer we were at the Sweet Chalybeate with our families. The Johnstons occupied a two-story cottage, and one morning we were chatting together on the upper portico and the general was narrating something with interest, when a wild shriek of fright came from the walk below. He looked over the railing, and in a moment had resumed his narration, when he was again interrupted by a yell. This happened the third time, when he looked down upon the frightened shrieker and called out to her fiercely, "Why don't you run away?"

I remarked, "That is fine advice to come from a great commander." He turned upon me. "Well, sir, if she won't fight, the best thing she can do is to run away, isn't it?"

Mrs. Johnston, with her hearty laugh, put in, "'That used to be your plan, I know, sir." His fierce face relaxed into a hearty laugh, in which we all joined. A young woman in a red cloak and a turkey gobbler were the cause of the interruptions. The gobbler ran at her; she stood still and shrieked, which repulsed the turkey. Then he turned and charged her again, and she, making no effort to get away, shrieked and shrieked again, till at last assistance came.

Johnston and I had traversed in Texas the beautiful Wild Rose Pass of the Guadalupe Mountains, through which for many miles the Lympia Creek finds its way. In places, the bare cliffs of basaltic rock rise twelve or fifteen hundred feet above the little stream. In other parts, beautiful wooded slopes stretch away for miles, so that the Lympia Cañon has been for years the beautiful wonder of the route from San Antonio to El Paso. One day I asked him how he explained the power of that little stream to make a way for itself through the great mountain barrier, expecting some profound geological solution. I was answered when he said, "I presume the Power that could make the stream could make a way for the stream to pass, sir."

In the last year of his life, he consented to be godfather to my little granddaughter, and we went to Richmond and occupied neighboring rooms at the hotel. I have rarely seen the general brighter or more cheerful. He played with the little child, ran up and down the halls with her, and held her in his arms during the entire service, after which he and the venerable pastor, the beloved Dr. Peterkin, stood long together by the chancel, in deep and earnest conversation. As he turned away, the general's eyes were moist. They both felt they were near the bourne they so soon passed. The

Count de Paris and his suite were in Richmond at the time, and were honored with a reception at the home of Colonel Archer Anderson, who invited us to meet them. The general and the count soon drew off to one side, and for more than an hour were absorbed in earnest discussion of the vexed questions of war.

After our return to Washington, I visited him frequently, and he told me several times that his visit to Richmond was the happiest week he had enjoyed for many years. One day I found him reading an ancient folio, the writings of Tamerlane, Timour the Tartar. He read to me many pages, with great interest to us both. On another day he was reading Thiers' history in the original, and read aloud with much feeling the narrative of the last days and death of Napoleon. Soon after, he contracted a dangerous cold, and gradually sank.

Five or six days before he died, I called to see how he was. As I entered the room, he beckoned from the lunch-table for me to come and sit by him. Open on the table near him lay the memoirs of Du Guesclin. He was quite ill then, and soon took to his bed, from which he never arose, and where he calmly and serenely received the last sacrament of the church. As I bade him farewell, I said "Good by," as cheerfully as I could, adding: "I go to Texas to-morrow. We will soon meet again."

"Yes," he replied, with marked emotion, "we surely shall meet again"; and, drawing me to him, he kissed me twice.

CHAPTER XIII

N leaving Manassas, I went to Richmond and procured an assignment to the army of Fredericksburg, with headquarters at Brooke's Station. General Holmes was its commander.

I was much impressed by the excellent drill and discipline of the troops and the ability and high accomplishment of the officers. I had never seen as good drilling in any infantry troop or artillery of the United States army as I found in these volunteers. The officers a few months before had been in their law-offices, or in their counting-houses, and the rank and file in their various civil vocations, but already they were in excellent condition for the active service. They were eager to learn and work. Perhaps the Fortieth Virginia Infantry, Brockenborough's, was in the most complete state of efficiency. The Georgia Regiment of Colonel Simms, the North Carolina Regiment of Colonel Pettigrew, one of the ablest soldiers and most cultivated gentlemen who fell in our war, and the regiments of Colonel Stokes, of Colonel Gaston Mears, of Colonel Tew, were all in fine order. Every one of these able commanders was killed in battle, and had made a command worthy of him. Two fine regiments of Texans came along on the route to Dumfries; the Fourth Texas under Colonel Hood, and the Fifth under Colonel Archer.

The only survivors of that roll of able and brave colonels are Colonel Fagin, then of the First Arkansas Regiment, since a prominent general; Colonel Bates, since governor, and now senator of Tennessee; and Colonel Ransom, of North Carolina. Another Texas regiment was afterwards added to the Fourth and Fifth to make up the famous Texas Brigade under Hood, which was accounted invincible. The Fourth Texas had over four hundred native-born Virginians in it. It was this Texas brigade which caught Lee's bridle when he wished to lead it to the assault at Spottsylvania, and said, "You go to the rear, and we'll drive them to hell."

After the victory of the first Manassas, both armies lay quiescent for many months. Johnston, commanding the Confederate forces, was confronted by McClellan, commanding the great Army of the Potomac. In February, 1862, General Earle Van Dorn was made commander of the Trans-Mississippi Department, and I was ordered to proceed at once and report to him as Chief of Staff of the Department. While a distinguished honor, this was a sore trial to me; for it took me far away from my wife and mother and from my native State, Virginia, when my chief ambition was to fight for her.

I overtook Van Dorn and his staff at Jacksonport, in Arkansas. With him were several officers of the old army, with whom it was my destiny to serve through more than one campaign. The story of the war has been so often told that I shall give only the prominent events in which I bore my part, and of which I have personal knowledge, omitting reports and battles of campaigns heretofore published.

After our defeat at Elkhorn, we remained several weeks

in Van Buren, resting and refitting the army. One night it was reported that forty men had died in the hospitals, poisoned by morphine, given to them through mistake for quinine. A box, marked quinine, had been smuggled in from St. Louis. All of the bottles were labelled quinine. One, as the fatal result proved, was morphine, and was administered in quinine doses. We had no means of ascertaining whether the mistake was the result of accident or of a cruel fraud. There was no remedy and no appeal. The government of the United States had declared medicines contraband of war. In all the wars of history, Wellington alone in his Spanish campaigns had proclaimed this inhuman war measure.

Restless at this enforced inaction, Van Dorn told me that he would send a dispatch to General Sidney Johnston that he would join our army of the West to Johnston's forces at Corinth, destroy Grant's army at Shiloh, and clear Kentucky and Tennessee of the enemy. General Johnston desired this to be done, so we put our forces at once upon the march, while we hastened on in advance to consult with General Johnston about our plans.

The battle of Shiloh was fought before we reached there, and Buell rescued Grant before our fresh troops could complete Johnston's success. We brought about 16,000 men to reinforce Beauregard, holding the works about Corinth, against which Halleck was very slowly and timidly advancing with overwhelming forces. Three times we moved out of our works, and invited Halleck to attack, but each time he drew back. Finally, our troops suffered so much from bad water and a bad commissariat, that we evacuated the lines on the night of May 30th, and retired by slow marches upon Tupelo, where we had good water, fresh provisions, and plenty of time for drills, reviews, etc.

On the night of our evacuation of Corinth, I commanded the rear guard of the army of the West. The splendid Missouri Brigade, Wade's or Bledsoe's battery, and two fine regiments — one the Third Arkansas, and the other the Sixth Texas — made up my command. We marched at 1 A.M., and by daybreak had taken up a strong position just beyond the Five Mile Creek. We felt that the whole army could not drive us from that position. We waited unmolested until about 10 A.M., when a staff-officer came back from Van Dorn with orders for the rear guard to close up with the army, which was halted for the day in battle order about six miles beyond us. We were neither followed nor molested by any one, yet next day General Halleck sent a telegraphic dispatch, announcing to the country that General Pope reports the capture of 10,000 rebels and 20,000 stand of arms. Had he come across that creek, he would have found nearly 3000 of us, and would have probably thought we were 10,000. At sunrise, I sent two couriers back by the road over which we had marched, with instructions to General Beal, commanding the cavalry left in Corinth, to destroy all stores. Those couriers met nobody upon the road. Pope had a very general reputation amongst army people of mistaking his imaginations for facts.

Meanwhile, my family had found protection and generous friendship from Mr. Dick Clarke, an old Virginian, who had greatly prospered, and lived at Verona. He had a new and spacious residence, and for several months they were his guests; for he would never permit me to pay him. Our affectionate relations with him and his household have continued always. When the army moved away towards Iuka, I pressed Mr. Clarke to permit me at least to remunerate him for our mess-

bill.   He firmly declined, and said : " General Maury, I
am a money-making man.   If you were to put me on an
island in the middle of the ocean, I should find some way
to make money.   But I thank God I always can use my
means to help deserving people.   And now you must leave
Mrs. Maury and the children here with me, while you
go on into Kentucky, and feel sure she will be in every
way as well cared for as if she were in her own father's
home in Virginia ; and in case you are made prisoner
and taken sick, you may need money.   Here are letters
of credit to my correspondents in Kentucky, which will
protect you."

At Iuka, Rosecrans struck us a heavy blow.   Grant
failed to co-operate, fortunately, and we got back to
Tupelo considerably worsted.   We had marched north-
ward because we had information that all of Grant's
forces had crossed into Tennessee to join Buell.   We
found they hadn't.   Then came the terrible Corinth business, which has been fully written up heretofore.

When I was at Brooke's Station, a very likely negro boy,
named Jem, was employed about the stables.   He was a
native of Fredericksburg, and was born free, yet he
didn't seem to know it, or to care about it.   His unfailing good-humor was equal to any tax upon his exertions
or any disregard of his dignity or rights as a free man.
He did whatever he was told to do, but did it in his own
way.

My own boy was not able to accompany me on so long
and arduous a journey as that before me, so Major Seth
French called up Jem and told him to go with me to
Arkansas by next train, and he went as my body-servant,
and for three years we took care of each other.   That is,
I took care of Jem, and Jem didn't take care of me or
my things, that I was ever aware of.   At Chattanooga, I

left Jem on the platform of the depot in charge of my baggage, etc., while I went to attend to some business matters. When I returned, my fine elk robe, blankets, and camp bedding were all gone, and Jem seemed very much surprised, quite innocent of any responsibility for it, and imperturbably good-humored under my remarks about it, which were caustic.

When we reached Memphis, I left Jem in charge of my room and effects while I went off for a short time. On my return, Jem placidly informed me, " Colonel, somebody done took bof dem pistols of yourn when you was gone."

Another time, he left my ambulance and team of lively mules, hitched ready for a trip, while he amused his leisure moments. The team started, the bar over the top of the stable-yard gate was too low for the carriage to pass under it, and the mules went through, taking the body of the ambulance, the top of it remaining under the gateway. Jem's only emotions were of surprise " that them mules is sich fools."

He was about six feet two inches in stature, of a most joyous and happy disposition, and a ready wit, which made him a great favorite with all about headquarters, whether black or white. I cannot recall that I ever saw him show any anger or resentment, or wear a jacket. When he was summoned from the stable to go with me to Arkansas, he came right along just as he was. Nor can I ever remember seeing him use water, or take a bath, except when our canoe upset in Black River, Arkansas, when he had to swim for his life.

Dick Holland was my first cousin. When I was made brigadier-general for conduct in the Elkhorn campaign, I found Dick at Corinth, after Shiloh, sergeant-major of a Mississippi regiment. On my application, he was appointed captain and aide-de-camp to me; and a more genial, gallant fellow never wore a sword than Dick. He was the model of an aide-de-camp, — knew everybody worth knowing in the army, and made a friend of every man who ever came to headquarters.

My staff were all bright, harmonious, and active young fellows. We had one large mess, and care was taken to keep up a comfortable table, to which every gentleman, whether a general or a private, was welcome and sure of a good dinner. Dick looked after all this, and had a peculiar aptitude for finding good things to eat and good places to rest for himself. His success in making himself comfortable while he was helping all of us, made him the subject of many a joke amongst us.

I had a very fine horse which I never rode because he was too tall for me. He suited Dick exactly, and he quietly appropriated him, until Jem spoke of him as "Marse Dick's horse." Once while Dick was off on a furlough, a very gallant and able officer, Major Brown, reported to me on the eve of a little fight. He asked my permission to go into it, which I gave, when he said, "General, my horses are not up yet; can you mount me?" I called to Jem to catch his Marse Dick's horse for Major Brown. The engagement was a skirmish with Sherman's rear guard on his retreat from us at Chickasaw Bluff, and before long I saw Brown coming back, carrying his saddle and bridle, and on foot. I said, "Major, what's the matter?"

"Well, sir, I was down on the levee, when a shell from a gunboat knocked that horse's head off. So I thought the best thing for me to do was to bring the saddle and bridle back."

Some days after Dick returned from his trip, all the staff gathered about him to hear his experiences and to tell him of ours. Jem selected his opportunity and made his way to greet him, saying : " Sarvant, Marse Dick. I'se mighty glad to see you safe back. Ah, Marse Dick, if you had a been here, dat horse would never have got killed in dis world." Dick joined in the laugh, and the staff told the story over town ; and the papers having announced that Major Brown, of General Maury's staff, had his horse shot under him, the girls called Dick Major Brown ever after.

In the winter of 1862–63 we were on the Tallahatchee, holding Grant's army in check, when news came that I had been made a major-general. Jem was much elated at this increase of rank, and swaggered over the other headquarters darkies accordingly. The weather was bitter cold, and he was making up my camp bed next morning. I said : " Jem, you must tuck in those blankets better at the foot of the cot. My feet stuck out last night and were almost frozen." With an indescribable air of humorous impudence, he turned towards me and said, " Why, you ain't growed no longer 'en what you was, sir, is yer, since yer been promoted ? "

Jem's stature exceeded mine by about one foot. He used to brag over the other negroes because he was a " Virginny nigger," and had been in the terrible battle of the first Bull Run. In his opinion, " Thar is no soldiers like them we all left in Virginny. The privates dar was better dan some of dese yer kurnels," and there never was service so dangerous as he had seen in the battle of Manassas.

It was on the evening of the critical fight for the passage of the Hatchie, after our two days' fighting about Corinth, that I sent a courier to the rear to bring up a fresh horse. The bay mare I was riding had been under saddle all of the two previous days of action, and it was

time to relieve her. Jem came galloping up to me on
my finest horse, Roy. It was against orders for him ever
to mount him. He had his " own mar'," and he informed
me that " mor'n one man had dun shuck two hundred
dollars at him fur dat mar' " ; which, considering the easy
terms on which he had acquired her, would certainly have
been a good speculation. She had strayed one morning
into the field where my horses were, and Jem took her
in there and then.

He was shifting the saddles ; Roy was bridled and sad-
dled, and I mounted him and found he had cast a shoe —
was dead lame. Just then a shell burst in the trunk of
the tree a few feet above us. I turned to tell Jem to give
me back the mare, but he was gone at full speed, lying
close down on the mare and urging her on. He was
about to throw his saddle on her when the shell burst.
He dropped the saddle and away he went.

Two days afterwards Jem made his appearance in the
" avalanche," looking as chirpy as if he had won the
battle. He gave his experience since his sudden disappearance with his usual fluency.

" Gen'l, when dat shell busted de mar' runned straight
away." I had seen the flight ; the rascal didn't stop to
put her saddle on, but went off head down on her crest,
with legs pounding her sides. " Ole Gen'l Price an'
'bout a dozen of dem colonels of hisn, dey was back dar,
— 'bout a hundred yards behin' whar we all was, — and
she busted plum thro' 'em. De Gen'l did cuss ! ' Stop,
you black rascal ! Somebody kill dat nigger ! He'll
stampede dis whole army ! ' Now, Gen'l, I always 'lowed
Gen'l Price had mo' sense 'en dat. Dat warn't no time
to stop, an' Gen'l Price ought to ha' knowed it. De mar',
she never stopt nuther — not till plum at de avalanche —
and I got in de avalanche, and ain't leff it sense, cause I

knowed you hilt me 'sponsible for yo' things what was in the avalanche." Investigation showed the mess-chest to be empty, on which Jem evinced much surprise and indignation at the want of integrity "of dese here Southern soldiers."

After this episode Jem lost credit as a fire-eater; but his loyalty to me never faltered, and he stayed with me until the very last moment, when we parted affectionately. He went to Mobile just in the flush cotton times, and when I last saw him he was the prosperous owner and driver of a cotton flat. I heard that he had become quite a politician in the reconstruction times of Alabama.

CHAPTER XIV

THE battles and military operations in which I was concerned have heretofore been fully written about and published. The only application for service I ever made during the war was for service in the field in the army of northern Virginia. This I made when Pemberton was placed in command of Mississippi and its forces, and I renewed it by every influence I could bring to bear, until I became absorbed in the active operations of my own department. At any time I would have given up the higher position I held in the service to take command of a division in the army of northern Virginia. General Early kindly explained to me that it would have been felt an injustice to the generals who had been so long and actively engaged in Virginia, to place me over their heads, as would have been the case with several of the major-generals of that army.

Great as was the compliment and the opportunity, I deplored my promotion to the trans-Mississippi department, and did all I could properly do to have the order suspended. As soon as I joined Van Dorn, I told him that while I would do everything in my power to organize his forces, I was not willing in such a war to do only office work. In his hearty, generous way, Van Dorn replied, "I appreciate your soldierly feelings, and assure you I will not disappoint you by keeping you in an office any longer than may be necessary for the organization of my army, when I will secure for you a proper command in the field." I was accordingly promoted to brigadier-general after the Elkhorn campaign, and had an opportunity to make up a fine brigade, and very soon after a fine division.

When General Van Dorn and I went to Corinth to confer with General Albert Sidney Johnston, Van Dorn said to him: "General, I met upon the river a fine Texas regiment, the Second Texas, Colonel John C. Moore commanding. I ordered it to come at once to you for this impending battle. Please remember that it is to be one of the regiments of the brigade I am going to make up for General Maury." General Johnston replied: "I will remember; but I wish you would leave Maury with me now, and I could at once make up a good brigade for him." Van Dorn said he could not spare me then, and so I escaped the disastrous battle of Shiloh. General Johnston was a high and great man. No man could have met him without feeling respect, confidence, and love for him.

It was on the day before Christmas, 1862, that the news came to us at Granada of the complete success of Van Dorn's bold dash around Grant's army and of Grant's precipitate retirement from our front. On Christmas Day, a prominent and prosperous gentleman of Granada, Mr. Mister, a native of Maryland, gave a grand dinner to General Price and his generals, and a sumptuous table it was that we sat down to. All were in fine humor to enjoy it, for Grant was gone and there was no one to make us afraid.

We had just taken our seats, when a courier arrived
with a telegram from General Pemberton, ordering
Maury's division to march at once to reinforce General
Stephen D. Lee at Vicksburg, who with only 2300
men was attacked by Sherman with a corps of 30,000.
General Price handed the dispatch to me, and I arose
at once, bade farewell to Mr. Mister and his brilliant
company of generals and colonels, and proceeded to
put the First Division in motion to succor Lee, as
noble and gallant a soldier as ever bore that name.   We
had to go by rail to Jackson, thence to Vicksburg, over
the very worst line of road in the State.   It was dark of
the next day before we rolled into Vicksburg with the
advance train, bearing only 400 men; the rest of the
division were distributed along the route from Jackson.

The train bearing the Thirty-fifth Mississippi and
Bledsoe's battery was detained in Jackson several hours.
Colonel Barry and Captain Bledsoe were capital fellows
and good friends.   Barry was one of the most popular
and eloquent men of Mississippi.   Genial, gentle, and
humorous, he never seemed to harbor an unkind thought.
Bledsoe was one of the most distinguished battery captains of Price's Missourians.   They were convivial that
night, and occupied a box-car together, in which, after
some hours of congenial enjoyment, they rolled themselves in their blankets and slumbered.   Bledsoe was
about six feet three inches tall, and paid but little
attention to any elegance of attire.   He wore boots of
extraordinary size and length, which came half-way up
his long legs, and were innocent of any coloring save
the native yellow of the unpolished hide.   Barry awoke
first, and seeing Bledsoe's great boots standing by, called
a negro and gave him a dollar to black them.   The
darky performed his task well, replacing them carefully.

Then Barry aroused Bledsoe, told him it was time to be up, and lay chuckling as Bledsoe searched the car for his yellow boots.

When at last he realized that the freshly blackened pair before him were his own, and that he had furnished fun for the company, his wrath arose against Barry, and he challenged him to a duel. But that jovial colonel declined to fight him because he "was only a captain, and he could not think of waiving rank." Poor Barry died of consumption soon after the war, loved and lamented by all classes of people. Bledsoe, when I last heard of him, was a prosperous business man in Missouri, where every one respected him.

I met Stephen Lee upon the battle-field from which he had driven Sherman. The night was black as a wolf's mouth, a cold rain was falling, and all around us lay the dead and wounded, whose piteous moans went out for help to the surgeons and litter-bearers, the flickering light of whose battle lanterns appeared here and there about the field.

On reaching Vicksburg, I said: "Lee, I am here with only four hundred men, but the whole division will be up soon after daylight. Please dispose of my force where and how you think best, for though I rank you I don't know anything about the conditions here. I don't know where your line lies, I don't know where the enemy is; in fact, I don't know where I am. I entrust everything to you with the assurance that you shall have all the glory, and I will be responsible if anything goes wrong." This surprised and pleased him, too. He said, "General, that is very generous, and I thank you"; and he went to work accordingly, my only suggestion being to urge him not to expose himself so much as he continually did.

Stevenson came up in a day or two with a large force — over eight thousand men. We had carried on a light skirmish with Sherman until all of Stevenson's division arrived, when we resolved to attack the enemy; but at early dawn we discovered Sherman's smokes along the Yazoo as he retreated. I sent Lee with six or seven regiments to worry his retiring forces. Lee won great praise for his admirable conduct of this expedition, and after my warm endorsement and earnest request was promoted to major-general. He is a splendid fellow, and is now president of the admirable Agricultural College of Mississippi.

The day before Sherman's retreat, a flag of truce brought us a letter requesting permission to bury his dead. The letter was signed by General Morgan, and the permission to bury was signed by Lee, who immediately after the fight had attempted to remove Sherman's wounded, but had been forced to desist in his humane efforts because his people were fired upon by the enemy. His litter-bearers therefore retired until after dark, when all of the Federal wounded were brought to our hospitals.

I did not realize the good name of Price's corps until, on one occasion when Grant seemed to be preparing a descent in force upon our lines, General Stevenson ordered me to place two regiments of my division on picket to defend the expected point of attack. After the usual tour of twenty-four hours, I was informed that the rations were all gone, and went to see Stevenson about relieving them with some other troops. He said confidentially, "We are not willing to entrust any other troops with the defence of that point."

"Oh!" said I, delighted; "just let me tell them that, and they will stay there till Gabriel blows his horn," and galloped off to tell the colonels to let their regiments know that they held the post of honor.

In organizing that division, Van Dorn appointed Generals Moore, Cabell, and Phiffer, excellent disciplinarians, to command its three brigades, and in the campaign against Grant in September and October at Corinth they had shown great tenacity, being in action three days. They went in with 4800 Rifles the first day, and on the third three-fourths of their number were gone, yet the remaining 1200 fought from 10 A.M. to 4 P.M. with unfaltering devotion. General Rosecrans himself paid a marked and generous compliment to the bravery of that division. When Van Dorn, after the battle, detailed a party under Colonel Barry to bury our dead, Rosecrans courteously replied that "he could not admit them within his works, for reasons which General Van Dorn could appreciate, but that the latter might rest assured that all possible care would be bestowed upon the wounded and all respect showed the dead, especially those who fell so bravely as the men of Maury's division."

Rosecrans was a great soldier and a generous gentleman. He had been my instructor at West Point, and our relations had always been of a very cordial nature. After the battle, he sent me a message through one of my most gallant battery captains, Tobin, who was captured that day, bidding him, "Tell Maury, with my regards, I never used to think when I taught him, a little, curly-headed boy at West Point, that he would ever trouble me as he has to-day." Rosecrans buried Colonel Rogers of the Second Texas, which led the assault, with the honors of war, and marked and enclosed his grave.

On our retreat before Grant, down through Mississippi,

our rear guard had a skirmish with his advance at Coffee-
ville.   My division was ordered to march at 4 P.M., to
send all baggage, etc., to a station ten miles below us,
and to bivouac there for the night.   A cold, sleety rain
fell upon us until 10 A.M., when the head of the column
halted at Mr. Brooks' large and comfortable plantation
home.   He was a thrifty planter, and his fields and
fences were in good order.   On his large lawn about his
house stood several dozen bee-hives, all well stored
with honey, and on both sides of his long lane, for a
mile or more, high worm fences guarded his broad fields
of cotton and corn.   The division filled the whole lane.
It had been carefully trained to respect private property, and especially never to burn rails, but as soon as
we halted I ordered Flowerree, my chief of staff, to send
along the line the order that "the division will burn
rails to-night."

A great shout, a genuine Confederate yell, roared
along the line, as they charged those fences.   In a few
minutes, both sides of the lane were cleared of rails, and
huge, blazing fires cheered our wet and weary men.   The
fence around the yard disappeared too, and the bee-
hives vanished, and nothing was left but the stile blocks,
over which old Mr. Brooks had been passing for forty
years, and over which he still uncompromisingly climbed
as he came in to report some fresh disaster, though
nothing was left to bar his passage through his fenceless
yard.   I heard of no colds or pleurisies caused by that
night's march.   I told the old gentleman to make out a
liberal account of the damage to his property and it
should be promptly paid, and a few days after he
brought in a bill of damages amounting to six hundred
dollars.   The quartermaster paid it at once, and at that
time Confederate money was about as good as green-

backs, so Mr. Brooks was happy in receiving ample value for his losses and I was glad my men escaped much illness.

The old gentleman and his wife were as kind and hospitable as could be, and we were sumptuously entertained at supper and breakfast, and comfortably bedded all of that inclement night. There were more than a dozen of us, generals and staff-officers, who received liberal hospitality at the hands of that old Virginia family.

One night about eleven o'clock I was roused from my slumber upon my saddle blanket under a bush, by the trampling, almost upon us, of a horseman who called out to know, "Where is General Maury?" Flowerree scratched a match and read, "General Maury will turn over the command of the rear guard to the next officer in command, and proceed at once to the head of the army, assume command of the First Division, and march punctually at 2 A.M." It was my third successive night without sleep. The good and great Father Ohannon, chaplain to Price's Missourians, was near me. He is now in high favor with the Pope, as he ought to be, for he promptly said, "General, you are very tired; take a drop of the cratur'; 'twill do you good, and then you can get a nap till half-past one." The good Father never drank a drop himself, but he was indefatigable in his care for his wounded and wearied people, and always carried into battle a quart canteen full of good whiskey.

Accordingly I was aroused at half-past one, and proceeded to hunt up my new command. I found them peacefully sleeping, the lines of white blankets looking weird in the flickering light of the camp-fires. We had some trouble in arousing five thousand men under such circumstances. One fierce old Texan called

out to me, "Somebody'll shoot you directly, ef you
don't quit goin' about here makin' so much fuss!"
But we got them into the road at last, and marched
punctually at two o'clock. We expected to encounter
the enemy at daylight.

This Texas brigade was one of the finest bodies of
men ever seen in any service, but had no idea of accurate discipline. Their colonel was a very handsome,
poetical-looking young fellow, with voice and manner
gentle as a woman's, and the heart of a true soldier of
Texas, and the head to raise him afterwards to the
Executive Chair of his great State. May Heaven soon
send him there again! He had not then the least con-
ception of discipline; so I and my staff devoted ourselves to Ross' brigade, for every potato patch and
green apple tree drew them from the ranks until we
drove them back again. On the march, I usually
dressed in an old suit of corduroy and a light felt hat,
and these Texans had never seen or heard of me before.

I heard one fellow say: "I wonder who that little
fellow is, in that white coat, anyhow? Where did he
come from? He's goin' to keep us closed up, you bet;
he keeps on at it." Another called out to his comrades
plundering a melon patch, "Look out, boys! Here
comes the *pro vo!*" A third informed Ross, confidentially, to whom he was giving some green peas just
foraged, "If that little fellow don't quit his foolishness,
he'll git the stuffin' knocked out of him, first thing he
knows."

I devoted especial attention to this brigade for nearly
a month, and they hated me accordingly. But after we
had been into action together, they used to cheer me
whenever they saw me, and called me "Little Dab."
One thing in my favor with those Texans was my fine

horses, and the way they would carry me over places when some of the staff would have to ride around. That brigade and Ector's brigade of Texans, and the famous Missouri brigade, organized, instructed, and fought by General Henry Little of Maryland, and my Louisiana brigade might have taken the contract for the conquest of the Soudan, and would have kept it, too. It is very certain they would never have formed a square in an aggressive campaign or made, before battle, all of their preparations for defeat. They would never have murdered a wounded man, or destroyed the Abb-bhu-Clea wells when defeated there and compelled to retreat, for they were true men and self-reliant soldiers. Each man with his repeating rifle was a small fortress.

After Ross had remounted his brigade, he one day caught a Federal gunboat on the Yazoo River, lying in security with all her fires out. He placed a section of his battery above her and another below, smashed every boat on her, and, driving her people all under deck, compelled her to surrender. He had no boat in which to board her, so the sergeant of the battery — it was an Arkansas battery — and twelve men stripped, swam out to the steamer, and, stark naked, received the surrender. She was armed with six twenty-four-pound bronze howitzers, which were sent to me at Mobile, and did great service in the defence of Spanish Fort. Ross has now become one of the leaders in politics in his State. He is gentle as ever, and has always been an example of how the gentlest are ever the bravest. He is a man of culture, too, "an excellent thing" in a governor.

After we drove Sherman from Vicksburg, in December, Grant, having been defeated in his invasion of Mississippi by Van Dorn's brilliant *coup*, was permitted to organize a great army for the capture of that city.

He brought Sherman back there with him, and meantime we had assembled all available forces, over thirty thousand effectives, to resist his attack. Our army extended from Haines Bluff, seventeen miles above the city, to Warrenton, ten miles below. General Johnston thought that this was a faulty disposition. His view was that a strong fort should have been made, commanding the river at the turn above the city, to be garrisoned by two or three thousand good troops, and the rest of the army left to operate in the field.

General Carter L. Stevenson, a veteran and most complete soldier, commanded Vicksburg and all of its dependencies. He assigned me to the command of all of the forces above the town, including twenty thousand men, while General Barton commanded all below the town, about ten thousand men. Stephen D. Lee commanded all of the artillery of the place.

During the period of high water, all of the streams were in flood, and Admiral Porter availed himself of the opportunity to pass with his light-draft steamers up into one of the tributaries of the Yazoo, get above Vicksburg, and cut off communication with its back country. Sherman supported the movement with a large body of troops, and it seemed very near to success, when General Sam Ferguson, a vigilant and daring young officer, intercepted it, stopped Porter's advance, and caused his abandonment of the whole enterprise. Along my part of the line we could note the progress of the expedition by the smoke of the steamers above the tree-tops, eight or ten miles in my front. Ordering Featherston's brigade to reinforce Ferguson, I sent Stephen Lee in a skiff through the overflow to see if it were practicable to throw a force behind Sherman, and so capture the whole expedition. If he found it impossible to move a sufficient force to accomplish this, then Lee was to make a demonstration and create the impression that he was there in strength, and cause the information to reach Sherman, so as to lead him to retreat. This was all that could be done in his rear; Ferguson had done all possible in his front. Had Ferguson been reinforced and left in command, it seems probable we should have captured that whole expedition instead of only defeating and driving it away.

Our plan was successful, and the whole expedition was a failure, and retreated precipitately out of the country. Ferguson reported the abandonment by the enemy of ten fine boats left on his hands, including the commodore's gig, which he sent to us at Vicksburg, and which we found useful as a flag-of-truce boat. This was Sherman's second failure with which Lee and I had to do. But for Ferguson's fine conduct, Porter might have reached the Yazoo.

Soon after this General Quinby came down through the Yazoo Pass, with a corps, intending to get into the Yazoo River at Greenwood. Loring repulsed and detained him there until I could get to him with a force of four thousand men from Vicksburg. The rivers were out of their banks, the lowlands were under water, skiffs were moored to doors of the farm-houses, and buffalo gnats swarmed over the horses and cattle. I lost twenty-four mules one night from their poisonous bites. In repulsing Quinby's advance, Loring used the famous Second Texas sharp-shooters, who fought in water up to their waists. I could scarce find dry land enough on which to form a line of battle, and smokes were made all along the line that the horses might stand in them and in some measure be protected from the gnats.

General Lloyd Tilghman was a very gallant brigadier

from Maryland, whose brigade joined my right. He proposed that we should try and break up the enemy's headquarters about a mile away from our front. Tilghman had been a civil engineer, and he had a county map showing the position of the farm-house where Quinby had his headquarters. He trained his guns by the compass, while I sent in a body of sharp-shooters through the woods upon the enemy's right. We opened at the signal, and broke up the whole establishment, which retreated hastily for the Mississippi by way of the Yazoo.

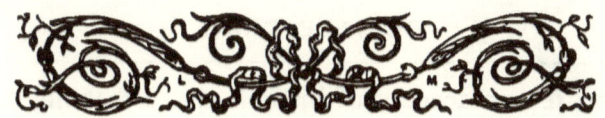

CHAPTER XV

Mysterious Disappearance of Young John Herndon Maury — Grant and Porter aid in the Search for him — Conjectures and Theories regarding his Fate — A Christening under Fire — Anecdotes of Dr. Lord — A Magnificent Spectacle when Porter ran the Vicksburg Batteries — An Interrupted Ball

T was about a month after we had driven Sherman's forces away from our front that an event occurred which plunged my family and staff into the deepest and most anxious suspense, and which furnished one of the most unusual and inexplicable mysteries in the many tragedies of all the sorrowful period of our Civil War.

One morning in the latter part of January, I, accompanied by my chief of artillery, Colonel Burnett, and my young aide-de-camp, John Herndon Maury, son of Commodore Maury, rode to General Stevenson's headquarters, and, after the conclusion of my business there, sent these two gentlemen of my staff to make a reconnoissance near the Big Black Road. This was about ten o'clock in the morning. I have never seen my young aide-de-camp and kinsman since that moment, nor have I ever been able to ascertain what was his fate.

Burnett returned to dinner at headquarters and reported that at about one o'clock P.M., having finished their business on the Big Black Road, young Maury left him in order to ride down to a point opposite the canal, and observe what the enemy were about there. No uneasiness was felt on account of his non-return that night, but when ten o'clock next morning had come and Johnny, as every one called him, had not yet been seen nor heard of, a vague anxiety manifested itself among us. This was soon increased by hearing that on the previous evening, about three o'clock, Generals Stevenson, Barton, and other officers familiar with John Maury, had seen a riderless horse, resembling his gray mare, on the far side of a crevasse in the levee on the plantation of Mr. Smeeds, about four miles below Vicksburg.

On learning this, I, accompanied by several officers and couriers, rode to the point, and found John's horse, with saddle on and bridle hanging loose. A strong levee had been built by Mr. Smeeds from the highland, more than a mile distant, in order to shut out the waters of a bayou which in some seasons would otherwise inundate his plantation. Recently this bayou had torn its way through the levee, making a breach of about twenty yards in width, through which the water was now running deep. The trail of the mare led from the highlands along the levee, entered the bayou at the crevasse and passed out at the other side; but from the point of exit the mare had been running back and forth so much that we were unable to follow the trail further. We concluded, however, that Maury had been drowned in attempting to cross the water, and immediately procured boats and proceeded to search for his body.

This was continued without discovering anything which might tend to confirm our belief that he was drowned, until next evening, when Colonel Burnett, an experienced Texan hunter, reported that he had been carefully examining the tracks of the mare, and that from his observations she was evidently mounted when she emerged from the bayou beyond the crevasse; that she had been ridden at a trot along the levee to a point not far from the river; that at this point her footprints upon the levee ceased, she having turned off from it into the overflow, made a detour and came up on it again nearer the crevasse ; that from the point where she had thus come up on the levee she had galloped, riderless, back to the brink of the crevasse, near which she remained until we found her. At the point where the mare had turned off, he found the paper cases of several cartridges different from those used in our army, and also a fine piece of india-rubber, such as the Confederates could not procure, which had been used to cover the cone of a rifle. There were also evidences of a struggle on the brink of the Mississippi River, a few hundred yards distant, where he found the edge of the bank freshly broken off, and signs that several men had embarked there in a small boat.

The space in which the young officer's body must lie had he been drowned, as we at first supposed, was small, and as no trace of it had been found in the course of our thorough search, we decided, on hearing Burnett's report, that he had been captured by some scouting party from the army across the river, and had been borne a prisoner to the other shore. The anxiety of his friends was at once allayed, and some of them even ventured on a laugh at his expense; for this was the second time he had experienced capture while reconnoitring alone. Some of Grant's army had made him prisoner in November, near Holly Springs, and he had only been back with us a month. No one doubted that he was now safe and in good hands, and that his exchange would soon be effected.

Next morning Major Flowerree, adjutant-general of my division, was sent under flag of truce to General Grant to make inquiry about Lieutenant Maury. To our grief and surprise, he returned in the evening with the report that nothing was known of him by the Federal commander; but with courteous assurances from General Grant and Admiral Porter, who knew young Maury well, that they would take all possible means to ascertain if he had been taken prisoner by any party of theirs, and would communicate to me the earliest intelligence they could procure. Thus we were again thrown back upon the fear that he had been drowned in crossing the bayou, and for two weeks the locality where his mare was found was watched, cannon were fired over it, and all the space was carefully dragged.

About this time other kindly messages were received by me from General Grant and from Admiral Porter and other naval officers, assuring me that great pains had been taken and careful inquiry made after Lieutenant Maury, but that they had ascertained nothing calculated to remove the painful belief that he had been drowned. General Grant had been my own schoolmate and comrade in arms, and my young cousin was well known to Admiral Porter and other officers of the United States Navy, who had met him while he was a boy at the Observatory, of which his father was so long the chief. The conviction was then positive, and is now, that those officers were sincere in their efforts to find him and to aid me in my search.

Some months had passed, when reports came to me from several sources that a young officer named Maury, an aide-de-camp, had been captured near Vicksburg, and had been seen in Memphis and at other places in the spring, on his way to the prison at Johnson's Island. Returned prisoners from Johnson's Island reported to me that they had seen and conversed with my young cousin there, and so many points of identity were established that hope revived once more, but only to be lost again by learning that a young gentleman named James Fontaine

Maury, while serving in the battle near Grand Gulf as aide-de-camp to General Bowen, had been made prisoner in May, and sent to Johnson's Island. A very remarkable personal resemblance between John Herndon Maury and James Fontaine Maury, their common family ties, and identity of rank and of age — they were both nineteen years old — frequently caused them to be confounded with each other, and gave rise to the rumor that the former was still alive.

Soon after the fall of Vicksburg, when in Mobile, I received a letter, ill-written and from an evidently uneducated writer, informing me that John had been made a prisoner and had died of pneumonia the third day after his capture, on board a Federal gunboat lying off Vicksburg. At the time very little importance was attached to this letter, but not long after, Colonel Underhill, a gallant young Scotchman, who had resigned his commission in the British army to serve in that of the Confederacy, wrote to me a very clear and consistent narrative which he had received from Captain Smith of the Thirteenth Iowa regiment.

Colonel Underhill and Captain Smith were from the same county in Scotland, and met during a truce between the lines at Vicksburg, Underhill then being aide-de-camp to General Stephen D. Lee. During their sociable conversation on this occasion, Smith told Underhill that on the 27th of January he had crossed from the mouth of the canal with a party of four or five men to the levee on Smeeds' plantation, in order to ascertain if we were constructing any batteries there; that soon after reaching the levee, he observed a Confederate officer riding down it toward the point where he and his party were concealed, and, lying close, they waited until he came up and dismounted. While he was looking through his field-glasses at the Federal works on the opposite bank, Smith and his men sprang upon him and secured him. The mare broke away from them, ran out into the overflow, and, remounting the levee, galloped back to the point whence she had come. As soon as it became dark, Smith and his party recrossed the river with their prisoner and sent him to Grant's headquarters, where he believed he was when my flag of truce came to inquire for him two days after. Captain Smith showed Underhill the field-glass which he had taken from his prisoner and retained as a trophy of his exploit. It was one that I had loaned John that morning, and was marked with my name and rank.

There are several points in this narrative which render it worthy of belief. It agreed in the main with Burnett's observations and the theory deduced from them, of which neither Smith nor Underhill had ever heard. There was never any evidence procured of the drowning, and capture was the probable alternative. The field-glasses seemed to fix the latter fact, while the respectable standing of the two gentlemen, and the absence of any motive or object for such a fiction leave us no right to question any part of their story. As to Smith's belief that young Maury was at Grant's headquarters while that general was denying all knowledge of him, we must remember that Smith could only know that Maury had been sent to the headquarters; while Grant, having just arrived at the army with large reinforcements, and being occupied in reorganizing his forces, could not be expected to be interested or even informed of the capture of a lieutenant. I have never doubted the sincerity of his desire to aid me as far as possible in my efforts to unravel this sad mystery, and believe he would have gladly done anything in his power toward it.

The writer of the letter I received at Mobile stated that

my cousin died of pneumonia three days after his capture. Soon after Underhill's testimony reached me, I received a verbal message from a lady in Vicksburg, who knew me and my young kinsman. She stated that a lieutenant of the Federal navy came to her house, accompanied by a man named Griffen, who had deserted to that service, and who had been employed about my headquarters, and who had known young Maury. Griffen told her this same story—of young Maury's being ill with pneumonia and dying on a gunboat within three days of his capture.

For more than fifty years the father, the uncles, and many other relatives of this young gentleman were well-known officers of the naval service of the United States. Having passed almost his whole life at the Observatory, he was himself well known to scores of naval officers. These circumstances, coupled with the further facts that he was a staff-officer of the general second in command of the army at Vicksburg, the immediate, active, diligent, and persistent search made for him, the cordial interest evinced by Generals Grant and Sherman, Admiral Porter, and Captain Breeze, and other officers of the Federal service in the investigations made as to his fate, combine to render the mystery which enshrouds it as extraordinary as it is inexplicable, while the beautiful traits, the fine intellect, the excellent attainments, and the gallant yet gentle bearing of the young soldier invest it to all who knew him with a peculiar and especial sadness. Thirty years have come and gone since the events narrated here took place, yet not once has the curtain which shrouds the actual facts in this pathetic drama of the war been lifted; and we who knew and loved the chief actor in it shall learn no more until we, too, have followed him and crossed to the other shore.

On my return to Vicksburg after the Yazoo expedition,

I found orders awaiting me to proceed at once to Knoxville and take command of the department of East Tennessee. This was an agreeable promotion, for I should escape the fate of Vicksburg, and be so far on my way to Virginia, where I still hoped to have a command in the field. Before leaving, we desired to have our little son baptized, and the good Bishop Green of Mississippi, who was in the city, kindly consented to perform the ceremony at my headquarters. General Stevenson was godfather, and the members of my staff all assembled for the occasion. The Rev. Dr. Lord, the dearly loved and very able rector of the parish, and his wife, were also present. While the ceremony was progressing, Grant opened a new battery upon my headquarters, and throughout the baptismal service the shriek of the falling shells sounded in our ears: one of them actually fell in the stable near at hand and exploded there; but the bishop went calmly on until the end, for Vicksburg had been under bombardment so long and without fatal results that all were accustomed to it.

Dr. Lord was one of the most remarkable men I have ever known. He was for many years the rector of the church in Vicksburg, where he won 'the confidence and affection of his people by his precept and example, too. His wonderful versatility of information and his charming conversational capacity made him a welcome guest in every home in his parish.

Some time after the war, while I was the guest of Major Flowerree in Vicksburg, Dr. Lord was invited to dine with me. The night before I had been to see Ben de Bar play Falstaff — the best Falstaff I have ever seen. Dr. Lord took up the subject, and made the most interesting discussion of Shakespeare's greatest character I had ever listened to. He plainly proved that Falstaff was no coward, and when I asked for his exposition of the difference between wit and humor, he recapitulated the history of the Fat Knight, showing where he was witty, where humorous, and where both witty and humorous. We listened to him, absorbed, for an hour, when he left us to attend to some parochial duty. As soon as he had gone, I said to Flowerree, " I have never had such a treat ; I seem to have struck upon Dr. Lord's specialty."

" You were never more mistaken in your life," he replied. " No matter what the subject is, he seems to have mastered it. Some years ago there was a club of intelligent gentlemen here in Vicksburg, who met to enjoy conversation. Dr. Lord was a member, and no matter what might be the question under discussion, he was the master of it. One day Dr. Crump received a new book upon whaling and other arctic experiences ; I believe it was called ' Three Years before the Mast.' He read the book and was charmed with it, and passed it around to several other gentlemen of the club, that they might also read it and introduce the subject at their next gathering, and for once know something with which Dr. Lord was not familiar.

" Accordingly, when the evening came, the subject of whale-fishing was taken up by these freshly informed gentlemen, with the expectation that their rector would for once be at a loss, but they reckoned without their host ; for in a few moments the reverend gentleman took up his parable, and instructed them all in facts about whales and the Arctic Circle, such as they had never heard of before, and finally informed them he had been a sailor on that very ship they had been reading about." He remained with his people during the severe trials and dangers of their terrible siege, and ever bore with him their affectionate and grateful memories.

On the night after the christening, my wife awoke about midnight, saying, " Dab, the pickets are firing on your lines !" I sprang up and called to Jem to saddle my horse. He seemed to be always awake, no matter at what hour he might be called, and he could " catch a horse " quicker than any one I ever saw. By the time I was booted and spurred, the horse was ready at the door, and I mounted and galloped off towards the firing. All of my staff were at a ball ; but as I passed my couriers' quarters I shouted for them to turn out and follow, and as I crossed the bridge I heard the clatter of horses' feet behind and found one of my smartest Texans was close at hand. He joined me, and together we mounted the hill overlooking the river in time to see the passage of Porter's whole fleet, as he came around the bend above the city and past its front, on his way down to unite with Farragut.

It was the grandest spectacle of my life. For four miles our batteries were in full play, blazing away at the line of gunboats making their way past them, and giving shot for shot as they went swiftly by. The whole landscape was as light as day, for before the first steamer swung round the point, our pickets across the river had promptly fired their calcium lights and had set torches to the huge piles of pine which stood ready at hand, and were then securely under cover. Porter gamely led, and hove to off the town to send a few shots along its streets, which stampeded the entire population, especially the ball, whence the gallant young officers dashed away to their posts, leaving the ladies to their own devices. These fled in their slippered feet and light robes for the nearest shelter. Vicksburg was well supplied with bomb-proofs, into which whole families might retire when a bombardment was hot, but some of the belles, panic-stricken, that night did not stop even there, but hurried over the muddy roads until they were out of cannon range, and took refuge in the nearest country houses.

Believing that Porter's whole fleet would join in the bombardment of the city, I sent a courier back to my wife, with instructions to get at once in the ambulance and drive out of the town until she reached a position beyond the reach of the enemy's guns, but she decided to remain where she was, and stayed serenely there, explaining to me afterwards that she "did not wish to take the baby into the night air."

The value of Vicksburg was now gone, for Grant could cross over below the city. Stevenson immediately ordered every man, except the guards of the batteries, to march at once below Vicksburg and defeat his landing. Pemberton countermanded the order, permitting only Tracey's brigade and Cockrell's Missouri brigade to go to meet him. These fine troops under General Bowen detained Grant a day or two; Stevenson's whole army would have driven him into the river.

Next day I went off to Knoxville, where I remained for about six weeks in command of the department of East Tennessee. Here, as elsewhere, we were the recipients of much kindness; Mrs. Sanborn, who had a lovely home in the suburbs, being especially hospitable to us.

CHAPTER XVI

T the end of six weeks I was ordered to take command of the Department of the Gulf, with headquarters at Mobile, altogether an interesting and agreeable command. No kinder or more generous people ever lived than these. Some time after our arrival, Judge Dargan came to me and, introducing himself, placed his furnished house at our disposal. It was elegant and comfortable, with ample lawn and garden, and here we lived until the end of the war. The judge occupied one room in the wing, and came every evening into our sitting-room to converse with us, and became a warm and lifelong friend of me and of mine. His own family had moved up to Tuskeegee for the war.

Soon after assuming command of the Department of the Gulf, I was notified that a steamer under flag of truce would arrive in Mobile Bay with the sick and wounded Confederate soldiers from Vicksburg. This was one of the many considerate and kindly acts of General Grant, who never made war upon women or other unfortunates who might fall in his power. Of this, and of all the other qualities of a soldier's charac-

ter, he has left his record in the grateful memories of
the Southern people.   We cordially welcomed our weary
and wounded comrades, and went down in steamers to
meet them and escort them to that charming bay-shore
resort at Point Clear, where the hotel and cottages
awaited their reception, and no soldiers of the Confederacy ever enjoyed a happier destiny than these in ex-
changing the damp and soggy climate of Vicksburg for
the fresh salt breezes and sparkling waters of Mobile
Bay, with its fishing and bathing and famous oysters,
and now and then a boat-load of limes and bananas and
other tropical luxuries brought in by the blockade-
runners.   .

As I went from cot to cot in my visits through the
wards of our temporary hospitals, I noticed a poor,
emaciated lad of not more than sixteen years, who
seemed very near to death's door.   I inquired of him
as to his name and home, and he replied, "My name
is Waymack, and I am from Hanover County, Virginia."
He had been a member of a Virginia artillery company,
and I did my best to make him feel that he was once
more in the house of his friends.   Under good care and
the healthful climate, he rallied, and as soon as his company was fit for duty I made it the headquarters guard of
my department.   I found great comfort in my Virginia
guard, and a sense of mutual good feeling existed between them and the members of my household, which
was not a little enhanced by my wife's invariable
remembrance of them at dinner-time.   A year or so
before the final engagements which terminated the siege
of Mobile, two battalions of "Galvanized Yankees"
were sent to me, to form part of my army.   They had
been captured in some recent battle, and being all Irish-
men declared that they would rather fight for us than for

the North, and were accordingly sworn in to serve till the end of the war, and duly enrolled and equipped. I sent them up to meet a raid into Mississippi, but no sooner did the rascals come in sight of the blue uniforms than they raised the white flag, and, going over in a body, surrendered at discretion.

One day, some months after this, Waymack came to my office and stated that he had something very important to tell me. He was very much excited and alarmed lest his interview with me should be known. I satisfied his fears, and he informed me that in the same fort in which his battery was then stationed, Fort Jeb Stuart, in a company of the First Louisiana . Artillery, there were two "Galvanized Yankees," who were preparing to desert to the enemy, and to take with them drawings and plans of the defences of Mobile. They were Germans, he said, and very powerful men, and one of them had been made a sergeant. A man residing in Mobile was their accomplice.

I assured the boy of his absolute safety, commended his zeal and courage, and enjoined on him increased vigilance as to the conduct, etc., of the spies. I then sent for General Cockrell, commanding the famous Missouri brigade, now a staunch and able member from Missouri in the United States Senate, and asked him to select from among his men a good and efficient detective from St. Louis, and detach him to report to me for special service, cautioning him and Colonel Fuller, of the First Louisiana Artillery, to make no comment on the irregularity of the order. I transferred the Missouri sergeant to the Louisiana company, where he soon won the confidence of the intending deserters, and, together with a trustworthy comrade of his own, entered into their plans. I was especially anxious to get hold of the citizen of Mobile who was their confederate in the proposed treachery, and the detective fully shared this desire, and delayed the time of their desertion until he found the spies impatient to be off, and, he thought, somewhat suspicious of him.

They got all of the plans of Mobile and its defences, etc., completed, and set out at midnight through the pines toward Pascagoula, near which the Federal army lay. The Confederate sergeant and his comrade bore them company for some miles from Mobile, when each man closed with his antagonist. Next day my two emissaries returned, bringing me the papers they had taken from the deserters. They would have been of inestimable value to the enemy in his attack upon the place. The Confederate sergeant told me that in all of his experience as a detective, he had never had to deal with so clever and dangerous a man as that German sergeant was. In the chances and changes of the years since then, I have lost sight of little Waymack, although I have tried to learn something of his whereabouts, but I hope he is alive and prosperous; for he was as game and true a lad as I ever knew.

Until Farragut's fleet entered Mobile Bay, the blockade runners were very active carrying out cotton and bringing in stores from Havana, and thus we were still in touch with the outer world, and Mobile was to our western armies what Richmond was to the army of Virginia. Spies, too, were active there, spies for us and spies for General Banks, sometimes for both at once. Many applications were made to me to permit the government cotton at Mobile to be traded with the Federal government for army supplies, but as I required the supplies to be delivered first, nothing was ever accomplished except that I was ordered by our government to send one thousand bales of cotton to New York to be used to buy overcoats and blankets for our prisoners. An agreement was entered into between the two governments, and General Beal, a prisoner of war, was released and stationed in New York to receive and sell the cotton, which was done with the fidelity of that most excellent officer and gentleman.

One day, in 1865, a man came to me with papers approved by Lincoln, Stanton, and Farragut, authorizing him to exchange army supplies with me for cotton. He was a pleasant-looking man, whom I will call S——. He said he was from North Carolina, and an ardent Southern sympathizer, a class which I have always felt would bear watching. I told him that many such propositions had reached me, but that no trade could be made, because his government wished to have the cotton before delivering the stores, and I must have the stores before delivering the cotton. He thought he could arrange to give me the stores first, and receive the cotton at Mobile in payment, so I told him to go ahead and see what he could do. The provost-marshal furnished him with passes to go and come between the Federal commander General Gordon Granger and myself, and at the same time had him closely watched, and he went back and forth many times, but made no progress in our trade.

Many weeks passed in these fruitless efforts, and meantime the enemy was making his grand and final preparations for the reduction of Mobile, and I, by my complete system of scouts, was daily posted as to his force and movements. One Sunday there was a ring at my door, and the servant announced that Mr. S—— wished to see me on urgent business. My wife, who was sitting with me, left the room, and he was ushered in, somewhat flustered by the import of his tidings.

"I am just from General Granger at Pascagoula," he said, "and Canby's army is actually marching against you." All of which I already knew. After I had heard him through, and had got all he could or would tell, he drew from his breast pocket a package of assorted kid gloves and handed them to me, "as a present for your lady." I kindly declined them for her, saying she was already sufficiently supplied with gloves. He seemed a little mortified that I did so, and retired at once. My wife came in to hear the news of the enemy, and I said to her, "Mr. S—— was very kind, for he brought you a dozen of Jouvin's kids." Beaming with delight, she said, "Oh, where are they?"

"I declined them, telling him you were sufficiently supplied."

"How could you tell such a story, when you know that I have not had a kid glove on for a year!"

"But," I urged, "remember that I may have to hang him to-morrow, and it would never do for you to be wearing those gloves then."

Sure enough, the next day a worthy young officer attached to my headquarters, Major Sam Duncan, of Natchez, gave me a letter brought to him by S—— from Duncan's father in New York, telling him the days of the Confederacy were numbered, that he must get out of it at once, and that a man-of-war's boat would receive him near Dog River and take him aboard of a vessel bound for New York, etc. Accordingly, S—— was closely watched, and that evening, fifteen minutes before the train left for Meridian, he was arrested and taken up to the prison there, to be dealt with when a court should have time to try him. A few weeks after, the surrender came, and he, with all other prisoners, was liberated, and so it happened I never hanged a man.

I never saw S—— until six or eight months after the
war.   I was on my way from the depot to the Battle
House, in Mobile, when I saw a man approaching me,
whom, as he drew near, I recognized as S——.   He came
straight for me, and I knew he was after me.   There
was nobody in sight, and I was convinced that a severe
beating was the least that I could expect; for he was a
very able-bodied fellow and had me in his power, I
being entirely unarmed.   What was my relief, as S——
drew near, to observe a kindly smile stealing over his
face, as he extended his hand to seize mine, saying,
"General Maury, I have come for the honor of shaking
you by the hand, and telling you that, by G—d, sir, you
are the only honest man that I met during the war from
Abe Lincoln down!"   I never shook a man's hand with
more sincere pleasure in all my life, and as soon as I
could I wrote my wife how those gloves had saved me.
Some weeks ago I went into the office of the Secretary
of the Navy, when a man sprang up from the sofa and
claimed acquaintance, saying, "I am S——, whom you
tried to hang in Mobile."   I informed him I felt glad
I did not do it.   On further talk he told me he was so
anxious to shake hands at our last meeting because he
was afraid of me.

During my command of that department, General
Bragg invited me to accept a fine command in his army,
which I declined, preferring to be directly under the
control of the War Department, as I then was.   Afterwards Hood applied to the President to have me appointed lieutenant-general, and ordered to a corps of
his army, but the President replied I could not then be
taken from Mobile, but he would promote me to the rank
of lieutenant-general.   He told General Taylor this, and
in Mrs. Davis' book she states that such was his purpose.

During all the period of my service at Mobile, my
kinsman, Colonel Henry Maury, was with me, and no
man in the community had more friends, perhaps, than
he. His handsome face, cordial manner, and ready
wit attracted toward him every one with whom he came
in contact. His courage was unquestioned, while his
loyalty to his friends, and his kindness of heart, won
him lasting esteem. He had gone from Fredericksburg to Mobile while yet a youth, and made his home
there. He entered the Navy as a boy, and was present
at the siege of Vera Cruz. Afterward he entered the
merchant service, and by the time he was twenty years
old had command of a barque. General Walker, the
filibuster, employed him to take a battalion of recruits
down to Nicaragua. Mr. Marcy, the Secretary of State,
sent a marshal in a revenue cutter to detain him in
Mobile Bay. Harry received the marshal courteously,
and acquiesced in his own detention. He took him
into his cabin, and entertained him with lavish hospitality, when he persuaded his guest to sleep aboard the
barque, urging that he could not possibly escape with
his ship, for the cutter was lying close by and he would
show a lantern from the barque's peak all night, all of
which the marshal understood, and retired to sleep.

After some hours, all being quiet aboard both vessels,
Henry shifted the lantern from the peak to the end of a
long spar which he let down into the mud of the bottom.
The wind favored him, he slipped his cable, dropped
down the bay, and by daylight was out of sight of land,
and well on his way towards his destination. It was
not until the second day that he met a vessel bound for
the States, to which he courteously transferred his guest,
with an apologetic letter to the Secretary of State for
having been compelled to take such a liberty. He was

short-handed, his filibusters could aid his crew but little in the stormy weather they encountered, and the *Susan* was wrecked off the island of Ruatan. None were lost, and the British governor treated them with so much kindness that his government recalled him.

After the close of the troubles in Nicaragua, a Captain Henri de Rivière, who had been dismissed from the French army and had cast his lot with General Walker's expedition, returned with the surviving adventurers to Mobile, and became a favorite in the gay society there. His impudent deportment aroused Henry's indignation, and a duel resulted. A steamer took the duellists down to Pascagoula. Doctors Knott and Ross went along as surgeons, and a great many gentlemen of Mobile, who desired "to see Harry shoot the Frenchman."

I was told by several eye-witnesses the remarkable history of this curious affair. The ground was near the residence of the proprietor, and a hammock was swinging in the veranda. Captain de Rivière advanced to Captain Maury and asked if he might take an hour's nap in that hammock, as he felt very nervous. His request was granted, and his second aroused him at the end of an hour. He arose apparently quite refreshed, and took his place for the duel. They were to begin firing with revolvers at twelve paces, to advance a pace after each shot, and to stop if either fell. At the first shot, the Frenchman staggered backwards and seemed about to fall. His antagonist lowered his pistol, but kept his thumb upon the hammer and his eye upon his enemy, whom he detected in the act of cocking his pistol, but before he could raise it and fire Maury shot him in the mouth. He was taken to the home of a gentleman in Mobile, whose sympathetic wife and beautiful daughter cared for him during some weeks.

When he had recovered sufficiently to travel, he departed, accompanied by his devoted nurses. The head of the family went in pursuit of them, reaching Havana just after they had left for Nassau, and arriving at Nassau after they had sailed for New York. In New York their escapade was arrested by a lady who came out of a convent and claimed Captain Henri de Rivière as her lawfully wedded spouse. Then at last the bereft husband and father recovered his delinquent family, and returned with them to Mobile. Towards the close of the war between the States, the Marquis de Rivière died in France, leaving his great fortune to his younger brother, Captain de Rivière. The head of the enamoured family still living in Mobile assented to the urgent request of the new marquis that he would escort his wife and daughter to Paris, where the latter became the Marquise de Rivière. They lived in great splendor till the Franco-Prussian War, when the marquis was killed in battle.

During the war between the States, Colonel Maury commanded the lower defences in Mobile Bay. One day he went up to Mobile in the steamer which plied between Fort Morgan and the city. He reached the evening boat too late, but persuaded a boatman to take him down the bay in his skiff. The wind was blowing half a gale and rising, and the little craft bounded over the heavy seas, sometimes half hidden from the view of the anxious watchers on the wharves of the city. The approach to Fort Morgan was more anxiously watched by the garrison, all of whom came out upon the wharf. They feared their colonel was in that boat, knowing well his daring nature. When the dingy reached the landing-place it was impossible to land, so violent was the rush of the water seaward. The colonel sprang into the

raging sea, and, swimming to land, called for volunteers
to man the launch and go with him to the rescue of the
boatman, who was being rapidly borne out to the Gulf,
where he would inevitably perish.   The launch, steered
by his own steady hand, soon overhauled and rescued the
poor fellow.   This was only one of the many noble
feats of daring which marked his whole life.

General Gordon Granger was stationed with his corps
at Pascagoula a month or two previous to the attack on
Mobile.   Thence he detached a brigade to a narrow but
deep creek about half-way to Mobile, and I ordered
Colonel Maury with three regiments of horse to go
down and force the brigade back into Pascagoula.
Soon after he marched, a courier came in hot haste,
bearing a dispatch from Colonel Maury, reporting his
progress.   I think that when he sent it he was about
three miles from town.   I thought it very unaccountable
until several other equally unimportant bulletins arrived,
when I said, "Henry is drunk, and nothing will come
of his expedition"; and so it was.   Next day he came
back, having done nothing, and I was not surprised
when charges of drunkenness were preferred against him
by officers of his command.   I ordered him under
arrest, and to be tried by the military court of the department.   To my surprise, he was acquitted, and I
asked the president-colonel-judge how it happened.
He said, "Three officers of high intelligence and character swore that he was drunk, and we all thought that he
was done for and deeply deplored it, for we all love
him; but bless your soul, sir, Harry produced six officers of equal character, who swore, point-blank, that he
was sober, and we had to acquit him!"

When I sent Colonel Maury into Jones County to
break up that secession movement, he dealt with the

traitors very roughly, so that after the war he was pursued very actively by the survivors, and his fine horses were seized. The aid of the United States troops was invoked, and would have been employed, but that I went to see General Canby about it, and he at once peremptorily forbade it. Meantime the colonel went to Selma and secured the protection of the Federal commander there, a kindly old Scotchman, who, like many other good and sensible people, was charmed by Henry's wit and *bonhomie*. He invited the colonel to a sumptuous lunch, at which there was a big Federal major, who seemed inclined to quarrel with Henry, who never needed two invitations to a fight. Toasts and songs went round, and the major made several flings at the colonel, who treasured them up, until presently Colonel Maury was called upon for a song. He said if the company would accept the change, he would offer a conundrum instead of a song. The proposition was vociferously applauded, the big major being among the most enthusiastic. "Why are the Confederates like Lazarus?" asked Maury. The major gave a contemptuous solution. "No," said the colonel, reaching across the table to indicate and emphasize his reply; "because we have been licked by dogs!" The Scotch general loudly applauded, swearing "he had not read so good a conundrum in the newspapers for a year."

The genial and witty Bishop Wilmer, of Alabama, was a warm friend and admirer of Harry, and greatly enjoyed his conundrum; and when, after the war, he went to New York to invoke assistance for the churches so desolate in our Southern country, he was induced to relate this incident. A clergyman present, who was not pervaded by that Christian spirit which all bishops and the clergy especially should illustrate, said with much heat, "Well, sir, if that is your feeling, why do you come to us now for aid?" "Oh," said the bishop, "to get a hair of the dog!"

The bishop himself sometimes left a lesson by a witty repartee, as he did once when the train in which he was travelling rolled down an embankment. As he picked himself up a rough fellow near him, who had been annoying the passengers by his coarse and profane talk, said to this old Virginia gentleman, "Well, Bishop, we all like to went to hell together that time!" "Speak for yourself, my friend," was the ready response. "My ticket is for the other place." May God send him long life and strong health, that he may continue to teach all other bishops how potent is the influence of gentleness and unfailing good temper in them above all other men. Ever a father to his people in the cruel war we endured together, we respect and love him and trust him now.

While colonel of the Thirty-second Alabama, then a part of Johnston's army, and stationed at Jackson, Colonel Maury was wounded in the right breast by a rifle-ball. He was relating an anecdote to a group of appreciative brother-officers when this happened, and coolly finished his story before turning to one of them, to whom he said, "Please put your ear to my chest and see if you hear any noise in there." "No." "Then, boys, I'm good for a ninety days' furlough." Several years after the war, he died from the effects of that very wound.

I was living in New Orleans at the time his death occurred, and the circumstances which attended it and my own connection with it were very curious. I may state at the outset that I am not at all a superstitious person, and that I have no theory to advance or explanation to offer with regard to the following facts. Henry was then residing in Mobile, and when I had last heard from him he had been in his accustomed health and spirits. One morning, in the spring of 1868, I awoke and started up, saying, "Where is Henry?" My wife, aroused by my voice, replied, "You are dreaming!" "No," I said emphatically; "I am not dreaming. I saw Henry standing by my side, and he was about to speak to me, when suddenly he disappeared." She argued with me, as was natural, that it was all a dream, but I could not shake off the conviction of its reality. As I stepped into the car to go down to my office after breakfast, a gentleman who was reading a paper looked up and greeted me cordially, saying, "General, I am glad to see you, for I just thought I had read of your sudden death," — handing me the paper in which was a telegram stating that "General H. Maury had died in Mobile early that morning." Henry had been promoted to the rank of brigadier-general just at the close of the war. Our personal relations were very warm and affectionate, and I was his nearest of kin in that part of the world.

CHAPTER XVII

Recollections of General Forrest — His Personal Appearance and Traits — His Characteristics as a Commander — Never surprised or attacked — Ignorant of Tactics, but Great in Strategy — Instances of his Aggressive Self-Reliance, his Rapidity of Movement, and his Personal Power over his Men — The Fort Pillow Episode

DURING my command of the Department of the Gulf, I was constantly occupied in strengthening the defences of Mobile and in driving out raids which were made into Mississippi and Alabama by Generals Grierson, Straight, Rousseau, Davidson, and Sherman. In each effort of mine to intercept the progress or thwart the intentions of these expeditions, I was ably seconded by General Nathan Bedford Forrest. Indeed, I relied so implicitly upon his skill and judgment that I never hampered him with especial instructions. His natural qualifications as a soldier were phenomenal, and our association together was such that I am able to bear personal testimony to his great ability as a military leader, which deserves full recognition and appreciation at the hands of his people.

Forrest was born in 1821, in one of the counties of Tennessee, upon its southern border. He was the eldest of twelve children, and when his father died he was sixteen years old, and at once assumed the care of his family. He had had but little opportunity for learning, because even elementary schools were rarely found in that wild country, and he scarcely read before he was a grown man. And even during the war, when he had become the greatest soldier of his time, he dictated all of his correspondence. It lacked nothing in force and clearness, however deficient he was in his syntax, and etymology. His early life was a period of privation and a hard struggle to maintain his mother and his younger brothers. He went early into active life, and from the very outset evinced those extraordinary capacities for business and that wonderful self-assertion which were the marked characteristics of his career. He became a horse-trader and a negro-trader, and made a large fortune in these avocations, while maintaining a character for strict probity and for kind and fair dealing rarely ever found in such callings.

When the war broke out, Forrest was in the prime of his mental and physical powers. Over six feet in stature, of powerful frame, and of great activity and daring, with a personal prowess proved in many fierce encounters, he was a king among the bravest men of his time and country. He was among the first to volunteer when war broke out, and it was a matter of course that he should be the commander of the troopers who flocked to his standard. From the very outset he evinced his extraordinary capacity for war, and in his long career of great achievements no defeat or failure was ever charged to him.

When I first met him, the army of the West had been moved out of the lines about Corinth to offer battle to Halleck's forces, which was declined by that general. Forrest, already famous, had gone alone into one of the abandoned redoubts, whose only garrison was the chaplain of a regiment whom, with his horse, he brought out with him. I observed him with great interest, and felt the influence of his wonderful self-reliance. He could never brook the dictation of any commander, and he conceived and executed his own plans, moving when and where he saw work was to be done, and reporting only the successful result, which was always surprising to his enemy and to his commander. In all his long and arduous campaigns and scores of battles, he never was surprised or attacked. His successes were achieved with forces much inferior to his enemy. With unfailing daring and circumspection, he would make his tentative attack, or, as he expressed it, "I will give 'em a dare, anyhow." He was a great poker-player and illustrated some of its principles and technicalities upon the battle-field. When he found his enemy too strong for him at the point of attack, he would pull out and find a weak place, where he never failed to make in and win his fight. When once asked how it was he always succeeded in his battles, he replied, "I don't know, but I reckon it's because I always get there first with the most men." Unknowingly, he had announced and illustrated Napoleon's great principle of success in battle. When he found an enemy he could not attack with any hope of success, as was once the case with a strong blockhouse garrisoned with negro troops and commanded by a stout-hearted Dutchman, who firmly declined to surrender and dared him to attack, he temporized and invited a parley. Forrest knew he could not carry the place without heavy loss, and that a large reinforcement was coming on the railroad to the enemy. In twenty minutes he convinced the stout-hearted colonel that he would certainly carry his works, and that if he had to do so he could not restrain his men, who would take no negro prisoners, and the whole garrison was surrendered without firing a shot. Meantime he had sent a detachment down the road, derailed the train, and took in the reinforcements.

His insubordination was only excused by the wonderful success he constantly won while having his own way. In April, 1863, Bragg's army was up in Tennessee. Van Dorn commanded all of the cavalry, some eight thousand horse. Forrest commanded a brigade, and captured a Federal brigade commanded by General Coborn. Bragg sent orders through Van Dorn to Forrest, to turn over all his captured horses, arms, etc., to the ordnance and quartermaster officers of the army. The property not being forthcoming, the general wrote peremptorily to Van Dorn to call on Forrest to obey the order, and explain his delay in doing so. Van Dorn sent for him to come to his office, and in a tone of authority demanded of him immediate compliance, saying, "Why have you not turned in those captured horses?" Forrest replied defiantly, "Because I haven't got 'em." Van Dorn said, "That statement differs from your written report, sir." Forrest, white with rage, said, "General Van Dorn, the time will come when your rank will not protect you, and you shall account to me for this outrage!" Van Dorn, with his blue eyes blazing, retorted, "General Forrest, my rank shall never protect me from any man who feels aggrieved by me, and I await your pleasure now, sir." Forrest slowly passed his hand over his face; then he said: "General Van Dorn, I think there are Yankees enough for you and me to fight without our fighting each other. I am sorry for what I said, and respectfully ask your pardon." Van Dorn replied: "General Forrest, I am glad to hear you speak so. No man can ever doubt your readiness to fight any man or any thing, but while under my command you must obey my orders, and I

have important orders for you to execute at once." He
then ordered him to pursue the raiding party of Colonel
Straight, which had just passed down into Alabama.

This was the last interview between these two celebrated men, alike in their wonderful courage and energy,
while very unlike in their persons. Forrest, with his
powerful frame, high cheek-bones, light gray eyes, and
straight black hair, was in physical powers superior to
all men. He had probably slain more men in battle
with his own hand than any man living. Van Dorn,
with his light graceful figure, florid face, light waving
hair, and bright blue eyes, seemed formed for love and
war. Not over five feet six in stature, he would have
encountered Forrest or any other man. I believe they
were two of the bravest men living who stood face to
face that morning. They never met again. When
Forrest returned from his splendid pursuit and capture
of Straight's command, Van Dorn had fallen a victim of
private vengeance.

When Forrest, with about twelve hundred men, set
out in pursuit of Straight, he was more than a day behind him. Straight had several hundred more men in
the saddle than Forrest, and, being far in advance,
could replace a broken-down horse by a fresh one from
the farms through which his route lay, while Forrest,
when he lost a horse, lost a soldier too; for no good
horses were left for him. After a hot pursuit of five
days and nights, during which he had lost two-thirds of
his forces from broken-down horses, he overhauled his
enemy and brought him to a parley. This conference
took place in sight of a cut-off in the mountain road,
Captain Morton and his horse artillery, which had been
so long with Forrest, passing in sight along the road
till they came to the cut-off, into which they would turn,

re-entering the road out of view, so that it seemed that a continuous stream of artillery was passing by. Forrest had so arranged that he stood with his back to the guns, while Straight was facing them.

Forrest, in his characteristic way, described the scene to me. He said: "I seen him all the time we was talking looking over my shoulder and counting the guns. Presently he said, 'Name of God! How many guns have you got? There's fifteen I've counted already!' Turning my head that way, I said, 'I reckon that's all that has kept up.' Then he said, 'I won't surrender till you tell me how many men you've got.' I said, 'I've got enough to whip you out of your boots.' To which he said, 'I won't surrender.' I turned to my bugler and said, 'Sound to mount!' Then he cried out, 'I'll surrender!' I told him, 'Stack your arms right along there, Colonel, and march your men away down into that hollow.'

"When this was done," continued Forrest, "I ordered my men to come forward and take possession of the arms. When Straight saw they were barely four hundred, he did rare! demanded to have his arms back and that we should fight it out. I just laughed at him and patted him on the shoulder, and said, 'Ah, Colonel, all is fair in love and war, you know.'"

Forrest learned after the surrender that Straight had sent off a detachment to destroy our stores and works in Rome, Georgia, not very distant from where they were, and immediately caused Straight to send a staff-officer to recall that detachment, Forrest sending one of his staff along with him. The recall was in good time, and Rome was saved.

Hard riding had reduced Forrest's force to four hundred mounted men. Straight had lost a number in the collisions which had occurred during the pursuit. I believe thirteen hundred was the number of prisoners which I forwarded with their gallant colonel to Richmond. He was a very daring and able soldier, and soon made his way out of prison and escaped with a large part of his command.

When Forrest, in fierce pursuit of Straight, had come near to the bridge over the Estananla, a little girl of fourteen or fifteen summers appeared in the road before him and signed to him to halt. She said, "The Yankees have halted at the bridge, and will fire upon you if you go within sight."

"Is there not a ford above here," asked Forrest, "where we can cross?"

"Oh, yes! A little more than a mile above is a good ford."

"Well, can't you guide me to it?"

"Yes, indeed," she said. "Take me up behind you. I know the way very well, and will show it to you."

So she got upon a stump, and sprang up behind him, and pointed out the route he must take. And so they pushed on together, that fierce warrior, gentle always with women, and the bright little girl, excited and glowing with pride in her noble action and in being of such important service to the most famous of all of the brave men of that stirring time.

After going nearly a mile she said, "Now you had better stop here. For after you pass that timber, they can see you from the ford; for by this time they may have sent some soldiers up there, and they will shoot at you if you pass that point."

So Forrest dismounted, and, accompanied by several of the officers at the head of the column, advanced to the timber, and was peering around it, when the enemy

at the ford opened fire upon them. He was amazed
and alarmed when the little girl darted past him, and,
spreading out her little frock, cried, "Get behind *me!*
Get behind *me!*" He snatched her up, drew her back
to a place of safety, tenderly and laughingly too, mounted
and charged the enemy, clearing the way for his column
in a few minutes. The little girl was named Emma
Sanson. The Legislature of Alabama gave her six hundred and forty acres of good land, and she has now been
married many years to a worthy man, and is the mother,
we hope, of many sons worthy of such a mother.

When retreating, Forrest would often ride back some
distance in the rear of his command, in order that he
might reconnoitre the enemy for himself, and form his
own estimates of his progress, etc. On one of these
occasions, while crossing upper Georgia, he was galloping in haste to overtake his men, when an old woman
came out of a house, and, waving her sunbonnet at him,
called out, "Stop, you miserable coward! Stop and
fight!" adding, as he hurried past, "If Forrest was
here, he'd soon stop you!"

In 1863, General Sturgis moved out from Memphis to
occupy the prairie country of Mississippi, that large
fertile region upon the Mobile and Ohio Railroad,
where the great cotton and corn fields lay as yet un-
tracked by the hoofs of the invader. Forrest fell upon
him on the Tishomingo Creek, with less than twenty-
five hundred horse. The army of Sturgis is estimated
at about fourteen thousand men of all arms, and was
completely equipped. His negro troops were in front.
Upon these the Confederates made a deadly charge,
which completely routed them. The survivors fell back
in confusion upon the advancing artillery, which was
thrown into disorder, and the whole command broke up

in utter panic and fled back to Memphis. Sturgis lost all of his artillery, three batteries, his wagon train, and a great number of killed and wounded. He reached Memphis without any command, and ever after held Forrest in profound respect, and when he would hear of an expedition going out to capture him would remind the commander that he once did that.

General Tecumseh Sherman, when in command of the District of Mississippi, fitted out a formidable expedition for the capture of Mobile. He moved out from Vicksburg with twenty-two thousand infantry and artillery. General Sooy Smith left Memphis with seven or eight thousand cavalry, intending to join Sherman at Enterprise, on the Mobile and Ohio Railroad, and thence the combined forces would move to capture Mobile. General Smith's cavalry was considered invincible by all the Confederate forces. Forrest had about two thousand men not far from West Point. He fell upon Smith near Okolona in the open prairie, put his command to utter rout, and, like Sturgis, General Smith reached Memphis without his command. On this memorable field Colonel Forrest, brother to the general, fell, bravely leading his men. When General Forrest saw this, he sprang from his horse, caught his dead brother in his arms, kissed him tenderly, and with streaming eyes led his redoubtable bodyguard in a charge, broke the enemy, and commenced his rout. Sherman, on hearing of the destruction of Smith's column, retreated in haste to Vicksburg, pursued by the Confederates, under Stephen D. Lee, who had recently defeated Sherman in the battle of Chickasaw Bluff.

Forrest understood well how to patch the lion's with the fox's skin, and to supplement force with stratagem. In the winter of 1864, I was commanding the department of Alabama and Mississippi. Forrest, with about forty-five hundred horse, was in north Mississippi, and I charged him with the defence of north Mississippi and west Tennessee, and, knowing his peculiar sensitiveness when under control, I wrote to him to this effect: "In placing you in the command of this district, I wish you to feel sure I shall not interfere with your exercise of it. I will be responsible if anything miscarries, and you shall have full credit for all the successes I am sure you will accomplish. I cannot spare you a single soldier, but will promptly respond to your demands for supplies of every sort." This gave Forrest great satisfaction. It was the first time he had been so unhampered by any of his commanders, and he ever after regarded me with gratitude for the confidence thus reposed in him, and with respect for my intelligence in showing that I realized he understood his business better than I did.

About this time a heavy corps was sent out from Memphis to occupy the State of Mississippi, under the command of General A. J. Smith. The rains and the roads were very heavy, and Smith's army could move but slowly. Forrest kept a large force close in his front, while he, with two thousand men, remained quietly about West Point, getting his horses in good order upon the fine forage there.

Farragut was bombarding Fort Powell, with the intention, as I anticipated, of getting an army and fleet into Mobile Bay. Forrest telegraphed me in cipher to this effect: "The enemy has twenty-seven thousand men; has more cavalry than my whole force; I cannot check him, but with your permission will pass behind him into Memphis and destroy his stores, and thus compel him to retreat." I replied: "Go, but come back quick.   You are all I depend upon for the safety of north Mississippi."

It was more than a week before he moved.   He then made a rapid march across to Oxford, and with his whole force drove back the enemy's advance, and at 4 P.M. Friday, dashed off to Memphis with two thousand horse and four guns.   Saturday I first knew of his movements from the telegraph operator at Senatobia in about these words: "General Forrest just passed here at a gallop, bound for Memphis."   At dawn, Sunday, came this: "Heavy cannon-firing about Memphis."   He had marched ninety-four miles in thirty-six hours.   Three rivers were out of their banks.   He tore down houses and fences near by and bridged them and crossed his guns safely over.   At crack of day, Sunday, he dashed into Memphis, and occupied the city.   The commanding general fled in his night clothes from his bed, leaving his uniform, sword, etc., to the Confederates.   The garrison of infantry threw themselves into the Irving Block, a strong building, from which they could not be dislodged without loss of many men.   Forrest's object was fully accomplished by destroying stores and by spreading panic throughout the city, which was soon communicated by telegrams and couriers to the whole department and army of General A. J. Smith, who, on hearing that Forrest had occupied Memphis, threw up his hands, crying, "We are gone up!" and at once retreated out of Mississippi.   Forrest drew his men out of the place, and by 4 P.M. was ready to go back to his own country.

In telling me of this, he said that a fine-looking staff-officer came to him, requesting the restoration of his general's uniform, with the assurance that its return would be acknowledged by a present of a bolt of the finest gray cloth to be found in Memphis.   The major, whom Forrest described as a very "sassy fellow," said, "General W. desired me to say he will catch you before you get back." "You may tell the general from me," rejoined Forrest, "that I am going back by the same road I came by, and if we meet, I promise to whip him out of his boots." — "When I told him that," continued Forrest, "I allowed he would not believe me, and would send all of his forces to intercept me on the other road; but after the major had gone off with this message, I began to think he might believe me and attack me on my same homeward road, and I got scared, and ran back as fast as I came." The Federal general did as Forrest hoped he would, disbelieved him, and made all of his arrangements to catch him where he wasn't. Thus again he had saved the State of Mississippi, and this time by his finesse and energy alone.

When I wrote him my acknowledgment of this great service, I told him he should come down to Mobile and take a few days' rest, and asked him to send me one of his brigades; for I thought that the enemy on hearing, as he surely would, that Forrest and his command were in Mobile, would delay the attack then under consideration. My wife wished to entertain him, and gave him a dinner, inviting some lady friends who were desirous of meeting this great hero. His natural deference to the sex gave them all much pleasure. He was always very courteous to women, and in their presence was very bright and entertaining. He had for women that manly courtesy and respect that marks the truly brave man. Under all circumstances he was their defender and protector from every sort of wrong. His wife was a gentle lady, to whom he was careful in his deference.

The enjoyment of our dinner was enhanced by young Colonel Aleck Chalmers, one of Forrest's regimental commanders. He was a handsome young fellow, as gallant as he looked, and full of humor. He described for our great amusement the descent of his command upon the Gayoso House at Memphis. At dawn of the morning, they rode right into the great hall of the office, dismounted there, and clattered up the broad stairway to the corridors above, where they found the first-class boarders, officers and their families. He said: "We went along the hall knocking at the doors with our sabres or pistol-butts. The doors would fly open and the occupants of the beds come forth accoutred as they were. Sometimes it would be a man, sometimes a woman, sometimes both, all in appropriate costume. One beautiful young lady sprang from her bed, threw her arms around my neck, and begged 'For God's sake, sir, don't kill me!' 'Not for worlds, madam,' said I, returning tenderly her embrace." Which he illustrated with the proper gestures. He was a fine young fellow, and survived the war, to die after of the swamp fever of the country.

General Frank Armstrong was much with Forrest, and was an able cavalry commander — one of the very ablest in the Confederate service. He says Forrest was never disconcerted by any event in battle. On one occasion Forrest, with Armstrong's and Starnes' brigades, was operating in Tennessee against Gordon Granger's command. Armstrong was in front, with his skirmishers pressing Granger's skirmish line, when two couriers came galloping from the rear, yelling at the tops of their voices, "General Forrest! General Stanley has cut in behind you, has attacked Starnes' brigade, has captured the rear-guard battery, and is right in Armstrong's rear!" Forrest immediately shouted so that all could hear him, "You say he is in

Armstrong's rear, do you? Damn him! That's just
where I have been trying to get him all day, and I'll be
in his rear directly. Face your line of battle about!
Armstrong, push your skirmishers forward — crowd 'em
both ways! I'm going to Starnes. You'll hear from
me in about five minutes!"

Off he dashed with his bodyguard, and in a few minutes loud cheering was heard. He recaptured the battery, recovered all of the prisoners lost by Starnes, and
captured a large number of the enemy, driving his forces
back. To this day Armstrong's men believe Forrest had
laid a trap for the Federals, into which they fell; whereas
Forrest was as near frightened as he could be in battle,
and Armstrong believed "they were all gone up."

Forrest knew nothing about tactics — could not drill
a company. When first ordered to have his brigade
ready for review, he was quite ignorant, but Armstrong
told him what commands to give, and what to do with
himself. He had an excellent memory, — remembered
everything exactly, — and was so pleased with his success
that he often afterwards had reviews.

I once asked him about the charge so often preferred
against him of the murder of his prisoners at Fort
Pillow. He said the negroes brought it all upon themselves; that after the white flag had been raised, and
while it was flying, they continued to shoot his men,
who, much infuriated, shot the negroes; that he stopped
it as soon as he could, but not before many had been
shot. It created a great terror of him ever after among
the negro troops. He knew this and, as in the case of
the Dutch colonel, he used it as a caution against resistance, and an incentive to prompt surrender when dealing with the commanders of negro troops.

Sometimes, on the eve of a battle, convalescents and

released prisoners would join him and he would say, "I have no arms for you yet, but fall in here behind, and you shall have plenty of good Yankee arms presently." He told me he had twenty-eight horses shot under him. He was shot only three times, which is quite remarkable when we remember how many battles he fought, and how continually he exposed himself.

In his last fight at Selma, he was in the telegraph office with General Dan Adams, when a little boy came running in and said, "The Yankees are coming!" They ran to their horses, which were tied to the fence. The enemy, led by a big yellow-haired Dutchman, were close upon them. Forrest said: "Dan Adams was on a smart horse and got off. The big Dutchman closed upon me, and had a smarter horse than mine, and he kept cutting me over the head and arms with his sword, which wasn't sharp, but it made me mighty mad, and I kept dodging it, for my pistol got hitched, and I could not get it out till he had hit me several times. When I did draw it, I dropped my reins, caught him by his long hair, and fired two loads right into him!"

One evening we were sitting together in the veranda of my headquarters at Meridian, when his bodyguard came by on their way to water. I said, "General, that is a fine troop of men and horses." "Yes, it is; and that captain is the eighth captain who has commanded it. The other seven have all been killed in battle!" Such was the influence of his success and fame, that there were always daring applicants for vacancies in Forrest's bodyguard.

CHAPTER XVIII

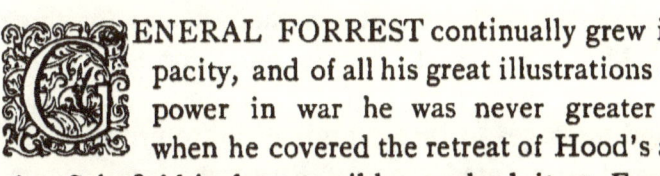ENERAL FORREST continually grew in ca-
pacity, and of all his great illustrations of his
power in war he was never greater than
when he covered the retreat of Hood's army,
after Schofield had so terribly repulsed it at Franklin,
and, with Thomas, had routed it at Nashville a few
days later, and now hung upon its rear and pressed it
to the very brink of the Tennessee River. Hood, in his
sore calamity, gave charge of his rear guard to Forrest
and General Walthall. Forrest had about two thousand
horse, and Walthall, in command of the infantry, was
allowed to select eight brigades, numbering only two
hundred rifles each! Walthall told them of the severe
work before them, and personally inspected each brigade, calling upon any man who desired to fall out to
do so. Not a man of those sixteen hundred Confederate veterans responded. They were all volunteers for
that desperate service. Forrest was in chief command,
and would have chosen Walthall from all that army for
his second.

Forrest will always stand as the great exponent of the
power of the mounted riflemen to fight with the revolver

when mounted, and with the rifle on foot. His troops were not dragoons "who fought indifferently on foot or horseback," nor were they cavalry who fought only mounted and with sabres. Few of his command ever bore sabres, save some of his officers, who wore them as a badge of rank. None of Forrest's men could use the sabre. He himself had no knowledge of its use, but he would encounter half-a-dozen expert *sabreurs* with his revolver.

In the great battle of Chickamauga, Forrest's division fought upon the right of Bragg's line. They were all dismounted, and did not see their horses for three days. After the retreat of Rosecrans, Forrest pursued up to within cannon-shot of Chattanooga. He sent repeated messages to Bragg, urging him to press on the flying and disordered army of Rosecrans, and occupy Chattanooga. Had this been done, there would have been no foundation for the claim that Chickamauga was a great Federal victory. It was the hardest stand-up fight ever made by the Confederate and Federal armies of the West. For two days the battle raged. At the close of the second day, the Federal army was driven from the field in rout. Thomas alone held his division in hand; the rest in confusion ran towards Chattanooga. Bragg's whole force numbered forty-six thousand men. When the battle ended, eighteen thousand of them lay killed and wounded. No army of modern war in the Old World or the New ever suffered such a loss and won the field. The enemy's losses were very great, including five thousand prisoners. His own reports show that he began and fought the battle with forces superior to Bragg's. The reason given by the latter for not following up a victory so signal was, in Forrest's opinion, not justified by the facts of the condition of the two armies when the battle ended by the retreat from the field of the Federal army. And no one was more competent to judge of the condition of the two armies at that time than Forrest. That it was a great opportunity lost by Bragg, a great victory unimproved, has been generally admitted. That it was a defeat of the Confederate forces or a great Federal victory, history can never record.

On the 13th of May, 1865, Forrest's command was paroled. His farewell address to his men was full of common-sense, and he himself set an example of entire acquiescence in the new order of things. Many of his negro slaves were employed as teamsters, etc., for his own command. The Federal authorities did not interfere with his plans, and he took these, now free, with teams sufficient, and moved at once to his plantations in Mississippi, where he went steadily to work. The negroes were fond of him, and worked for him as for nobody else. Some time after the war a turbulent negro came to his house threatening him. Forrest killed him before he could execute his purpose. I heard of no more trouble upon his plantation.

I was in Mobile when Admiral Semmes was arrested, and happened to return to my home in New Orleans upon the steamer with him. As I stepped upon the gang-plank, Semmes, in charge of an officer and guard-of-marines, had just passed on board. He said to me, in a loud voice: "You see, General, they have me in arrest. They are going now to disregard the paroles of all of us." The marine officer in charge was a considerate and gentlemanly man, and said to him: "Admiral, this is a most unpleasant duty for me to have to perform. I wish to discharge it with as little annoyance to you as possible, and hope you will feel free to converse and

move about the boat at your pleasure. You shall be
subject to no unnecessary surveillance." So the admiral
and I occupied a sofa in the saloon, where we sat con-
versing till a late hour. He wore his characteristic
manner of brave composure, while he felt the gravity of
his condition. His only apprehension seemed to be of
mob violence in New York, when his presence there
should be known. He was taken next day to the St.
Charles Hotel in New Orleans, where he was detained
several days. His friends were allowed free interviews
with him. General Dick Taylor, Senator Semmes, Duncan Kenner, and other eminent friends were in earnest
conversation with him; for the occasion seemed very
grave, not only for Semmes, but for all others who had
been prominent on the Southern side in the war between
the States. He agreed with me in believing that Forrest would be the next Confederate arrested. The
Federal organs already were indicating him as the most
proper object of Federal vengeance.

So next day I went to Memphis and sought Forrest at
once, to tell him about all this and urge him to leave
the country. He was down at his plantation at work.
I could not see him, and sought Colonel Sam Tate, his
partner and chief friend (he was president of the
Memphis and Charleston Railroad), who showed a
deep interest in my story, and said: "Do you sit down
at my desk and write to Forrest what you have told me.
I will prepare letters of credit for him. He must not
delay his escape. By the time your letter is ready, I'll
have a trusty messenger to bear it."

Accordingly a fine young fellow, a captain of Forrest's corps, presented himself and took charge of our
dispatches. I left Memphis before I could learn the
result, and did not know of Forrest's action for some

weeks. His reply to our letters was: "This is my country. I am hard at work upon my plantation, and carefully observing the obligations of my parole. If the
Federal government does not regard it, they'll be sorry.
I shan't go away." Some weeks after, having occasion
to visit Memphis, he called upon the Federal commander and spoke to this effect: "General, I have
called to know what you are going to do about my case.
I understand you have arrested Semmes, and are probably going to arrest me." He then repeated the reply
he had made to Tate and me. The general assured
him there was no purpose to trouble him. Tate and
other acquaintances of President Johnson's had no doubt
procured from him assurances that Forrest would not be
disturbed. He continued for several years to work
with his accustomed energy. Finally, in undertaking
to make a railroad from Memphis to Selma, he failed.

My last interview with him was in his office in Memphis. He looked much aged and broken, and said to
me sadly: "General, I am completely broke up. I am
broke in fortune, broke in health, and broke in spirit."
But when, a day or two after, some of the men who had
"broke" him called to see him and didn't talk to suit
him, he spun round upon his revolving seat and gave
them a piece of his mind worthy of his most unbroken
days.

General John T. Morgan, the able senator from Alabama, was his close friend, and undertook his claim
against the railroad company. Being in Nashville,
Forrest wrote him to come and see him at the Maxwell
House, where he was ill in bed. I shall give Morgan's
account of that last and most touching interview with
the greatest soldier of this generation. Morgan had
put Forrest's case in such shape that it was only neces-

sary to have his signature to certain papers to insure the payment of the large sum involved in the suit. He found Forrest in bed, ill and much broken. He said: "I am a dying man. For more than a year I have been a converted man. I have joined the Presbyterian Church. It was the church of my dear old mother. She was the best woman I ever knew. I hope it has made a better man of me. I have led a life of strife and violence. I now want to die at peace with all men. My son is a fine young fellow; he will do well. I do not want to hamper him at the outset of his young life with litigation. I have sent for you to tell you to drop all further proceedings in that case. I will not sign the papers."

This is the last record we have of this great soldier. He was born a soldier, as men are born poets, and his whole warfare was Napoleonic. It has been sometimes said that if he had been educated as a soldier, he would have been the greatest general the war produced, as he fought more battles than any commander of his day, always attacked the enemy upon his vulnerable point, and was never attacked. He always defeated, routed, or captured his enemy, and he continually grew in power to the last, and was ever greater than his opportunities. I do not believe that four years' confinement under military surveillance at West Point would have made him a greater soldier than he was.

Another man whom I knew well was General Dick Taylor. About 1856, we travelled together with our families. Taylor had become a very successful sugar planter, had married a lovely Creole lady, Miss Bringier, of a distinguished Louisiana family. I had married Miss Mason of Virginia, and we were all travelling together on the Mississippi in the fine steamer *Empress*.

We were about a week upon the journey, and a more pleasant one I cannot recall. He was the life of the company. After this he took an active part in the politics of the South. He was never an aspirant for office, but was a power in his personal character. In the Charleston Convention, Taylor was very able and influential, and on the outbreak of the war he went at once to the field in command of a Louisiana regiment. His very interesting and trenchant book, "Destruction and Reconstruction," published only a few days before his death, is one of the most interesting and brilliant of all the works about the war, and leaves but little to be said as to the ability and wit of the author.

During my association with him during the war and after it, I had many opportunities of enjoying his charming conversation and pungent wit. Once a very bright and gay lady asked him if he thought a certain very steady general was a proper commander of an important post on the eve of an attack. Taylor replied: "He is the very best I could entrust that command to. What can you urge against him?" "Oh, he is so attentive to his wife, I don't see how he can conduct his official business properly." "Madam," said Taylor, "I can well understand how a man can be attentive to his own wife and his business at the same time, but I'll be d—d if a man can be attentive to another's man's wife and mind his own business." This struck home, for she was one of the other men's wives, as Taylor well knew.

After the little army of Mobile reached Meridian, it aggregated about forty-five hundred veteran infantry and twenty field-pieces. I organized it at once into a division of three brigades, and prepared to march eastward and join Johnston, then in North Carolina, opposing Sherman. But soon tidings came of his

capitulation and then of the capture of Mr. Davis, and
General Dick Taylor proceeded to make the best terms
possible with General Canby. They were very liberal
and kindly on Canby's part, who gave free transportation over the railroads to the Confederates of all of our
armies who were making their weary way back to their
unhappy people. A prominent official of one of those
railroads received permission from Taylor to pass into
Mobile on the business of his company. That city was
then occupied by Canby's big victorious army, and,
feeling himself no longer in danger of Taylor, the rascal
telegraphed to his agent at Meridian to "give no more
of those passes to Confederate prisoners of war." On
hearing this, Taylor telegraphed Canby, "Please send
that railroad official up here under guard to me."
What was the horror of the man when a corporal and
file of soldiers took him from his home and bore him
up to Taylor, into whose presence he came with well-
grounded fear, for report said the general had shot men
for less crimes than that. Taylor administered in his
fluent style such a tongue-lashing as only he could utter,
and concluded by saying: "You have often heard how
an honest man feels when he falls among rogues. Here-
after you will be able to tell how a rogue feels when
he falls among honest men; for General Canby and
I will teach you a lesson that will last you the rest
of your miserable life! If I were to serve you right,
sir, I would turn you over to those soldiers whom you
have attempted to wrong, and they would hang you as
high as Haman upon one of these tall pines. Go, and
at once countermand your orders!"

After the war Taylor went to Washington to see
President Johnson regarding his policy towards the
Southern people, and especially toward the Confederate

President, who was his brother-in-law, and to whom he was tenderly attached. He gives in his "Destruction and Reconstruction" a characteristic account of his interviews with Thaddeus Stevens and other extreme Republicans then prominent in Washington.

About 1875, Taylor went to England, where for some time he was the guest of the Prince of Wales at Sandringham, and was received with proper courtesies in the circle of the prince's friends. He never forgot that he was the son of a President of the United States, and a general of the Southern Confederacy, and he was so esteemed. He went with the prince to the Fishmongers' Annual Banquet. When some of the company aspersed Virginia for her failure to meet her obligations under the bonds held by the English, Taylor, a Virginian by descent and affection, in his terse and manful way defended her so well that he was invited to meet the holders of ten millions of Virginia's bonds in conference. They made a very liberal proposition in view of the revelation of Virginia's poverty, and authorized Taylor to bear their offer to the government of the State. This he did, but it was received with a coldness that argued no intention on the part of the Legislature of Virginia to pay what they had borrowed from the British bankers.

About 1870, Commodore M. F. Maury, feeling his threescore and ten drawing near, made a tour of visits to his kindred in the South. He came to see me in New Orleans, and as soon as it was known that he was there, many attentions were shown him. There was then living in New Orleans a very wealthy and kindly Southern gentleman, who had conceived the hopeless idea of reconciling the opponents in the war about his dinner-table, and whenever he gave a dinner he would

invite as many Confederate gentlemen as Federal. He
called to see Commodore Maury, and asked him to meet
some friends at his house at a dinner. At that time,
party spirit ran very high in New Orleans. The vials
of wrath of the dominant Federal party were poured
upon the unhappy people. A man named Flanders had
been elected, by bayonet rule and a rascally ring, mayor
of the city, and a Judge Durell was the Jeffreys of the
Federal courts. When we sat down to the table, we
found Durell on one side of our host, next to him Commodore Maury, then came General John B. Gordon,
and then the writer. Upon the other side of the table
were Mayor Flanders, Judge Wood, Dick Taylor, and
William Hunt. But for Taylor, it would have been a
sad and solemn feast; but from the first he amused the
company, otherwise silent and constrained, by his witty
chaffing of "his friend, Mayor Flanders." Presently Flanders said to Commodore Maury, "Commodore, to what
extent, in your opinion, do the developments of modern
science corroborate the revelations of Divine Writ?"
The commodore was an experienced diner-out and a
master of the power of language and of thought, and
went on in his peculiar and eloquent way to expound
the extent of the corroboration, until he felt that he
had occupied the attention of the dinner-table long
enough upon such a subject. Taylor saw it, and I
observed his dark eyes sparkling, as he broke in, "And,
Commodore, if you will excuse me for interrupting, you
remember how Job cried out in his agony, 'Oh, that I
had mine enemy by a ring'? Well, none of us ever
knew what Job meant, until the developments of modern
political science have taught us the power of a ring.
Everybody now understands that my friend the mayor
here holds this great city by a ring." This relieved

the commodore and the company, and old Flanders, throwing back his head and opening wide his great mouth, laughed with the rest. As we gathered about the buffet for a chasse of brandy, the commodore said, "Taylor, when did you and the mayor become such friends?" "I never saw him until to-night," was the reply. It was hard upon our good old host, but it may have been a lesson to him on "reconstruction dinners," as his were wont to be called.

Knowing my opinion of West Point, Taylor, one evening in New Orleans, delivered himself of his views on the education of officers for the United States Army as follows: "Take a boy of sixteen from his mother's apron-strings, shut him up under constant surveillance for four years at West Point, send him out to a two-company post upon the frontier where he does little but play seven-up and drink whiskey at the sutler's, and by the time he is forty-five years old he will furnish the most complete illustration of suppressed mental development of which human nature is capable, and many such specimens were made generals on both sides when the war began."

He once told me of a kindly old English duchess who was enthusiastic in her expressions of admiration for Mr. James M. Mason. She said: "Mr. Mason was a dear old man. I did love Mr. Mason! You may know how I loved him when I tell you that I even tolerated his eating his tobacco; and when he was coming to B—— Castle, I sent and got a lot of spit-pots, so that he could eat his tobacco all over the house."

Taylor's last illness was in the home of General Barlow, his warm personal friend, who had married one of the charming daughters of Mr. Peter Townsend, of New York. He was taken ill there soon after the publication of his book, and was nursed by his devoted sister, Mrs. Dandridge, of Winchester, one of the most intellectual and attractive women who ever presided over the elegant hospitality of the President's house. In her were blended the best traits of the gentlewoman of Virginia and Louisiana.

CHAPTER XIX

Last Day of Service for the Confederacy — Beginning the Journey Home — Hospitalities on the Way — Condition of the South after the War — Arrival at Richmond — General Lee's Opinion of the Oath of Allegiance — His Manner of administering a Rebuke — Other Aspects of his Character illustrated — Death of Mr. Mason

O resume my narrative, the final day of our service for the Confederacy was one of the deepest gloom to us. The little army of Mobile had held steadfastly together with the dignity of men who had risked all from a high motive, and we stood by each other to the last. My own deep sadness was cheered by the sympathy of the noble men who had been my comrades. Gibson's Louisiana brigade had been especially active and enduring in the defence of Spanish Fort; Ector's Texans, the Alabamians, and North Carolinians, and Massenbury's Georgians made up that steadfast little garrison. They were all around me now, and the Louisiana band, the only one left in the army, came to my encampment that evening and gave me their farewell serenade. The officers of the Louisiana regiments which had served with me longest came to my tent in a body and bade me an affectionate good by. The Federal major who relieved my quartermaster of his public property declined to receive my headquarters ambulance and team, and graciously urged that I should keep it for myself. This I declined to do; but when I

found that it would be of great value to my destitute
staff-officers, I approved of their accepting it, and
Flowerree, Dick Holland, and John Mason drove off
in it to seek their fortunes.

On the evening of May 14th, our surrender was complete. A train loaded with paroled prisoners of war
from Lee's army was going up the road that evening as
far as West Point, and a crate car was added to it for
me and my horse, all the property I then possessed.
The conductor told me it would not go further that
night than West Point, and that I would find hospitable
entertainment for the night in the house of a leading
gentleman of the town — Squire Collins. So just at
sunset, when our destination was reached, I left Roy
with the orderly who had faithfully remained with me
thus far to take care of the horse and to help me, and
set out to seek some shelter for the night.

I readily found the house, quite a handsome one, and
on the veranda were several young gentlemen and a
very handsome young lady in full conversation as I
approached the gate. I was ashamed to ask for shelter,
and had passed on, going some eight or ten paces
further, when I heard the gate latch rattle and a familiar voice call out, "General!" and I wheeled around
to meet a fine-looking young fellow, Captain Collins of
Armstead's brigade. With hands extended, and hearty
words of comfort and welcome, he claimed me as their
guest for the night, introduced me to his very handsome
sister (now Mrs. Dr. Curry of New York City), and
made me at home at once; and never was generous
hospitality more welcome. There was a sumptuous
supper with all the belongings of a well-appointed
table, an elegant bedroom, and a breakfast appropriate
to such an establishment, and, above all, the sympa-

thetic care of those charming people. It was the one green spot in all of that desolate time.

With many warm feelings we parted next morning, and I got again into my crate with Roy, and in an hour had reached Okolona, where I found one of our servants awaiting to conduct me to Mr. Clarke's residence, that kind friend having already sent for my family to stay with him until arrangements might be made for our future. As I mounted Roy, I raised my hat to the Confederates of Lee's army who filled the train, and they silently returned my farewell, showing deep sympathy and respect as I turned away. Our stay with Mr. Clarke lasted about two weeks. He was goodness itself. He sold Roy for $200 in greenbacks, the first I had ever seen. Roy was a noble chestnut sorrel of great power; he had cost $700 in gold, and was a present to me from an old friend, General Cabell. Mr. Clarke said: "Now, General Maury, I have no money at all, but there's near a thousand bales of cotton in my gin-house, and you just say how many you will accept to take you home and keep you till you find something to do; for you ain't going to be kept down long, and I will give you a certificate to my Mobile correspondent that you have that many bales in my hands and he will give you the money on it."

Of course our objective point was our home in Virginia. My father-in-law's home had escaped the general ruin and desolation, thanks to Burnside's kind heart, and all of his children and grandchildren were soon together there. My parole carried us meanwhile to New Orleans, where my good friend, Major Charles L. C. Dupuy, of my staff, met us, and also my kinsman, Mr. Rutson Maury, at whose house we were entertained. He had received instructions from his uncle, Mr. Rutson

Maury, of New York, to supply us with everything we might require. Commodore Maury, who was in London, had already sent me a generous check, when a noble-hearted Southern woman came to me and put into my hand ten gold eagles, but I would not take her little store, being already amply provided for by so many kind friends. Ten old friends and comrades offered me money. Some of these were personal strangers to me, but remembered some little kindness shown them in the days of my power. General Dick Taylor was one of these, and with him came Mr. Payne, the close friend of Mr. Davis. Mr. Richard Owen, of Mobile, insisted that my wife should share a little store of gold he had saved for an emergency, and the family of Vasser, of Aberdeen, who were much attached to her, contributed each a bale of cotton apiece, nine bales in all, worth then eighty cents a pound, and sent it to their commission-merchant to be sold for us; but we had already sailed, well supplied, and it was not until five or six years afterwards that I heard of this generous act.

Thank God, I can never arraign mankind for want of generosity, and it is with pride and gratitude that I record the hospitality and kindness which met me and mine on every hand throughout the war and at its close. It was not my personality which called it forth, but it was the spontaneous outcome of the spirit which pervaded the whole South in all that sorrowful time, and which distinguishes it even unto this day. Not even the cruel vicissitudes of that bitter conflict could chill the sympathetic hearts and close the beneficent hands of our dear Southern people. Brave men and tender women are these who in the past have nobly borne their part, and whose names will be written with the saints, for of them it may be truly said "that they loved their fellow-men."

I learned that the steamship *Constitution* would sail from New Orleans in a few days, and the quartermaster ordered transportation for us as far as New York upon her. There were a number of Federal officers who were passengers on her as well, and Captain Mehaffy, of the First United States Infantry, was the commander of the guard and of all on board. He showed marked consideration and courtesy to all of us who were his prisoners; insisted that I and my family should have first choice of seats at the table and also of the staterooms, and when he overheard a Federal chaplain on board talking unpleasantly about the war to one of my staff-officers, he cautioned him that if he again transgressed propriety in that way he would lock him up in his stateroom. The old captain of the ship imbibed Mehaffy's generous spirit and, finding that we were all Virginians, he took the responsibility of changing the ship's destination to Old Point Comfort, and landed us there instead of at New York. On parting, I formally thanked him and Captain Mehaffy for their considerate kindness in behalf of myself and my officers. Several times afterwards I met the latter gentleman and introduced him to friends in New Orleans, who were desirous of showing him courtesies. Mehaffy told me he had lived in Norfolk before the war, where his father owned a large foundry, and where he had learned to like Virginians.

On arriving at Richmond, I called to pay my respects to General Lee, then living in the house in Franklin Street, in which we afterwards established the Westmoreland Club. Captain William Lewis Maury, commander of the Confederate cruiser *Georgia*, went with me. I gave the general a written statement of my defence of Mobile, he having written to me with regard to it, and I felt it was proper to make my last report to him. At

the same time I told him that a few days before leaving
New Orleans, whither thousands of young Confederate
soldiers had flocked, seeking employment, a Federal
major on a street-car had said to me: "I understand
that these young men won't take the oath of allegiance
to the United States. They can't find employment
very easily until they do, and may get into trouble. I
think their generals should set them an example and
encourage them at once to take the oath and go to
work." He had no idea that he was talking to a
Confederate, for I had laid away all evidence of my
recent rank and calling. When the major left the car,
I continued in it until I reached General Beauregard,
to whom, as also to General Taylor, I repeated the
remark. They both earnestly agreed with his view, and
told me they would at once set an example to their people. When I had finished, General Lee said: "I am
very glad you did that. It is what we must all do, and
what I have already done." I said, "I will follow your
example."

General Lee had a quiet way of giving admonition
peculiarly his own. It was very effective sometimes,
although he rarely censured any one. One day he had
established his headquarters in the large country residence of a gentleman who had placed it at his service.
A distinguished commander arrived with his corps and,
accompanied by his aide-de-camp, reported to General
Lee, who told him to bring the latter with him to the
house, and to direct the rest of the staff to encamp on
the lawn with his own staff. Soon after, dinner was
served, consisting of bacon, and greens, and corn-bread,
to which was added a slice of fine roast beef sent to General Lee by a good lady of the neighborhood, on which
the general hoped to mend his fare. The three sat

down to dinner, and General Lee inquired of his guest, "General, what may I offer you?" "Some of the bacon and greens, thank you." Then came the aid's turn. "Captain Smith, what will you have?" "Beef, if you please, General." General Lee suavely transferred the slice of beef to the young man, who calmly ate it up.

More than a year afterward General Lee arrived at the headquarters of the commander who had been his guest upon this occasion. When dinner was served, there happened to be a fine roast upon the table, and the aforementioned young beef-eater was present. When his host inquired of General Lee what he would have, the latter looked at the unfortunate aide-de-camp, and smiling kindly replied, "I will thank you for a piece of that beef, if Captain Smith does not want all of it." He never showed temper in his rebukes, but they were all the more effective. On this occasion, he was as tender to the lad as if admonishing a son.

When General Lee did express displeasure, his method of administering a rebuke was usually salutary. During the fighting around Richmond, one of his officers, who had been placed in charge of certain lines, was frequently conspicuous by his absence. This was especially noticeable whenever there was heavy firing about his post of duty. His staff were much mortified and disgusted by the conduct of their chief, especially as they were aroused night after night just after they had fallen asleep, worn out with the hard service of the day, to receive couriers from their superior, comfortably housed in the city, demanding reports of the day's events. They had no idea that General Lee had observed all this, and were therefore surprised and delighted when one morning, as the recreant appeared, General Lee accosted him with intense sarcasm. "Good morning,

General Blank. Are you not afraid to trust yourself so far from the city, and to come where all this firing and danger is?" "Oh! General, I am somewhere upon the lines every day." "Indeed? I am very glad to learn it, sir. Good morning, General Blank!" And he turned from him with a scorn as withering as his words.

When one of his commanders, from want of promptness, permitted a corps to escape, General Lee was very indignant, and said to him: "General, I have sometimes to admonish General Stuart or General Gordon against being too fast. I shall never have occasion to find that fault with you."

A warm friendship existed between General Lee and a very gallant and handsome young officer, who was married to a lovely Virginia girl on the very night of the conflagration of Richmond. He did not see his old commander for some years after the war. When they did meet, General Lee greeted him with warm affection, and said, "How many children have you?" "Just four. —"Are they girls or boys?" "All girls." — "Well," said the general, "I love and revere and admire women, as you know, but do you go home and tell your wife she has done enough for the female line. I hope she will now go on and have four boys to fight for their restored country in the next war." The gallant young colonel and his dutiful wife faithfully executed their general's commands, and now four lovely daughters and four sturdy sons solace the evening of their days.

Lee was very averse to office work. Colonel Walter Taylor, who was his adjutant throughout his great career, found it difficult to secure his attention to the accumulating reports of the army. One day he took the general a bundle of documents, reports, etc., for his examination. After going over a few of them, Lee, with an

expression of impatience, tossed the rest aside, whereupon Taylor, whose own patience was exhausted, gathered
them up and was about to retire, when General Lee said,
in a gentle, repentant tone, "Stop, Colonel! When I lose
my temper, I do not think you should let that make you
angry," and forthwith addressed himself to the task before
him, which he completed thoroughly and carefully.

On one occasion his opinion upon Sherman's raid
through Georgia was invited. "I have never understood," he said, "why General Sherman has been so
much commended for that march, when the only question before him to decide was whether he could feed his
army by consuming all the people had to eat."

General Lee was very fond of Stuart, who was also a
great favorite with the young ladies of the valley.
Shortly before the battle of Brandy Station, Lee reviewed
his cavalry corps. The young ladies of Culpepper had
decorated Stuart's horse with flowers, placing a wreath
around his charger's neck. When he had saluted, and
rode up to take his place beside General Lee, the latter
remarked: "Take care, General Stuart! That is the
way General Pope's horse was adorned when he went
to the battle of Manassas."

Lee rarely drank any liquor. One day General John
G. Walker, a very able officer, reported to him with
regard to some service he had performed. He was very
tired, and could not refrain from glancing toward a very
inviting looking bottle which was very suggestive of
something comforting. The general observed it, and
said: "You look fatigued. Take a drink. It will do
you good." Walker cheerfully acquiesced, and taking
a bottle, poured out a tumbler of cold buttermilk, the
general smilingly enjoying his little sell the while.

The remarkable proclamation of amnesty promulgated

by President Johnson required us to respond to fifteen separate disqualifications for citizenship and trustworthiness. My application was to the effect that in begging for pardon I confessed that I was a graduate of the United States Military Academy at West Point, and a captain in the adjutant-general's department of the United States Army; and finally I was to state whether I was the possessor of $20,000! After informing His Excellency of my guilt in regard to the first two clauses, I stated, in order to thoroughly clear my skirts of the third, that I was the possessor of nothing save the ragged Confederate uniform in which I stood. I never heard from President Johnson.

About this time I received a letter from Admiral Buchanan, telling me he had not yet asked pardon because he could not bring himself to express regret for anything he had done. I showed the letter to General Joe Johnston, who said, in his terse way: "You don't have to express any regret. I have asked pardon and have expressed no regret. Oh, yes, I did, too. I requested that His Excellency would grant me a pardon, and expressed regret that I could offer him no reason why he should."

After this I set out to follow my family, who had preceded me to Mr. Mason's home. The railroad ran only as far as Hamilton's Crossing, the track having been torn up beyond that point, and not yet replaced. The whole country had been wasted by war, and the condition of the people was fearful. The poverty-stricken Confederate soldiers returning to their ruined homes found Federal garrisons in every county seat, sometimes white and sometimes negroes. All of our good men were destitute, and there were but few who were not cast down in heart and spirit.

A stage-coach awaited the passengers for Fredericksburg at Hamilton's Crossing, and into it I climbed with a Federal major and his wife, on the arrival of the train from Richmond. It had been raining, and the roads were very heavy. After a while the stage-agent came to the door, followed by a respectable looking negro woman, and said, hesitatingly, "Can't this woman have a seat in there? It's a long and very muddy walk to town." "No, indeed," said Mrs. Major. "No nigger-woman shall sit by me." "I will be d—d if she shall sit by me," said the manly major. "Come and sit in here by me, old woman," said I. "I've been riding by such as you for nearly forty years, and it is too late for me to put on airs now." And this little difference being amicably adjusted, we proceeded on our way.

I went at once to Mr. Mason's home, where I found all the family assembled. Many of the negroes had left, but a number of the field-hands remained and were at work, making and gathering the crops of wheat and corn. One day, while Mr. Mason was busy superintending the working of his wheat machine, his arm was caught and drawn into the machinery and dreadfully crushed. He realized his own condition from the first, and said: "I have been faithful to my wife and faithful to my friends. Whether I have been faithful to my God, a few hours must now determine." He asked me to read Gray's "Elegy" to him, which I did. It was a trying task. All of us children and grandchildren gathered about him until his death, which took place thirty-six hours after the accident. His presence and example were sorely missed, not only by those of his own household, but also by the large circle of friends and associates to whom he was ever an exponent of much that most adorns a man.

CHAPTER XX

The Classical and Mathematical Academy of Fredericksburg estab-
lished — Accepts a Business Offer in New Orleans — Engages in the
Manufacture of Resin and Turpentine — Disastrous Results of this
Enterprise — Preventing a Duel — Preservation of Southern War
Records — Organization of the National Guard — Recollections of
Senator M. C. Butler

T was decided by my friends and by me that,
as there was no school of standing in that
war-swept region, it was fitting I should
establish one. It was known that I was an
A. B. of the University of Virginia, and a graduate of
West Point, where I had also been for four years an
instructor. Encouraged by the recollection of these past
achievements in the field of knowledge, I determined
to establish in Fredericksburg a Classical and Mathematical Academy of a high grade. As soon as the
announcement was made, pupils came to secure admis-
sion, not because they knew anything about my attainments, but because I was a Confederate general, and
they had the utmost confidence in my qualifications.

As the engagements multiplied and the time for opening the academy approached, my own misgivings as to
these qualifications greatly increased. In fact, I felt
that I was working under false pretences, and I determined to practise my abilities as teacher and guide of
youth upon my daughter, modesty limiting my course
of instruction to the elements of arithmetic. My

efforts were distinguished by such signal failure and lack of intelligence on my own part, and by such sorrow upon hers, as convinced me that I must have a partner in the conduct of the Classical and Mathematical Academy.

There was a very clever teacher, named Buckner, who had managed the Fredericksburg Academy before the war with that ability and success to be expected of me. I sought Mr. Buckner and told him that I found it wiser to have a partner in this important enterprise, in case I should be sick or wounded; that I already had forty-five pupils engaged at $50 each per scholastic year; that I had heard of his capacity as a teacher, and thought it prudent we should work together; that I was willing to entrust to him the older and more advanced boys, who were learning the Latin and Greek and higher mathematics, while I would undertake the instruction and flagellation of the little a.b. abs. Buckner was a gentleman and a scholar, and a fine Confederate soldier as well, and joined at once as junior professor of the Fredericksburg Classical and Mathematical Academy.

One of the deciding causes of this arrangement of mine and Buckner's was the arrival at Cleveland of five boys sent to me from Alabama to be "plebs" of my school. My blood ran cold when I saw them, but I found an elegant gentlewoman bereft of her comfortable fortune by the war, who was willing to receive them into her family on very reasonable terms and to look after them, which she did for several years very kindly.

At this crisis I received a very lucrative offer of business in New Orleans. So I transferred to Mr. Buckner my responsibilities in our mutual institution of learning, and went to New Orleans to be an express-agent. Having been the quartermaster in the United States

Corps of Cadets, it was presumed I had peculiar fitness for all matters appertaining to transportation, etc., so I retired and Buckner managed the academy until his death, and a more faithful and accomplished principal it could never have had. For, since the days of Mr. Thomas Hanson, no man had won the confidence and love of pupils and parents, or deserved them more than he.

I always felt satisfied as to my connection with that excellent institution, for I was strictly honest in it all. I knew I had been in school from the time I was four years old until I was twenty-four, and ought to be competent to teach, but when the five boys arrived from Mobile, entrusted by confiding friends to my tutelage, I felt the gravity of the responsibilities, and instituted a rigid course of self-examination. It was true that for eight or nine years I had nothing to do but study Latin and Greek, but a careful private investigation showed that I had not for many years been able to tell one Greek character from another, and could not translate a line of a Latin author without a dictionary. As for mathematics, I had forgotten the algebraic signs, and after a while I began to doubt if I could even keep up with the a.b. abs.

I must have been a success as an express-agent, for soon after entering upon this business, the company raised my wages to $200 per month, and I sent for my family to join me in New Orleans. Not many months elapsed before I ascertained that the company was about to sell out to an older and richer one, and I was advised to consider the business of the manufacture of resin and turpentine. Naval stores were ruling at enormous prices, many times their ante-war rate, and the whole manufacture in America had ceased. I took counsel of as many friends having knowledge of such things as I could reach, and they unanimously advised me to go into the business. Pine lands were cheap, the process was simple, negroes were less averse to that than any other sort of labor. One generous-hearted gentleman of Mobile said, "General, I don't think you can fail, and if you will find a suitable place for the business, I will buy it for you." This was Colonel Jack Ingersoll.

Another, Captain John Gillespie, was in charge of an enormous fire and marine insurance business. He had never in his life made so much money, and he went on famously, making commissions of many thousands of dollars per month for some time. One brilliant stroke of his electrified his New York company, for he put a whole shipload of cotton into that company. The managers posted to Mobile in intense anxiety, but the ship arrived safely in Liverpool, and they made a fine premium. However, they begged Gillespie in future not to monopolize such a risk for them. Gillespie said: "General, you can't fail in this turpentine business. Go on with it, and draw on me for your expenses. You took care of me for four years; I'll take care of you as long as I have a dollar." And he did. He is now an eminent lawyer in Kansas City, Missouri, — Judge John Gillespie, as able as he is honest, and brave, and generous.

Another true and noble friend was my adjutant-general, E. W. Flowerree. He had attracted my attention by his manly and soldierly bearing at Elkhorn. On inquiry, I learned that he was a Virginian, and a graduate of the Virginia Military Institute. As soon as I was promoted to a brigadier, I selected him for my Adjutant-General, and he stayed with me until the end of the war, and was my dear friend the last day of his life.

I bought of Mr. Ben Turner, of Alabama, a place he owned and had profitably worked in Louisiana, in St. Tammany Parish. There was a comfortable residence upon it, and all of the apparatus necessary for the distilling of turpentine, and it was surrounded by great forests of the best sort of pine. By close attention I managed to have 70,000 boxes out by the opening of the season, which there opens two weeks earlier and closes two weeks later than in regions further north. Adjacent to my land lay a fine body of timber upon public land, which Mr. Turner had boxed and worked one season, so that in all I had 140,000 boxes, half of which would yield a fine white resin, then selling at fabulous prices.

The prices had tumbled before mine got to market, but I received $15 per barrel for a small lot, and turpentine also brought enormous values, selling at several dollars a gallon. I saw a certain fortune before me, and when an overture was made to me of the presidency of a railroad, with a salary of $10,000, I declined it, because I could not afford to accept it at the cost of giving up such business prospects. All went well with me for a little while. Every stilling gave nearly one hundred gallons of spirits and from fifteen to eighteen barrels of white resin, and I was in a fair way to reimburse Ingersoll and Gillespie their advances, when the latter, who had been over-generous to his friends, came to grief, and I had no capital to pay my hands or carry on my work.

For the rest of that year things went very badly with me; we were far from all human sympathy, surrounded by a very low order of people. The war had developed the fact that the worst class of our population was to be found in the vast region of piney woods that sweep along our seaboard from Carolina to the Sabine. They are also in the mountains of East Tennessee; the same so graphically described by Miss Murfree, and who have until now manifested the most vicious and cruel natures of any North American. Jones County, Mississippi, is in this piney woods belt, between Meridian and the lower Pearl River. Toward the close of the war, it was reported to me that the people of that county had declared their independence of the Southern Confederacy. It was said that a Confederate wagon-train passing through that section had been captured, and the officer in charge paroled as any other prisoner of war might have been. So I forthwith ordered the Fifteenth Confederate Cavalry to invade this *imperium in imperio* and reduce these secessionists to order. Colonel Maury, who was in command of the expedition, did his work very actively, broke up the cover of these malcontents, put several families into mourning, and scattered the military powers into the neighboring swamps and fastnesses, where his horsemen were unable to follow up the fugitives. Colonel Lowry, since governor, of the Third Mississippi, was sent to support Maury, and completed the work of the mounted men so thoroughly that the malcontents left the county in great numbers, and moved down toward the Delta or Pearl River.

It was into this community, where my name, as I afterwards found too late, was the red flag to the bull, that I, unwitting of my neighbors, came to seek my fortune. Threats were soon made against me, and one rascal was insolent enough to threaten me in my own house. I invited him out, escorted him through my gate, and warned him never again to set foot upon my property. On the next Sunday, about midday, I returned from New Orleans to find my greatest body of pine in a general conflagration. Seventy thousand boxes were burned out, and with difficulty the fences and buildings were saved. After that I never left my house unarmed.

It was, therefore, with a special relief that I welcomed the arrival of my kinsman, Jack Maury, from Fort Delaware. He had refused to take the oath of allegiance to the Federal government and, with a few other Confederate officers, was detained in prison until the late summer, when the United States refused to keep them any longer and bade them, as Dogberry did, to "go in God's name." About this time my wife fell ill, and we were very desolate, no human being ever coming near us; till one day there was a step upon the veranda, a tap at the door, and there stood that grand old gentleman, Dr. Louis Minor, late fleet-surgeon of the Confederate Navy, as gentle as he was brave, the Colonel Newcome of our time. He had heard in New Orleans of my wife's condition, had boarded a sloop on Lake Pontchartrain, and after a rough experience of forty-eight hours, reached us. He came like a minister of mercy, and was with us many days, and his patient was convalescent before he returned to his own comfortable home in New Orleans.

It became evident that our whole enterprise in St. Tammany Parish was a failure. The sum of $10 was the total balance in hand, and I took $5 and went to New Orleans to seek my fortune. At the Rigolet I boarded a sloop bound across the lake. Her captain and crew of two men were negroes, and the passenger accommodation appropriate. My passage money was $2.50, and on the second day when we landed I walked into the city with $2.50 in my pocket and went to the office of an old friend, General Simon Buckner. He told me the office of secretary of the Southern Hospital

Association had been created the previous night with a salary of $125 per month, and said, "Will you accept it?" "Accept it? Of course I will. That's $125 a month more than my present income." In a short time it was raised to $200, and I was able to be reunited with my family.

One bright Sunday morning in the winter of 1871, as we were returning from church, my friend Colonel M—— joined us, and after chatting awhile on various topics, touched my arm and turned away. I followed him, and he told me that the night before, while drunk, he had slapped the face of his old friend, Captain L——, and that he had been awakened on Sunday morning by Mr. Essling and Captain Adams, bearing a peremptory challenge; that Colonel Jack Wharton had agreed to act as his second, provided I would serve with him. Remembering that the challenger had a wife and children, and believing that I could prevent the duel, I consented to serve. The challenge was peremptory, and we accepted it, Wharton and I agreeing to fix a "long day," that time might be gained for the intervention of friends, and a peaceful solution reached. We fixed the following Wednesday as the date, Bay St. Louis as the place, and duelling pistols as the weapons. We then reported to our principal, to whom Wharton remarked, "Now you will have time to brush up your pistol practice." Raising his head proudly, Colonel M—— replied, "No, sir, I will not touch a pistol until I take my place upon the field next Wednesday." I said, "I am glad to hear you say so. It is just what I expected of you."

In that day, and especially in New Orleans, no man could refuse to fight a duel under such circumstances as these, and preserve his self-respect or the confidence of the community. The principals in this affair were both Kentuckians and soldiers of high courage. After accepting the challenge we set ourselves to find some mutual friend who could act as mediator. By this time the whole rotunda of the St. Charles Hotel was filled by the curious and anxious friends of the principals, who had discovered that a duel was in prospect. Late in the evening, General Tom Taylor, a friend of both parties, came to me — may God bless him for it! — and said, "General, these men ought not to fight." I replied, "I know it, but the challenge was peremptory, and no opportunity for apology was offered." He disappeared, and, as I expected, soon returned, saying the seconds on the other side desired to see us. As we entered the room, Essling said, "General, I am surprised that you seem so anxious for a fight." I said: "No other alternative is left us by the challenge. I am exceedingly anxious for a peaceable solution of the matter, if possible." "Well," said Essling, "if the challenge were withdrawn, do you think we could reach a solution?" "Yes," I said; "in that case we might." "Well, General, we will suspend the challenge with the understanding that if we can't satisfactorily adjust matters, they shall proceed as before arranged." I retired, outwardly grave and serious, but with a heart lightened of its deep anxiety, into a private room, where Wharton and I wrote an ample apology for the deadly affront offered Captain L—— by Colonel M——; and since that day I have had nothing to do with duels save to prevent them, although — to anticipate my narrative a little — the reckless opponents of Mr. Cleveland have censured him for appointing me United States Minister to Colombia, because I have "shot several men in duels."

On the last occasion of this mendacity, I wrote to

Mr. Cleveland, telling him that for myself I did not care; that my own people knew my character and history so well they had elected me a member of the Anti-Duelling Society of South Carolina. But, as the slander was published to injure him, I would take any measures to expose and punish its libellous authors he might advise. He replied with characteristic kindness, saying, "No one believes what that paper publishes, and unless it is reiterated I would not notice it." An eminent lawyer informed me I could successfully prosecute for such slander, but I decided to await further developments, which never came. Thank heaven, duelling among gentlemen has become almost unknown. The men who fought in the great war between the States have no need of such encounters to prove their courage or protect their honor.

To return to my story, whence the recollection of this threatened duel led me to wander, in New Orleans, in 1868, I determined to set on foot a plan for the systematic collection and preservation of the Southern archives relating to the war. General Dick Taylor cordially encouraged me, and in May of that year I called a meeting by quiet personal requests of nine or ten gentlemen in the office of Hewitt and Morton. After conversational discussion, it was agreed to meet at the same place in one week from that date. Meantime, each of us agreed to canvass among his friends and bring them in to help. Next week forty of us assembled, and the noble and able Presbyterian divine, Dr. B. M. Palmer, was elected president, and our work went on for several years, though without important result.

In 1873, a convention was called at White Sulphur Springs. It was attended by many able Southern gentle-

men, who evinced the most earnest interest in our work.
President Davis, Admiral Semmes, Governor Letcher,
and General Beauregard took leading parts.   The domi-
cile of the society was moved to Richmond.   Colonel
Wythe Mumford was appointed secretary and I chair-
man of the Executive Committee.   We occupied an
office in the capitol of Virginia, made acknowledg-
ments in the newspapers for documents received, and
arrangements for their publication.

The Executive Committee included the Honorable R.
M. T. Hunter and several other gentlemen of high character and ability, and so soon as we began to publish our
records, our membership rapidly increased; so that the
Secretary of War at length sought to procure access to
and the use of our archives.   We replied, "Open yours
to us, and ours will be open to you."   This ended the
negotiations.   The next Secretary asked access to our
papers with the same result.   Then Mr. Hayes obtained
the Presidency, and announced a conciliatory policy
towards the South.   He appointed General Marcus
Wright, who had already collected by his own exertions
many of our war papers, to the charge of that business,
and sent him to me to accomplish a free interchange
of documents between the War Records Office and the
Southern Historical Society.   To this I cordially assented, and opened our office with all of its great collection of papers to the free access of the office in
Washington.   Since then the interchange has continued,
until now the War Records Office can publish the
authentic facts of both contestants in the struggle.

Satisfied and proud of our prowess, so wonderfully
exhibited in the war, and with all our interest concen-
trated upon the South's financial prosperity, it was no
wonder that for a long time little thought was given to

the development of the military power of the Southern States. The contest of Tilden and Hayes for the Presidency caused some of us to apprehend civil war. During that political struggle and soon after the great labor riots in Baltimore and Pittsburgh, etc., I called a meeting in Richmond to consider how we might improve the militia of the State. We invited the co-operation of all the States in measures promotive of our military efficiency, and the matter was promptly taken up in New York and followed by the first convention and organization of the National Guard Association of America.

We succeeded in procuring from Congress a small increase in the annual appropriation for arming the militia, but, better than that, we aroused in every State such interest in this vital subject as has placed on foot the most efficient national militia in the world. Only a short time has passed since the great State of Pennsylvania called out her militia, and in twenty-four hours an army as large as that with which Scott conquered Mexico was thrown into a remote part of the State, where it arrested and crushed out the most dangerous and powerful organization ever yet in arms against the government. In setting this movement on foot, I had the active help and co-operation of Captain Chamberlain, Colonel Cutshaw, Colonel Purcell, and other gentlemen of Richmond.

Before bringing my narrative to its end with an account of my experience and adventures in Colombia, I wish to pay a tribute to my old friend, Senator M. C. Butler, of South Carolina. Senator Butler is a descendant of the best families of the Southern and the Northern States. The famous Commodores Perry of New England were his uncles. On his father's side he was of the Butler families of Virginia and South Carolina. That

noble Senator Butler, Andrew Pickens Butler, com-
peer of Calhoun, was his uncle. None who ever enjoyed
the pleasure of his acquaintance here forgot how
high a privilege that was. Judge Butler, R. M. T.
Hunter, and James M. Mason were for years the great
triumvirate of the United States Senate. They lived in
the same house, ate at the same table, and were close
friends, warmly attached and associated in their personal intercourse, and staunch allies in debate and influence in the Senate in those days when the true dignity
and influence of a Southern senator were at their highest.

It was once my delightful privilege to pass the Christmas holidays with Judge Butler and a company of bright
ladies and gentlemen, old and young, in Hazelwood, that
old Virginian home of the Taylors of Carolina. Young
as I was, Judge Butler and I became close friends at
once. We had a dinner party every day, and every
night had its delightful close in a dance at Gaiemont,
Port Royal, or Hazelwood. The house, big as it was,
had no vacant beds or empty places at the table, and
we young people greatly enjoyed the old people. I
remember a dinner of twenty or more sets, when we
young men and maidens listened with delight to the
witty and wise conversation sustained by Judge Butler,
William P. Taylor of Hayfield, and John Bernard of
Gaiemont. We young folks ceased our merry chat and
listened with rapt attention to the wisdom and wit and
charming narratives and wise discussions of this cultured
trio of refined gentlemen of the old school. In a long
experience I can recall nothing so elegant as was that
Christmas week.

Senator M. C. Butler is worthy of his high lineage.
He entered the Confederate Army at the outset of the
war between the States before he was twenty, and con-

tinually grew in his influence and his distinction.
He had every quality of a great soldier, and far higher,
a nobleness of nature which has made him till now ad-
mired and loved by all sorts of people, by the highest
the most. He has been a senator of the old-time
standard of his gallant little State, and a leader in all
that has been important in the councils of his country.
For more than fifteen years he has been in his high
office, and well will it be for all our people if he will
continue in it. It was not merely by his energy and
daring soldiership that Butler won the confidence
and admiration of all good men, but he has given an
example of self-sacrifice which for all time will be held
up for the emulation of future generations.

Butler bore an active part in the famous cavalry battle
of Brandy Station, in which he was seriously wounded
and maimed for life. In the early morning of that
fierce fight, in which more than twenty thousand horsemen contested the field from dawn till dark of a long
day in June, Butler and young Captain Farley had just
come out of action and were laughing together over
some amusing incident they had both noticed. Side
by side in the road, they were facing in opposite direc-
tions, when a cannon-ball from an unobserved battery
came bounding at them. It struck Butler's leg above
the ankle, tore through his horse, and cut off Farley's leg
above the knee. Down they all went. Butler began to
staunch the blood with his handkerchief, and advised Farley how to do the same. Captain John Chestnutt, Lieutenant Rhett, and other officers came running up to Butler's
help, but at that moment he observed that Farley's dying
horse was struggling and seemed likely to crush him.
So he told the officers who had come to his help to "go
at once to Farley. He needs you more than I do."

This they did, placing Farley in a litter. He asked them to bring his leg by him in it, and said: "Now, gentlemen, you have done all for me possible. I shall be dead in an hour. God bless you for your kindness. I bid you all an affectionate farewell. Go at once to Butler." That evening about five o'clock Butler's leg was dressed in the field hospital, just as poor Farley breathed his last. Butler had never seen Captain Farley before that morning, when Stuart sent orders by him to Butler. Henceforth we shall not need to go to Sir Philip Sidney for an example of noble self-sacrifice.

Butler is full of genial humor and ready wit, as of more sterling qualities of manhood. On one occasion, he was at a reception in a Western city. A coarse, vulgar doctor was introduced to him, whose graceful salutation was, "So you are the fellow that killed all of them niggers in South Carolina." With an infinitely humorous expression, in his mellowest tones, Butler said, "Doctor, I have no doubt you have killed more men than I have." The retort carried the audience, who despised the doctor, and enjoyed his discomfiture as he slunk away.

This foolish invention of an Edgefield massacre, published by politicians, who used to ride over us and try to keep us down, gave Butler another opportunity to show his mettle. A leading senator, who had announced that he was an advocate of settling personal difficulties by the "Code of Honor," had pressed this charge against Butler with especial virulence, and led in the effort made to exclude him from his seat in the Senate. After all the charges had been thoroughly disproved, and all honest men were satisfied that Butler had successfully striven to prevent bloodshed and violence in that business, this senator failed to acknowledge in any way

that he had done injustice, but soon gave an occasion
for Butler to bring him down from his perch, and
received at the Carolinian's hands such a castigation
as he had never before been subjected to.

Butler married Maria Pickens, the second daughter
of Governor Francis W. Pickens, the first war governor
of South Carolina. In a recent letter Butler says: "No
sketch of my life would be complete which did not mention the good woman, my wife, who has so much to do
with shaping my career. If I have had any success in
life, it is due more to her and my venerated mother than
all else."

Beside General Butler's name should be written that
of another South Carolina soldier, Colonel Haskell,
whose arm was so terribly shattered that amputation at
the shoulder was necessary. The surgeon was about to
administer chloroform when Haskell said: "Stop, Doctor! You have very little chloroform since the enemy
has declared it contraband of war. Is it not so?"
"Yes, Colonel." "Then keep it for some poor soldier
who needs it. *I* can do without it."

CHAPTER XXI

BOUT six years ago, I was appointed United States Minister to Colombia, and enjoyed exceptional advantages of observing this interesting people and their wonderful country. My visits to the Isthmus impressed me with the great destruction of life and property which attended the construction of the De Lesseps canal, and caused me to believe that a work of such magnitude could not soon be accomplished under the management then in charge of it.

An exception to the general inefficiency of the engineering work upon the Isthmus was found in the Grand Canal, excavated by the American Dredge Company. For more than twenty miles that company had made a canal, one hundred yards wide at the brim, and thirty feet deep, with the slopes of the banks securely sodded with wire grass; so that, should the scheme of an Isthmus canal ever again be agitated, the American half of the work will be found ready for service. I believe that our interests will be better served by the Nicaraguan than the Isthmian route, which lies out of the track of our commerce with the Pacific Coast, as well as of our trade

with China. We have, as yet, very little trade with the
eastern states of South America, but when our commercial relations shall have assumed their proper propor-
tions, the Nicaraguan route will serve our needs as well
as that of the Isthmus.

The hospitals upon the hills overlooking Panama relieve the general evidences of unthrift and incapacity.
All that can comfort the sick, or cheer and enliven
them, has been there assembled. Every chamber looks
out upon the enchanting scenery. The lovely grounds
are beautified by flowers, fruits, and shade trees, and
cooled by the breezes of the great Pacific, which breaks
upon the shore below. Panama and its lovely bay lie
before us there, and the verdant islands which gem it,
all lying within common range of the city and of each
other, seem tempting prizes for any maritime power.

During the past forty years, England and the United
States have endeavored to purchase one or all of them
from Colombia. Mr. Marcy offered $600,000 for one
of them, but the constitution of Colombia forbade the
alienation of any of its territory, nor would the sensitiveness of that proud people assent to it. The constitution adopted about six years ago excluded the
prohibition of sale of Colombian territory, and contained a clause permissive of the alienation of it. But
the susceptibilities of the people were so great that no
administration would venture even to mortgage or lease
one of these little islands, which are strategetic points
essential to any power seeking to control the Isthmus.
The Congress soon repealed the permissive clause of
the constitution, and re-enacted the clause prohibiting
the alienation of Colombian territory, and if ever the
United States entertained the idea of establishing a
coaling-station or of erecting fortifications there, the

opportunity has passed, we fear.   Let us hope that when
the treaty of 1846 between New Granada, now Colombia, shall be revived, proper provision will be made for
the occupation by the United States of such points on
or near the Isthmus as are essential to its defence, which
the United States has pledged herself in that treaty to
maintain.

We made the run from Colon, once Aspinwall, to
the mouth of the Magdalena River, on a fine British
steamer, in about twenty-four hours.   She was commanded by Captain Woodworth, a typical English
sailor, master of his profession, intelligent, kindly,
and humorous.   He is widely known in those waters, and
is trusted and liked by all who know him.   Among his
crew was the original of Dick Deadeye, whom no
man who has seen the opera of "Pinafoie" has ever
failed to recognize.

A railway some twenty-five miles long took us up to
Barranquilla, a busy town of about twenty thousand
people.   It is the principal port of Colombia.   I went
from Barranquilla in another British steamer to Cartagena, to pay my respects to President Nuñez, who,
after his stormy political life in Bogotá, retired to this
his favorite city.   I found him enjoying his *dolce far
niente* in his beautiful villa, charmingly situated on the
beach of the Caribbean Sea beyond the walls of the
city.   In stature and general appearance Nuñez reminded me of General Mahone.   Unlike Mahone, he is
a poet, and no soldier.   He asserts that a strong government is essential to the peace and consequent prosperity
of Colombia; that the people are not educated or intelligent enough to govern themselves; and that therefore he will govern them, and meantime educate them,
until they shall be capable, as we of the United States

are, of having a free government. His army is well
equipped and held in strict discipline, and so distributed as to quickly crush any attempt at revolution.
When one remembers that for a long time civil wars
recurring every three or four years have stopped the
progress and wasted the resources of this rich country,
one cannot withhold approval of Nuñez's policy, so far
as it can preserve peace throughout the country.

About a year after I saw him, he came up to Bogotá,
relieved Vice-President Payan, to whom he had entrusted
the duties of the office, temporarily, of the presidency,
exiled thirty-six of the important leaders of the opposition, and issued a decree restraining the liberty of the
press. He then retired to his retreat in Cartagena,
leaving Payan again in charge of the government.
Nuñez had not long been gone before Payan recalled
the exiles, and repealed the laws restraining the freedom
of the press. Thereupon Nuñez hastened from Cartagena, and re-enacted legislation requiring a censor-
ship of the press. He did not revoke the pardon of the
exiles, but he sent Payan into exile himself, and the
latter went away into a distant province, where he lived
in elegant retirement for a year or so, when he was permitted to go to his own home in Cauca.

The city of Cartagena is one of the most interesting
in this hemisphere. It was the especial favorite of old
Spain in the day of her pride and power. Its great wealth
attracted the cupidity of the daring buccaneers who for
so many years roamed these seas in Elizabeth's day, and
for a long time after. Hawkins, Morgan, Drake, and
others were the leaders of the pirates of that day.
Hawkins was the pioneer of negro slavery, which so
pleased his royal mistress that she knighted him and
gave him a negro's head for a crest, and until the colony

of Virginia was emancipated from English thrall, great numbers of negroes were seized in Africa, and sold in Virginia, and this in disregard of the protests of her people. Cartagena was the object of the chief desire of the freebooters of that day, and was often attacked by them. It was also an especial point of interest to the king of Spain, who spent $60,000,000 upon its fortifications, which stand to-day a monument of the wealth and engineering skill of the old Spaniards.

In 1741, during the war between England and Spain, a large expeditionary force was fitted out against Cartagena, and entrusted to the command of Admiral Vernon. A year or two before Vernon, with a fleet of six English ships, had made an unexpected descent upon Porto Bello, capturing it and bearing away great spoils. Lawrence Washington, eldest brother of our great George Washington, was a lieutenant under Vernon, for whom he had so warm an admiration that he named his home in Virginia Mt. Vernon, after him. This estate after his death became the property of his brother George.

The expedition of Vernon against Cartagena was prepared with great ostentation and parade. One hundred ships and fourteen thousand men sailed and debarked before the place. Vernon's long and conspicuous preparations gave due notice of the object of his attack, and he found the Spaniards had not been idle or unprepared. In those days, no troops were so good as they, nor were any officers so proud and skilful; for they were in constant wars and rarely met defeat. The fighting was fierce and long. The defenders displayed heroic valor, and Vernon's laurels, won at Porto Bello, withered beneath the walls of Cartagena. Disease and Spanish valor destroyed his army, and after more than forty days' constant fighting, he re-embarked his shattered forces, and sailed away, leaving many trophies in the hands of his enemies. The most curious of these were the medals, which Vernon, in his vainglory, had prepared in England, to be presented to those of his officers who should distinguish themselves in the capture of Cartagena. Those medals are now preserved in the libraries of Bogotá.

The Bay of Cartagena is one of the most beautiful in the world. In its expanse it is like the Bay of Mobile, but has greater depth, extending up to the very walls of the city. The entrance by the Boca Chica is very narrow and easily defended by the strong forts erected by the Spaniards, which have more than once turned back the tide of war. On one of the islands in the bay is the Lazaretto, where hundreds of lepers are quarantined. No Father Damien has ever yet found his way to them. They live and die in their dreadful isolation, in full view of the shipping of the great city and the people of the busy world they can never enter more. A canal ninety miles long, called the Dique, connects Cartagena with the Magdalena River at Calamar. Steamboats run up this canal into the river and thence up to Honda, at the base of the Andes.

The Magdalena is a miniature of the Mississippi. Its densely timbered banks are only varied by the many wood-yards, occasional hamlets, and small plantations of bananas, corn, sugar, cocoa, etc. On the sandbars we saw many alligators. We counted one hundred and ten on one bar, and our only amusement during our seven days' run was shooting them. The sport would be wanton, but that the creatures are very prolific and dangerous to human life. The only vulnerable spot is the eye or the point where the jaw joins the throat. A ball, even from our Winchesters, could not penetrate any other part of their armored bodies. When struck elsewhere, or when startled by the passage of the bullet, the alligator flounders with great to-do into the river, but when fatally hit his tail quivers, and he lies still until some native takes his skin and fat. We never got closer to them than two hundred yards, and rarely within four hundred.

About twenty-five steamers do the freighting of the Magdalena. They are like the small stern-wheel boats that used to ply the Ohio River. They draw two and a half feet, and as the navigation is very dangerous, they tie up every night. The trip from Barranquilla to Honda is usually made in from seven to eight days when the river is high. The down trip is made in from three to five days. The boats are reasonably comfortable. Mosquito nets are sometimes necessary, and one's own mattress, for the staterooms have only cots, which are bare and very hard. The price of passage up to Honda is $35. Going back, it is less.

At Honda we took mules for Bogotá, for which we paid about $5 each; this includes the *arriero* or muleteer. These men are entirely trustworthy. At dawn they catch the mules, which have been grazing all night, and saddle and pack them with great dexterity, and move off, on foot, as soon as they are ready, without waiting for the traveller, who comes on at his leisure and does not see his baggage till he has reached the appointed place of halt for the night. No apprehension need ever be felt as to the safety of one's luggage. The usual duration of the trip from Honda to Bogotá is three days. A railway from near the crest of the mountain runs into Bogotá, about twenty miles distant, and takes one into the city in an hour and a half. All along the route up

the mountains, one is enchanted with the grand scenery.
They are verdant from base to summit, and covered
with small farms of bananas, corn, barley, etc., all cultivated by the hoe,— for no plough can work on their
steep sides, — and along the whole road, which was paved
by the Spaniards, one is never out of sight and sound of
the pack trains passing up and down.

The cries of the muleteers are not unmusical, and
cheer their animals, while they lend life to the road.
They also keep all wild animals away, and serpents,
too. I never saw in all of my hunts and travels one of
those dangerous and tremendous snakes of which such
terrible accounts are told. I know that in some regions
they are to be found; for many gentlemen told me so,
and I have seen enormous skins of constrictors and
venomous serpents, as well as of rattlesnakes, which
last are not so large as we have in Texas or Florida.

There are towns, and hamlets, and homesteads all
along the route, where meat and drink for man and beast
are plentiful and cheap. Hundreds of packs, "car-
goes," pass daily along the road, a "cargo" weighing
250 pounds; and when I was there the government
derived a great revenue from this freight, about $5 per
cargo. The mules are not the only pack-animals;
oxen are often employed, and men and women bear
large burdens up these mountains. There were many
sugar-plantations along the way, and the sound of the
grinding was pleasant to hear. They use horse-power
to work their mills. On the Rio Negro, where there
are many sugar-mills, they have a water-power which
could run all the factories in Manchester; and though
a short ditch would do the work better, for generations
these gentlemen have used mules.

As we ascended to 4000 or 6000 feet, we came upon

the coffee-plantations. I visited one of over 200,000 trees, which was in fine condition. It was well equipped with every appliance of the business, and was in good bearing. The raising of coffee is the most lucrative business, and as it is always conducted in a healthy region, well up the mountain, is very tempting to foreign capital. The trees do not bear until they are four years old, and during that time the expenses are heavy, and there is no return. After that, for ten years or more, the crops recur. Every winter yields one pound of coffee to each tree, and every summer about half as much. The trees are planted some four feet apart, or about 1000 to the acre. The cost of clearing and planting a coffee-plantation is estimated at $100 per acre. Nothing can be more charming than a fine coffee-plantation. They are always on the mountain slopes, in the midst of a beautiful scenery and delightful climate. The trees grow ten feet high, and their dark, evergreen foliage mantles the entire surface of the plantation. The proprietors are the grand señors of the country. On one plantation of 200,000 trees in full bearing, the residence of the proprietor was a vast, two-story building, elaborately and thoroughly constructed by his own laborers, of timber and stone from his own estate. Wide corridors ran all around every story. A handsome chapel was in the lower story. The establishment was completely furnished, yet the manager told me that the proprietor resided in Bogota, and spent about three days annually in this lovely home. The grounds were beautified by fruits and flowers of the temperate and tropic zones, and a crystal stream ran through the place and supplied a large swimming-bath.

Mr. Wheeler, the very able chargé d'affaires of Great Britain to Colombia, has passed many years in travelling over that country, and is probably better informed about its resources and conditions than any other foreign resident of it. His reports to his government on the agricultural conditions of the country, and upon its trade and resources, are full of reliable information on these subjects. They present a strong array of the natural advantages of Colombia, and a correspondingly strong arraignment of the people who possess but do not develop them. He says the following is a list of the chief agricultural products of Colombia: Cocoanut palm, cocoa, date palm, cotton, indigo, rice, yucca, sugarcane, anise, plantains and bananas, tobacco, olives, maize, aloes, caoutchouc, coffee, arrocucha, apples, eucalyptus, wheat, cinchona, cochineal, potatoes, and barley. All of these can be raised at little cost. Colombia is the home of the potato. They are raised there in fine quality and in great abundance. Wheat and corn yield two crops a year, yet the largest export from the United States to Colombia is of wheat flour.

Mr. Wheeler states that the total exports from Colombia amounted, in 1887, to over $14,000,000. Of these, the United States received a little over $3,000,000. The imports the same year were $8,719,297. England's share of this was $3,611,775, the United States getting only $9737 worth of goods. The tobacco of Colombia is easily grown and of excellent quality. There is a cigar factory in Ambulema, which employs 500 hands, and makes excellent cigars at $1 per hundred. They are preferred by some to those of Cuba.

The country abounds in fine cattle and good, active horses. On the plains of Bogotá are the largest cattle I have ever seen. Mr. Edward Sayers, a gentleman of English descent, sent me a fine cut of beef from a cow that netted 800 pounds of fat and 1200 pounds of lean.

In butchering beef, all the flesh is cut from the bone, so that the viscera, hide, head, and bones made the gross weight of this animal over 3000 pounds. He had on his estate a number of cattle of equal size fattened on blue grass, the seed of which he procured from Kentucky. The native grasses are excellent.

On a neighboring estate, owned by Mr. Alexander Urdanata, I saw twenty-five Durham cows milked every morning. One of them gave six gallons besides what was left for the calf. But little enterprise has been shown in improving the breed of cattle or of any other stock, and Mr. Wheeler's report shows that from 1849 to 1878 the total number of bulls imported was only thirty, and of cows only twenty; and more of these were Durhams than of any other breed.

Mr. Vaughan has on his place of Santuario the only imported thoroughbred horse I know of. The native horses are rarely over fifteen hands high, and but few are of that height. They all pace from their birth, and are active, enduring, and gentle. The method of breaking young horses is very cruel, but it is effectual. They are tamed forever after. There are a few imported coach-horses in Bogotá, but they are very clumsy, heavy-footed beasts.

CHAPTER XXII

The City of Bogotá — The Clergy, the Military, and the People — Trade
Relations with the United States — Social Life in Town and Country —
Duck Shooting — Mineral Wealth of the Country — An Exciting Dog-
Cart Drive down the Andes — General Henry Morgan — Return to
the United States

HEN the Spaniards came to Bogotá, the
capital of the country was a large Indian
village. It is now a large city, its population being estimated at over 80,000. The
head of the Catholic Church in Colombia resides there.
The President and his cabinet are there, and once in
two years Congress assembles there.

There are few cities I know of that are more elegant
and luxurious than Bogotá. Wealthy men from all parts
of Colombia make it their home, and England, France,
Germany, Italy, Spain, and the United States have their
legations there. The city is well built, of adobe and
brick, as well as of stone. There are many houses of
two stories, and some few of three. Within, they
have every modern improvement, — gas, water, electric
bells, telephones, etc. The streets are paved, and the
sidewalks are flagged. When I left, the electric light
was replacing gas and kerosene. The institutions of
learning are numerous and excellent. The chief of
these is a Catholic College of the Priesthood. These
young ecclesiastics occasionally passed my house in
columns of twos. I was struck by their attention to

personal neatness. They were in exact uniform, with broad hats, long black gowns, and low shoes with shining buckles, and manifested by their appearance their belief in the maxim "Cleanliness is next to godliness."

The clergy of Bogotá are men of ability and dignity. The good Archbishop Paul died just before I left there. He was a man worthy of the love of all his people. A vast concourse followed him to his grave, and as the imposing procession moved along the streets, the people in their homes wept for him. Around his grave the voice of sect was silent, and all men mourned the good man gone from them to his eternal rest.

The medical college at Bogotá is well conducted, and the graduates are a high class of gentlemen. There are usually five battalions of troops in the city: one of artillery and four of infantry. They were well equipped in all respects. Armed with breech-loading rifles, uniformed in blue coats and scarlet trousers, with belts well filled with cartridges, they were always ready for action. Their discipline is exact. I never saw one of them drunk. Many of them are young boys not five feet high. In one of the fiercest battles of the late revolution, these little fellows fought with great stubbornness, 4000 of them withstanding all day the assaults of 7000 government troops; and when at sunset a truce was called and peace was made, 800 dead were buried on the field, the loss in killed and wounded aggregating 4000 men. The guns of the artillery were light pieces, mountain howitzers, gatling, etc., and were all drawn by the men. The generals were fine-looking fellows of high social standing and influence. Their uniforms were gorgeous, and they were well mounted, but when they moved off at a pace the dignity of the occasion was lost in the eyes of a cavalryman trained in our school. There is a mili-

tary academy there, organized by Lieutenant Lemley of
the Third United States Artillery.

The people of Bogotá are very kindly and courteous,
and no women I have ever seen surpassed these in the
grace and dignity of their manners or in the purity
of their lives. They are devoted wives, mothers, and
Christians. If Colombia does not increase her population by immigration, she has a sure dependence in her
home production. One noble matron of Antiochia, who
was married at thirteen, contributed seven daughters and
thirty sons to the population of her State. They were
all living when I last saw them.

It is quite remarkable that a country so surpassingly
rich should continue in this age so secluded and unde-
veloped. With a sea-coast of vast extent on her eastern
and western shores, she has harbors and bays of absolute
safety, and the healthfulness of her seaports is at least
equal to our own. Yet we have no trade there, and
except the Pacific Mail Line, we have no American
steamers plying thither. The English, German, and
French do most of the transportation. Mr. Wheeler
states that thirty-two steamers visit Colombia every
month, of which fifteen are British and only three
American.

The social life of Bogotá is very attractive; the
dinners and balls are sumptuous and elegant. At one
of the latter I saw several hundred ladies and gentlemen, and many of the dresses were from Worth. The
races are always largely attended by the ladies. A military band of music is on the ground, and a battalion of
troops lines both sides of the track for half the quarter
stretch, to prevent accident. There were sixty coaches
occupied by families, which were all made to keep in
line and at a safe distance from the track. Several

hundred gentlemen, well mounted, galloped at pleasure about the field; but the racing was very poor, both horses and riders being untrained.

We had good shooting in Colombia. On one occasion I was invited to the hospitable hacienda of Mr. Urdanata, to shoot ducks. His house is one of the finest on the plain. He and his wife speak English perfectly, as do many of the well-bred Colombians. Not long before our visit, they had entertained over one hundred guests for three days in their home. There were several handsome parlors, and the usual sitting-room contained a small library. In this room I counted twenty-five guns of various sorts. My host bought his shot-guns in England, and his rifles in the United States. In the presses of that room were stores of ammunition sufficient to blow up the whole establishment. Urdanata's especial gun weighs about fifteen pounds, and is calibre No. 8. The charge is six drachms of powder and three ounces of shot, and it sounds over the water like a small cannon. I repeatedly saw him kill a duck at two hundred yards' distance. While we were with him, we usually bagged one hundred and twenty-five ducks daily, and he always got more than all the rest of the party together. On a hunt made after we left him, he told me he bagged seven hundred ducks in six days. I thought our Colt guns shot much better than his Lancasters. On the water it was easy to compare the ranges.

My intercourse with the government was always of the most agreeable character. President Holguin is a gentleman of most affable and attractive manner, and a man of eloquence and ability. His appearance is very pleasing and graceful, especially on horseback. In my long intercourse with him and the Minister of Foreign

Relations, Dr. Restrepo, I rarely proposed any measure of common interest to the United States and Colombia which was not acceded to, unless the claim was for money, when I was invariably postponed or denied; for they have no more money than they need themselves.

The emerald mines near Bogotá are the finest and probably the only emerald mines now worked in the world. Not far from them is a vast salt mine. Both of these enterprises are the property of the government, and yield a good revenue. There are also large iron and coal mines near by, and a foundry employing six hundred hands. Gold mines are numerous in many parts of the country, and most of these are owned by English capitalists. The aggregate yield of gold is only $6,000,000 annually. There are also silver, copper, and lead; and lately quicksilver has been discovered. Very unwisely, the government exacts a heavy tax on all mining machinery brought into the country.

The important question now is, Why have we not trade with this most beautiful and fruitful of all the regions of the earth? and what can be done to promote our commercial relations? The Spanish language, with which for many reasons we should be familiar, is rarely taught in our schools. There is not a school that I know of south of Mason and Dixon's line in which Spanish is taught. Most of us have spent eight or ten years of our boyhood in learning Latin and Greek, and to what end?

This Colombian trade must be worked up by commercial travellers who can speak Spanish well. American merchants should have sample-rooms in Bogotá and other large towns. Taxes should be adjusted to encourage commercial intercourse between the countries. The packing of goods for the Colombian trade is peculiar.

Flour for that trade is sent out in bags coated inside
with a paste of their own contents. Yorkshire hams are
protected by water-tight and air-tight cloths, and keep
for a long time sweet and good. Dress-patterns and dry-
goods must be of a certain length, no more and no less,
and every pack should weigh one hundred and twenty-
five pounds, or half a cargo. There are many other
practical details essential to this trade, as the commercial
traveller will learn. A railroad from the Magdalena to
the Plain of Bogotá is of vast importance, and will
pay well. The mail facilities are few and very insufficient. Sixty days are needed to send a letter and receive an answer, and a large part of the business of
the Legation is crowded into one or two days. Being
of an active temperament, I occupied much of my
leisure time in excursions throughout the country,
posting myself as to the people, productions, etc., and
going up and down the Andes many times by the different routes to the Magdalena.

One day Mr. Vaughan came up from the Magdalena
in his dog-cart. The road was new, and his was the
first vehicle that had passed over it, but the grading was
uniform, and a good horse could trot up or down it.
Vaughan and I messed together in Bogotá for about two
months. When he first arrived, he invited me to go
back with him in his dog-cart, down this Cambao road
to his country home. I promptly accepted his invita-
tion, and he was never satisfied after that until he had
me safely landed as his guest in his comfortable establishment. The down trip was much more dangerous
than the up. The road, for the greater part of its length,
was six feet four inches wide, and several times we left
our wheel-tracks over the brink of the mountain down
which we might have rolled over two thousand feet. We

had in harness a great clay-bank brute with white legs, who was as big a fool as Sam Patch, and would have jumped with him down the falls of Niagara. Just as we began to descend the mountain, a peacock paraded himself in front of us, and elevating his tail lifted up his voice in that terrible cry which is characteristic of that bird. At the first note our clay-bank spun around and darted at full speed up the mountain, until he met our pack-train coming calmly down behind us. Vaughan was then able to stop him and turn him back. Fortunately, the road just there was broad and good, or we should have all gone to Sam Patch.

That evening we halted for the night at a large spring of fine water in a fertile valley surrounded by mountains ten or twelve thousand feet high. Many of them were dotted with farms and pastures extending to their very summits. There were several adobe houses clustered together near the spring, and we rented one of them for the night. The family moved out with all their belongings, swept up the rooms, and we took possession. Swinging our hammocks, we took our dinner of cold fowl, tongue, etc., lighted our cigars, and made ourselves easy for the night. About ten o'clock a row broke out among the peons outside, of whom there were about twenty of both sexes, who were clamoring and fighting. The blows and imprecations fell fast and furious, and the fray grew more violent, until Vaughan sprang out of his hammock and took his pistol, saying, "I must put a stop to that." He spoke Spanish well. I couldn't speak much Spanish, but I could shoot. So I took my pistol and followed Vaughan, with a vague idea of doing whatever he might tell me. Just at this moment the police arrived, and quieted the combatants, by carrying off one of them who had been on the ground for some time. We then retired to sleep well until morning, when we paid our rent of five cents, and moved on.

We reached the river at Cambao that evening before sunset. The river is about four hundred yards wide there, deep and rapid, so we were ferried over in large canoes, our horses swimming by their sides, and landed quite safely and easily on the other shore, where we spent the night very comfortably. During the night a vampire sucked my horse, leaving a small mark upon his neck, from which a drop or two of blood had oozed. We mounted our dog-cart at daylight, and drove ten miles over a level road to the fine establishment of Santuario.

Vaughan had excited my interest the night before by his account of a tiger that had roamed the woods through which we passed. Perhaps his vivid narrative may account for the urgency with which I insisted on going no further that night. Near the roadside, he pointed out the tiger-trap, some ten yards away. We were very comfortable at Santuario, where my son joined us, and we spent several days very pleasantly. The young men killed some pheasants, pigeons, quail, and a couple of the pretty little deer of the plains. The mountain-sides and pastures were all burning, but we saw no snakes. From Santuario we drove over to the town of Ambulema, where are the cigar factory and fine residence of Mr. Vaughan. This was the largest establishment I was in while in the country, and was perhaps the handsomest house. The parlors, bedrooms, library, and billiard-rooms were all paved with marble. The china and silverware bear the name of the estate, and the excellent table is supplied with wines, sauces, and canned luxuries from London. An ice-machine gave us ice.

Here I waited several days for an up-river boat, on

which I went up to Giradot. The river was very low, and at some of the rapids the whole crew went overboard with a hawser, which they fastened to a tree on the bank, and then proceeded to warp the boat up the rapids. As there were only two feet of water, this was very slow work, but we reached Giradot the second day by noon, and General H. E. Morgan, an old Virginian, was waiting on this shore to take me to his hospitable and comfortable home, where I passed the night. Next morning he ordered a train to be ready by eight o'clock and accompanied me to the terminus of the railroad, now at Las Juntas, at the foot of the mountains, where he detailed a bright Lieutenant Gomez, his aide-de-camp, who speaks English, to escort me to Bogotá.

This is the pleasantest of all the mountain roads. There are several little towns on it, where good quarters can be had, and beautiful brawling streams cross and run along it; and, except for a short distance, it is practicable for wagons, and affords the best route for a railroad. Several reconnoissances have been made, but the government and the contractors have never yet come to terms so definite as to lead to this great result. We found comfortable lodgings in the little town of Annapoyma, and by midday next day I was met by my friend and Secretary of Legation, Mr. Boschell, with a coach, and by eventide was back in my own quarters. I do not believe that any dog-cart has been down the Cambao road since. It was a trip of great interest and some excitement to us, especially to Vaughan, who felt responsible for me, and never drew an easy breath while I was in the cart with him.

General Henry Morgan, now Enrique Morgan, was a native of Morefield Valley, Virginia. His family is well known and esteemed in that region. When sixteen years old, he enlisted in Stonewall Jackson's corps, and served in it throughout the war between the States. On the surrender of Lee, he went away from Virginia to seek his fortunes in some country where he would feel freer than in his native land. From California he went down to Colombia, where he soon found employment. He liked the country and the people, and became a citizen of it. He served his adopted land with distinction in three revolutions, won the grade of general, and is now commander-in-chief of all the engineer troops, five battalions, of the Colombian Army. His courage and fidelity have won for him the confidence and love of the people.

The ladies of Bogotá wear black upon the streets, with mantillas, often of costly black lace, on their heads instead of bonnets. Only occasionally are the latter worn by some one who has been in the United States or Europe. Many of them have small and beautiful feet and hands. They are usually of the brunette type, and have very gentle and winning manners.

There is a large asylum for foundlings, that of St. Vincent de Paul. It is in excellent discipline and organization, under the care of the sisters of the church. The Lady Superior and her second in command accompanied us in our visit to the various departments of the building, and seemed much pleased with my commendation of their good work, as with the small donation which I left as a climax to my praise. I said on leaving, "There is no such institution as this in my country." They replied, "Mil gracias, Señor"; when I added, "Because we Protestants are too good to need such an one." At which preposterous statement these ancient virgins shook their ample sides with convulsions of incredulous laughter. All of the children are of mothers of the lower classes, to whom the institution is so great a boon as to be considered by some people a very doubtful factor in the cause of morality.

My own home in Bogotá was as comfortable and complete as was possible when so far away from my nearest kindred. It was presided over by the lovely wife of my Secretary of Legation, and these good friends, more than any others, contributed to the happiness of my stay. The business of the Legation was conducted in such a manner as to receive the cordial approval of our government, repeatedly expressed, and when the result of the presidential election was known, the Secretary of Foreign Relations called at the American Legation to inform me that measures had been taken by his government to urge upon the government of the United States that no change should be made in the personnel of that legation. Surprised and gratified as I was by a tribute so unusual, I cherished but little hope of its influence upon the result.

The party axe fell promptly, and when I met my successor, Mr. John T. Abbot, of New Hampshire, I felt that in this case no injury could ensue to the public weal. He is a gentleman of high ability, self-reliant, courageous, and generous. My removal caused him genuine regret, and he and his gentle family showed their warm interest and sympathy, and he accompanied me in person on my lonely journey from Bogotá to Honda, an arduous six days' mule-ride for him, because he could not bear to see me go alone and friendless then.

www.ingramcontent.com/pod-product-compliance
Lightning Source LLC
Chambersburg PA
CBHW031952060726
47497CB00016B/1466